FOCUSING ON PEERS

The Importance of Relationships in the Early Years

DONNA S. WITTMER

ZERO TO THREE®

National Center for Infants, Toddlers, and Families

WASHINGTON, DC

Published by

ZERO TO THREE

National Center for Infants, Toddlers, and Families
ZERO TO THREE

(202) 638-1144
Toll-free orders (800) 899-4301
Fax: (202) 638-0851
Web: www.zerotothree.org

The mission of the ZERO TO THREE Press is to publish authoritative research, practical resources, and new ideas for those who work with and care about infants, toddlers, and their families. Books are selected for publication by an independent Editorial Board. The views contained in this book are those of the authors and do not necessarily reflect those of ZERO TO THREE: National Center for Infants, Toddlers, and Families, Inc.

These materials are intended for education and training to help promote a high standard of care by professionals. Use of these materials is voluntary and their use does not confer any professional credentials or qualification to take any registration, certification, board or licensure examination, and neither confers nor infers competency to perform any related professional functions.

The user of these materials is solely responsible for compliance with all local, state or federal rules, regulations or licensing requirements. Despite efforts to ensure that these materials are consistent with acceptable practices, they are not intended to be used as a compliance guide and are not intended to supplant or to be used as a substitute for or in contravention of any applicable local, state or federal rules, regulations or licensing requirements. ZERO TO THREE expressly disclaims any liability arising from use of these materials in contravention of such rules, regulations or licensing requirements.

The views expressed in these materials represent the opinions of the respective authors. Publication of these materials does not constitute an endorsement by ZERO TO THREE of any view expressed herein, and ZERO TO THREE expressly disclaims any liability arising from any inaccuracy or misstatement.

Cover design: Michael Brady Design
Text design and composition: Black Dot Group

Library of Congress Cataloging-in-Publication Data

Wittmer, Donna Sasse.
    Focusing on peers : the importance of relationships in the early years / Donna Wittmer.
        p. cm.
    Includes bibliographical references.
    ISBN 978-1-934019-27-6
1. Social interaction in infants. 2. Infant psychology. 3. Social interaction in children.
4. Toddlers—Psychology. I. Title.
    BF720.S63.W58 2008
    305.231—dc22   2008026326

For permission for academic photocopying (for course packets, study materials, etc.) by copy centers, educators, or university bookstores or libraries, of this and other ZERO TO THREE materials, please contact Copyright Clearance Center, 222 Rosewood Drive, Danvers, MA 01923; phone, (978) 750-8400; fax, (978) 750-4744; or visit its Web site at www.copyright.com.

10 9 8 7 6 5 4 3 2
ISBN 978-1-934019-27-6
Printed in the United States of America

Suggested citation: Wittmer, D. (2008). *Focusing on peers: The importance of relationships in the early years*. Washington, DC: ZERO TO THREE.

Dedication

I dedicate this book to all of my peers. Life is more meaningful and fun with your support, friendship, and love.

Table of Contents

Acknowledgments vii

Introduction 1

Chapter 1   Turning the Lens to Infants' and Toddlers' Peer Relationships 5

Chapter 2   The Power of Relationships on Relationships 23

Chapter 3   So Much More Than Parallel Play 53

Chapter 4   Becoming Prosocial, Making Friends, and Experiencing "Glee"—
                 The Joy of Relationships 81

Chapter 5   Of Course, There Are Conflicts—And Then There Is Biting 101

Chapter 6   Children Who Feel Challenged 119

Chapter 7   Developing a Community of Caring in Infant and Toddler Programs 141

Acknowledgments

I would like to acknowledge all who care about infants and toddlers. They nurture infant–toddler peer relationships because they appreciate the importance of the daily emotional and social experiences of infants and toddlers, understand that satisfying relationships are an essential ingredient of rewarding lives, and value young children and adults living in caring communities.

My work focusing on the importance of peer relationships began when Dr. Alice Honig was my PhD advisor at Syracuse University. Dr. Honig inspired my life-long passion for infants and toddlers. Her knowledge is immense, her intellect is brilliant, and her skill at teaching others is renowned. She continually inspires families and professionals to improve the lives of young children with her excellent articles, books, annual summer course, and consulting. I was also privileged to study with Dr. Ron Lally, whose lifelong work on the Program for Infant/Toddler Care (PITC) has enhanced the lives of infants and toddlers in child care and provided those who care about infant–toddler relationships with enlightening videos, informative educational materials, and life-changing learning opportunities. I am thankful for and indebted to Alice Honig and Ron Lally. They were my professors and now they are my friends, and they will always be my mentors.

My relationship with the organization ZERO TO THREE, which began when I was a fellow in 1982 and 1983, has been one of the most influential in my life. ZERO TO THREE represents and illuminates all that we know is best for infants and toddlers. I thank the board of ZERO TO THREE, Rebecca Shahmoon-Shanok, and Emily Fenichel for supporting my work on this book. Rebecca recommended that I do a research plenary on the topic of infants and toddlers' peer relationships at a ZERO TO THREE conference in the fall of 2004. Emily Fenichel encouraged me to write this book and cheered for *Focusing on Peers in the Early Years* until her untimely death. I am so grateful that I knew her, and I continually miss her. She had a boundless desire to improve the lives of young children and their families by providing professionals with edifying tools, and I hope that she would consider this book one of those.

I would like to acknowledge Sandy Petersen as her friendship means the world to me. A quote by Donna Roberts says it all, "A friend is someone who knows the song in your heart, and can sing it back to you when you have forgotten the words." Her insightful reflections on the importance of the early years also broaden my knowledge and motivate me to continue my work.

There are many who contributed to this book. It would not have been possible without the constructive and priceless editorship of Jennifer Moon Li, Director of Production for ZERO TO THREE Press. Her infinite patience and outstanding guidance were extremely important to me and to the quality of this book. The proofreading by Kathleen Kelly Halverson was exemplary. Anne Brophy, Production Editor, deserves a big thank-you for her excellent work on the photos in the book. I also would like to thank the photographers Deanna Wittmer Clauson, John Clauson, Ashante Butcher, Carla Mestas, Linda Enger, Mark Herlinger, Emily Petersen Adams, Manzanita Fine, Kristi Rieken, and Nicole Smith for the beautiful photos of infants and toddlers and the families for giving permission to use them. The photos capture the essence of adult–child and peer relationships.

The acknowledgments are not complete without a heartfelt thank-you to my husband, daughters, son-in-law, grandson, mother, other family members, and friends whose relationships are central to my life. My husband, Dennis, provides unconditional love that I cherish in the "time that is ours to be."

To infants and toddlers everywhere—I hope your eyes are dancing with love, friendship, meaning, and fun.

INTRODUCTION

As adults, we know that relationships are a source of joy to us. They are a fundamental element in the human experience. (Shanok, Wittmer, & Capatides, 1997)

The Scope, Focus, and Purpose

The focus of this book is on infants' and toddlers' joys and challenges as they negotiate peer interactions and relationships and the central role that adults play in facilitating children's peer development. There are three purposes for the book. One purpose is to increase parents' and professionals' appreciation for the remarkable capacities of infants and toddlers to enjoy meaningful relationships, have social goals, use many strategies to relate, become prosocial, and negotiate conflict with their peers during the first 3 years of life as they learn about the "self" and the "other." The second purpose is to emphasize the importance of the first 3 years of life to create strong adult–child and peer foundations for children's relationship success throughout their lives. The third purpose is to improve the quality of peer experiences for young children in early care and education settings by sharing the dimensions of responsive adult interactions, the environment and materials, and the structural variables (e.g., ratios, group size, teacher training) that facilitate infants' and toddlers' optimal social development.

In each chapter, I explore how children come to understand *self* and *other* (theory of the mind; Bullock & Lütkenhaus, 1990; Carpendale & Lewis, 2004; Dunn, Brown, Slomkowski, Tesla, & Youngblade, 1991; Flavell, Green, & Flavell, 1995; Gopnik, Meltzoff, & Kuhl, 1999; Hay, 2006; Imbens-Bailey & Pan, 1998; Trevarthen & Aitken, 2001). As infants and toddlers begin to consider the significance of others' perspectives, goals, desires, and behaviors they are thinking about the other in relation with the self. Evidence abounds that infants and toddlers can think, much earlier than many have thought, of the "other" and not just of their own "self" and that they actually discover self through their interactions with others (Bigelow, 2001).

The terms *infants, toddlers, 2-year-olds, peers, teachers, family child care providers,* and *early interventionists* are used frequently in the book. I use the term *infants* to refer to children from birth to 12 months of age, *toddlers* for children from 12 to 24 months of age, and *2-year-olds* to refer to children who are 24 to 36 months of age. Whenever possible, when citing research results, I share the exact ages of the children who are the focus of a research study. A *peer* refers to a child who is of a similar age or stage of development to

1

another child or to a child who is in the same play group, center care and education group, or family child care home. The term *teacher* refers to a professional who works with infants and/or toddlers in center care and education programs. The term *family child care providers* refers to adults who care for children in their own home, although they are not only providers but also teachers of children. *Early interventionists* are professionals who work with children with disabilities and their families.

Significance and Unique Features

The unique features of this book include a focus on the experience of the young child from the child's perspective, an interpretation of research, and illustrative vignettes that inform and inspire the reader to think differently about the complexities and importance of peer interactions and relationships.

With the increase in both parents working outside the home during the past 2 decades, infants and toddlers are spending more time together in early care and education centers and family child care homes. To ensure that these are quality experiences, this book focuses on how to enhance children's peer experiences through responsive adult–child relationships and through environments that support optimal peer development.

The approach highlighted in this book is a focus on the importance of relationships as central in the child's development (Emde, 1988; Hinde, 1992).

> A relationships approach involves the recognition that children must be seen not as isolated entities, but as forming part of a network of social relationships; and requires a delicate balance between conceptions of the child as an individual and as a social being (Hinde, 1992, p. 252).

As we know, the role of the adult in the adult–child relationship is crucially important. Emily Fenichel (2002) described the importance of adult–child *close* and *dependable* relationships in the following way: "Children grow and thrive in the context of close and dependable relationships that provide love and nurturance, security, responsive interaction, and encouragement for exploration" (p. 49). Chazan-Cohen and Jerald (2001) emphasized the importance of adult–child *secure* and *responsive* relationships as the foundation for mental health in the early years.

> **A secure and responsive relationship between the [child] and his or her primary caregivers is the foundation for mental health in the earliest years and the context in which healthy social and emotional development continues to flourish. (Chazan-Cohen & Jerald, 2001, p. 7)**

This book emphasizes the importance of adult–child relationships, as they provide the foundation for children's healthy emotional and social development. Each chapter offers evidence for how the quality of children's relationships with both adults and peers is an organizing principle for children's optimal development and sense of well-being.

This book also emphasizes that infants and toddlers have a relational capacity; that is, a capacity and desire to relate to others—both adults and peers (Nash & Hay, 2003; Selby & Bradley, 2003)—with each relationship "having distinct features and functions" (Nash & Hay, 2003, p. 223). Babies are able to establish relationships with a number of others simultaneously (Nash & Hay, 2003).

This book summarizes a comprehensive research base that examines infant and toddler peer development, play, conflicts, and competence; individual differences; temperament influences; aggression; the influences of family characteristics and parent–child interaction on peer competence; and the importance of responsive teacher strategies. The results of this extensive research review reveal that infant and toddler peer interactions are much more complex than they were traditionally thought to be and that there is information that may change the way in which adults view the meaning of peer experiences.

Researchers, professionals, and parents know a great deal about what it takes for young children to be socially successful. For example, "Well-liked children display positive affect" (Carson & Parke, 1996, p. 2218). In addition, a children's ability to regulate challenging emotions (Carson & Parke, 1996) and to recognize others' emotions influences their positive social interactions. Hay, Payne, and Chadwick (2004) identified the skills necessary for successful social interactions as follows:

- Joint attention

- Emotion regulation

- Inhibition

- Language

- Imitation

- Causal understanding

As young children develop, empathy and perspective taking are also important skills. As adults learn more about how socially successful young children navigate their social waters, they can put research knowledge into action to support children's social and emotional intelligence.

I wrote this book for a variety of audiences. Experienced and advanced professionals will have references, an extensive bibliography, and a list of resources to use for further reading on topics. Research examples and vignettes are interspersed throughout each chapter in a way that is meaningful to practitioners and administrators. Educators/trainers and undergraduate and community college professors can create discussion questions for each chapter to facilitate the readers' learning. Graduate students will enjoy reading the extensive research literature and thinking about the implications of the research for infants, toddlers, and 2-year-olds, and for the adults who care for them. Although I am not targeting the book to parents or policymakers, I hope that parents will enjoy reading the whole book, while policymakers will benefit from reading the last chapter of the book.

The chapters of the book include the following:

1. Turning the Lens to Infants' and Toddlers' Peer Relationships

2. The Power of Relationships on Relationships

3. So Much More Than Parallel Play

4. Becoming Prosocial, Making Friends, and Experiencing "Glee"—The Joy of Relationships

5. Of Course, There Are Conflicts—and Then There is Biting

6. Children Who Feel Challenged

7. Developing a Community of Caring in Infant and Toddler Programs

References

Bigelow, A. E. (2001). Discovering self through other: Infants' preference for social contingency. *Bulletin Menninger Clinic, 65*(3), 335–346.

Bullock, M., & Lütkenhaus, P. (1990). Who am I? Self-understanding in toddlers. *Merrill-Palmer Quarterly, 36,* 217–238.

Carpendale, J., & Lewis, C. (2004). Constructing an understanding of mind: The development of children's social understanding within social interaction. *Behavioral and Brain Sciences, 27,* 79–96.

Carson, J., & Parke, R. D. (1996). Reciprocal negative affect in parent–child interactions and children's peer competency. *Child Development, 67,* 2217–2226.

Chazan-Cohen, R., & Jerald, J. (2001). A commitment to supporting the mental health of our youngest children. *Zero to Three, 22*(1), 4–12.

Dunn, J., Brown, J., Slomkowski, C., Tesla, C., & Youngblade, L. (1991). Young children's understanding of other people's feelings and beliefs: Individual differences and their antecedents. *Child Development, 62,* 1352–1366.

Emde, R. N. (1988). The effect of relationships on relationships: A developmental approach to clinical intervention. In R. A. Hinde & J. Stevenson-Hinde (Eds.), *Relationships within families* (pp. 334–364). Oxford, England: Clarendon Press.

Fenichel, E. (2002). Relationships at risk: The policy environment as a context for infant development. *Infants and Young Children, 15*(2), 49–56.

Flavell, J. H., Green, F. L., & Flavell, E. R. (1995). Young children's knowledge about thinking. *Monographs of the Society for Research in Child Development, 60*(1, Serial No. 243).

Gopnik, A., Meltzoff, A. N., & Kuhl, P. K. (1999). *The scientist in the crib. What early learning tells us about the mind.* New York: Harper Perennial.

Hay, D. F. (2006). Yours and mine: Toddlers' talk about possessions with familiar peers. *The British Psychological Society, 24,* 39–52.

Hay, D. F., Payne, A., & Chadwick, A. (2004). Peer relations in childhood. *Journal of Child Psychology and Psychiatry, 45,* 84–108.

Hinde, R. A. (1992). Ethological and relationship approaches. In R. Vasta (Ed.), *Six theories of child development* (pp. 251–285). London: JKP Press.

Imbens-Bailey, A., & Pan, B. A. (1998). The pragmatics of self- and other-reference in young children. *Social Development, 7,* 219–233.

Nash, A., & Hay, D. F. (2003). Social relations in infancy: Origins and evidence. *Human Development, 46,* 222–232.

Selby, J. M., & Bradley, B. S. (2003). Infants in groups: A paradigm for the study of early social experience. *Human Development, 46*(4), 197–221.

Shanok, R. S., Wittmer, D., & Capatides, J. (1997). *Peer play groups: Enabling individual growth in very young children.* Washington, DC: ZERO TO THREE.

Trevarthen, C., & Aitken, K. J. (2001). Infant intersubjectivity: Research, theory, and clinical applications. *Journal of Child Psychology and Psychiatry, 42,* 3–48.

1

TURNING THE LENS TO INFANTS' AND TODDLERS' PEER RELATIONSHIPS

PHOTO: ASHANTE BUTCHER

A lens of a camera provides a way to focus on the dimensions of an object or person and inspires a different view of the subject. By turning the lens toward infants and toddlers' peer interactions and relationships, we see very young children's social development in detail and with new perspective.

The term *turning the lens* (Shanok, Wittmer, & Capatides, 1997) describes a change in focus from adult–child interactions to the complexities of infant and toddler peer interactions. Adult–child interactions are the subject of much research—much more than infant and toddler peer behavior. However, there are parents' and teachers' perceptive observations, as well as many professionals' research results, that surprise and provide insight into young children's peer intentions and experiences.

Instead of diminishing the importance of adult–child relationships for the infant and toddler, a focus on peer relationships in the early years enhances our understanding of the centrality of adults' responsive care for young children's social well-being. As we center our attention on peer relationships we begin to see from a new angle how critically important thoughtful adults are in children's development of affirmative social and emotional dispositions and experience of positive peer relationships. Infants and toddlers need the strong foundation that protection, affection, and emotional connections with adults provide. It is with this foundation and continued support from thoughtful, gentle, and emotionally available adults that the social experience of infants and toddlers flourishes.

We turn the lens to understand peer interactions from the children's viewpoint, to understand their goals and strategies and how they are experiencing the moment. The lens focuses on how important, meaningful, and sometimes challenging peer interactions and relationships are to the children and how they learn about *self* and *other* in their interactions with peers.

There is a focus on children's competencies, as well as on their challenges. As they focus on peer interactions in the early years, teachers and other adults cannot help but notice infants' and toddlers' many skills as they actively construct their ideas about peers. Parents and teachers also observe the challenges that young children have with peers as they learn to communicate and negotiate sharing people, objects, and space. However, Lokken, with the following quote, summarized how recent research gives a view of infants and toddlers that is different from what the terms *parallel play* and *the terrible twos* indicate.

> In what ways does the knowledge documented in recent toddler peer research challenge existing cultural suppositions on which toddling members of a society are valued? The knowledge should challenge any view that toddler relations are rare, short-lived and often aggressive, and as such continuously in need of adult or older children's support. (Lokken, 2000b, p. 172)

As we focus the lens, four levels of social development that provide a framework for a microscopic and macroscopic view of peer behaviors in each chapter come into view. The following example demonstrates the four levels of social development defined by Robert Hinde (1979, 1987, 1995; Hinde & Stevenson-Hinde, 1976) and Rubin (1998): within-individual, within-interaction, within-relationships, and within-group factors.

> *As two toddlers play in the sand in their center program, the teacher observes them carefully. As they take turns dumping sand in a big pile with their buckets, one is quiet and the other is making loud sounds to enhance his fun. Although these two boys seem to have different personalities, they often play together and seem to miss each other when one is gone for the day. They play best when there is a smaller group of children in the room.*

The child's *individual* contribution includes temperament, biological capabilities, gender, experience with relationships, and "repertoire of social cognitions, skills, and competencies" (Rubin, 1998, p. 611). Successful peer *interactions* (actions with each other) require child skills that differ depending on the context. To add to the complexity of interactions, each child brings his or her individual characteristics to his or her social situation (Rubin, 1998). *Relationships* (which include past experiences with a person that influence the present and future interactions) include attachment to significant adults as well as the ongoing friendships of children. Relationships can have a positive, angry, or distressed tone. "Memories and expectations may serve to move either of the individuals to avoid (reject), neglect, or approach the other in positive, neutral, or hostile manners" (Rubin, 1998, p. 611). Interactions and relationships often occur in groups. **Group** dynamics include how children's peer personalities play out in a group setting. As many teachers have experienced, each group of children has its own unique character, with each child contributing to a dynamic and constantly changing whole that is a different quality than its parts. Cultural beliefs and norms influence all of these levels of social development including the types of interactions, relationships, and group dynamics that are acceptable and encouraged within each culture (Rubin, 1998).

As the focus turns on infants' and toddlers' peer relationships, the quote from Georgia O'Keefe reminds us to take the time to see young children's budding interest in peers, their growing ability to be a friend who cares about another, and the adults' role in facilitating young children's peer connections and relationships that enrich their lives.

> **Still—in a way—nobody sees a flower—really—it is so small—we haven't time—and to see takes time, like to have a friend takes time. (Georgia O'Keeffe Online, 2007)**

There are at least 10 reasons why it is important to "turn the lens" toward infants' and toddlers' peer relationships—to take time to see, with vision and clarity, the complexity and value of peers in the early years. I explain these reasons briefly in this chapter and describe them in detail in the remaining six chapters.

Ten Reasons to Focus on Infant and Toddler Peer Relationships

There are 10 reasons why it is important to focus on infant and toddler peer relationships for the benefit of the children, families, teachers, programs, and communities (see Box 1.1). The first one is that we need to care deeply about what infants and toddlers are experiencing in programs.

We Need to Care Deeply

Infants and toddlers are experiencing their peers more often in child care and education groups (Administration for Children and Families, 2007; Capizzano & Adams, 2000).

BOX 1.1 | **Ten Reasons Why It Is Important to Focus on Infant and Toddler Peer Relationships**

1. **We Need to Care Deeply**

2. **To Be Human Is to Be Social**

3. **There Is a Power of Relationships on Relationships**

4. **Social–Emotional Development in the Early Years Is the Foundation for Learning and Predicts Future Social and Academic Success**

5. **Infants and Toddlers Are Capable, Competent, Curious, and Complex**

6. **Children Build Each Other's Competence and Understanding of Culture**

7. **There Can Be a Joy in Peer Relationships—The Prosocial and Gleeful Experiences**

8. **Conflict and Biting—The Need for Proactive Strategies**

9. **When Children Are Challenged They Need Relationship Support**

10. **Day to Day the Relationship Way—Quality Programs Matter**

1.2. Infants and toddlers spend time with their peers in center and family child care and education programs.
PHOTO: ASHANTE BUTCHER

Leila began her group experience at 3 months of age in a family child care home and has spent most weekdays from 8:00 a.m. to 5:00 p.m. with her family child care provider and three peers of various ages. By 2 years of age, Leila, who really likes her playmates, is very sad when the oldest child moves on to kindergarten.

Children like Leila are spending more time with their peers in center or family child care programs while their parents work outside the home. Approximately 53% of infants and toddlers spend some time in early care and development programs (Women in the Labor Force & U.S. Bureau of Labor Statistics 2005). In family child care homes, child care centers, Early Head Start, and kinship care (with relatives), peers are experiencing being around each other.

Fabes, Hanish, and Martin (2003), commenting on the studies of the National Institute of Child Health and Human Development (NICHD) Early Child Care Research Network, have argued that "there is a need to expand child care research by considering one of the most important, but unrecognized, contributors to child care effects—peers" (p. 1039). Because children are spending more time together with their peers, we need to care deeply about their experiences in child care and other early education and development programs. Just as our daily experiences are important to us, so are they important to infants and toddlers. We can thoughtfully ask, "What kind of peer day have the children had?"

To Be Human Is to Be Social

From everything that has been said, it can be seen how important it is to help children build their individual identities and, at the same time to find a sense of belonging. To be and to belong: these become one in defining growth. (Galardini & Giovannini, 2001, p. 105)

While a child's desire to express "self" is strong, so is the desire to be with others. We focus on peers in the early years because social experience is an essential human experience that begins in infancy and is crucial throughout children's lives. Social development among infants and toddlers is worthy of our attention.

Humans live together in communities, and although relationships can be a challenge, they generally choose to live with and near others. Most humans avoid isolation and loneliness and seek others to share joys, wonders, challenges, and sorrows.

Although a child's desire to become autonomous is a powerful force in a child's development (Mahler, 1975), there is an equally strong desire "to grow one's autonomy *with* connectedness" (Emde, 2001b, xiii).

Emde and Clyman (1997) observed that there are universal human motives for connectedness with others. Maslow (1968) identified a sense of belonging as a need that is high on the hierarchy of human needs; in fact, only survival needs and the child's sense of safety precede it. These strong human needs for individual identity within the context of connectedness and belonging manifest themselves in children's desire to be unique *and* social—"to be and to belong" (see Box 1.3; Galardini & Giovannini, 2001, p. 105). Emde (2001b) emphasizes that infants are primed for social interaction from the start.

Research indicates that there may be a genetic component to humans' willingness to cooperate with each other for the good of the group (Warneken & Tomasello, 2006). Brownell, Ramani, and Zerwas (2006, p. 803) summarized other researchers' ideas about the importance of human cooperation: "Indeed, cooperation may constitute a social imperative (Hartup, 1996) and it forms the foundation for human culture (Rogoff, 1990; Tomasello, 1999a)." The potential for cooperation and caring is within children. Children's ability to be compassionate with others begins early in their lives with adults who are empathetic and kind with them and promote their growth in human compassion.

Altruism (selflessness and helping others) is one of the most advanced human behaviors. Children as young as 18 months of age helped strangers (who were researchers) by, for example, picking up a dropped peg that the "clumsy" researcher had dropped but was now out of reach of the adult. However, Warneken and Tomasello (2006) noted that babies did not pick up items for the researcher if they believed that the adult was throwing something away. Warneken also commented, "These children are so young—they still wear diapers and are barely able to use language, but they already show helping behavior" (Max Planck Society, 2006, p. 1).

Because social experience is such a crucial part of the human experience, there is a consequence for children who are not successful with social relationships. Children who are not liked or who are rejected, isolated, or fearful in social situations are usually very unhappy (Rubin, 2002). Hay (2006, p. 40) noted, "Peer rejection has long-term effects on children's well-being (Deater-Deckard, Dodge, Bates, & Pettit, 1998; Woodward & Fergusson, 2000). Conversely, peer acceptance is a protective factor in development (Criss, Pettit, Bates, Dodge, & Lapp, 2002)".

Participation in family, peer groups, and the community is important for humans and is a right. Nations all over the world explicitly recognize this right as expressed in international documents such as the United Nations Convention on the Rights of the Child, which is available online at www.ohchr.org/english/law/pdf/crc.pdf. This convention emphasizes that all children have a right to participate fully in family, cultural, and social life. "Every right spelled out in the Convention is inherent to the human dignity and harmonious development of every child" (UNICEF, 2002). To participate fully, children need relationship dispositions and skills that lead to social competence.

Generally, human beings desire to live in homes, programs, communities, nations, and a world in which individuals have both a sense of self-worth *and* the ability to care about others. Adults can influence children's experience of tomorrow's communities through how they help them develop social feelings today. As adults focus on infants', toddlers', and 2-year-olds' peer relationships, parents and teachers can begin, in children's early years, to build a socially satisfying and humane future for them.

There Is a Power of Relationships on Relationships

Social and emotional competence is rooted in the relationships that infants and toddlers experience in the early years of life. (Robin Peth-Pierce, 2001, p. vii)

Talitha, a toddler, watched her peers play and then left her father's side to join the others as they explored the play center in the big mall. She often looked back and saw her father smiling at her. At times, she toddled back to him and touched his leg, as if to gain energy for her next move into peer land. She gave another toddler a hug when her "new friend" had to say good-bye. Talitha enjoyed playing with her peers, just as she enjoyed being with her dad.

Robert Emde (1988) enlightened professionals about relationships when he stated that there is an "effect of relationships on relationships" (p. 354). Children's sense of *self* and *other*, which they bring to their interactions with peers, begins to develop in their first relationships with significant adults. A self that is full of confidence, capable of being intimate with others, and convinced that others are likely to be enjoyable and responsive—or not—emerges from these first relationships. Infants and toddlers develop their beginning sense of other as kind, trustworthy, helpful, and fun in the embrace and enfolding (figuratively and literally) of the mother, father, and other special adults. Children learn "the other side of the relationship" in their interactions with the significant adults in their lives, and they then play out the behaviors and attitudes they learn with adults in their relationships with peers.

There is a "horizontal quality" (Russell, Pettit, & Mize, 1998) with the quality of parent–child attachment and children's sociability with peers. Toddlers view other toddlers with good relationship histories as attractive interactive partners (Jacobson & Wille, 1986). Social competence requires reciprocal interactions (Honig, 2002) that children learn in their first relationships with others.

In addition, a cultural style of interacting with others that has implications for peer behavior emerges in a child's first relationships (Chen, French, & Schneider, 2006; Vygotsky, 1978).

1.3. The toddler on the left shares his excitement with his friend.
PHOTO: CARLA MESTAS

Teachers cannot underestimate the importance of their relationships with infants and toddlers. Infants and toddlers need a satisfying emotional connection with their teachers that transcends physical caregiving and protection. The quality of the teacher–child relationship has a strong effect on the quality of the child's peer relationships (Howes, Hamilton, & Matheson, 1994; NICHD Early Child Care Research Network, 2001).

The parent–child and teacher–child relationships are a part of a network of other relationships that influence the experience of the child. The teacher–parent relationship, for example, influences the parent–child relationship *and* the teacher–child relationships.

As stated in its title, chapter 2 further explores the effect of relationships on relationships. The chapter delves into the effects of children's attachment with parents and teachers on children's emotional development, self-regulation, self-concept, and peer relationships; children's working models of relationships; and family, teacher, and peer relationship strategies that influence present and later social competence.

Social–Emotional Development Is the Foundation for Learning and Predicts Future Social and Academic Success

When considered within the context of a child's environment of relationships, the concept of school readiness is not exclusively a matter of fostering literacy and number skills but must also include the capacity to form and sustain positive relationships with teachers, children, and other adults, and develop the social and emotional skills for cooperating with others. (National Scientific Council on the Developing Child, 2004b, p. 6)

Our interest in infants and toddlers' social development is a key to their present and future social and academic success (National Scientific Council on the Developing Child, 2004b). How children behave socially as toddlers relates to their social competence at an older age (Hay, Payne, & Chadwick, 2004). Toddlers who are able to play well are more socially competent as preschoolers and less aggressive and withdrawn as 9-year-olds, whereas children who are more aggressive and withdrawn as preschoolers are more aggressive as 9-year-olds (Howes & Phillipsen, 1998). Children's rejection by peers can begin at toddler age (Hay et al., 2004; Rubin & Coplan, 2004) and continue into the elementary years if there is not adult facilitation of change (Farrington, 1995; Fox & Calkins, 1993; Rubin, 2002; Tremblay et al., 2004).

Early social competence and later academic success are related. Children need social competence to function well at school entrance and succeed in elementary school (Blair, 2002; Peth-Pierce, 2001). Children who are aggressive, do not have empathy, and cannot control their emotions with peers are not as likely to be successful in school. Others may not want to work or play with them, and their enjoyment of school suffers. Park and Welsh (1998) have described the Social Development Project, in which researchers have assessed more than 2,000 children from nine elementary schools, beginning when they were kindergartners. They reported that there is a strong link between social skills and academic performance. "Stable peer acceptance over the early school years protects children from early academic difficulties. Peer rejection presages early academic difficulties" (Park & Welsh, 1998, p. 32).

Howes and Phillipsen's (1998) discoveries concerning the continuity of social competence and challenges from ages 2 to age 9, coupled with research relating children's social competence to their academic success, should inspire parents and teachers to embrace fostering social skills among infants and toddlers who are in group care and education settings. Social and emotional development is a critical piece of school readiness.

It is important to remember that the early years are central to young children's later social, academic, and community success. The quality of their social experience is critical for their sense of well-being now and in their future.

Infants and Toddlers Are Capable, Competent, Curious, and Complex

We need to have "an openness to look for forms of communication, social influence, and coordinated action among young peers unlike those stressed for infant–parent encounters or even older peer encounters. . . ." (Eckerman & Didow, 2001, p. 328).

To figure out, to experiment, and to know—these are what infants and toddlers try to do. Infants and toddlers are discoverers on a voyage of peers learning how to communicate, make their needs known with peers, and learn the rules of physical contact and socialization. Children are constantly trying to make meaning in their lives and develop theories about how the world works through their active exploration (Piaget, 1936/1953). Infants and toddlers are making social discoveries from the beginning. Infants may crawl over another baby and are surprised when their mat mate reacts with a cry. They may think that other infants are just another object and try to taste their hair. They love to have their feet on each other and try to get another child's attention with their sounds. They explore cause-and-effect relationships with a poke or a squeal to make a peer cry out or laugh.

When we focus, we can see how curious infants and toddlers are about how their peers work, just as they are about how objects work, except that their peers are continually changing and are much more interesting than any object could be.

Infants and toddlers have many goals related to peer interaction, and they pursue these goals vigorously. An infant crawls toward another infant to check out a toy that he is waving in the air. Another tries to get his peer's attention through a series of yells. Another toddler has a goal of playing alone and crosses her arms to keep the other child out of her space. There often is a goal of being near another, even when conflicts come and go.

Toddlers are often "peer capable" and there is positive peer potential—much more than people may know. Imitation appears early and is an important factor in peer learning. Meltzoff (1985) and Bellagamba, Camaioni, and Colonnesi (2006) have demonstrated how able infants at 15 months of age are at imitating their peers and learning from them. Toddlers can adjust their social behavior to the age of their peer partner (Brownell, 1990). They use guided action (i.e., one child manages the interaction by guiding the activities of another child through prompting, demonstration, and affective signals in relation to a goal; see Eckerman & Didow's [2001] discussion of Verba's [1994] work). They engage in peer "conversations," which may be a series of glances, a kinesthetic dance (Capatides, Collins, & Bennett, 1996), or peer talk (Katz, 2004). Play emerges as an interest in each other and joins children together in cooperative and collaborative play by the end of the toddler years.

Adult knowledge of peer potential and development affects the adults' behavior with children. If adults do not know that children are capable of, for example, becoming empathetic with their peers, they may not provide the kind of support that children need to develop further their kindly attitudes. On the other hand, teachers who know that infants and toddlers are participating in an important social experience when they imitate others by pounding their small but mighty fists on the table, understand the learning potential of such experiences. If they know about development, teachers do not become upset when these behaviors occur and internally applaud and often even outwardly encourage these sometimes silly and meaningful behaviors, although at times the infant or toddler room may become noisy and the children boisterous.

Chapter 3—So Much More Than Parallel Play—discusses the intricacies of infants' and toddlers' development, social goals, and play. Topics include communication, coordination

(Didow & Eckerman, 2001), verbal and kinesthetic conversations (Capatides et al., 1996; Katz, 2004), and toddlers' social style (Lokken, 2000a, 2000b). The chapter provides specific strategies that support peer goals and promote peer expertise because, although infants and toddlers can be peer competent, curious, and capable, they need adult attention and support to support their budding skills (Honig & Thompson, 1997) and provide a peer-conducive environment.

Children Build Each Other's Competence and Understanding of Culture

> Interaction among children is a fundamental experience during the first years of life. (Malaguzzi, 1993, p. 11)

Tara, 12 months old, watches as Wanika bangs her toy on the floor with vigorous whacks. Tara picks up a toy and tries to smack her toy on the floor too. She looks at Wanika with a big smile on her face. This type of imitation of each other is an important way in which infants and toddlers learn.

AN IMPETUS FOR COMPETENCE

There is a movement that builds upon Vygotsky's [1978, p. 57] view that all the higher mental functions originate as actual relations between human individuals, such that every psychological function appears twice in development: first on the social level between people (intermentally) and then inside the child (intramentally). (Selby & Bradley, 2003, p. 198)

Play with playmates can lead to play that is more complex. The NICHD Early Child Care Research Network, commenting on Rubenstein and Howes' (Howes, 1990; Rubenstein & Howes, 1983) research, acknowledged that "play with age-mates, even among toddler-aged children, has been shown to produce increased positive affect and more complex interaction than solitary play, whether peer play occurs at home or in child care" (2001, p. 1480). As Brownell et al. (2006, p. 803) have noted, "[t]heorists have long maintained that critical social and cognitive developments are born in the context of cooperative play with other children" (Dunn, 1988; Garvey, 1990; Hartup, 1983; Piaget, 1936).

One of the ways in which children may improve their ability to control their emotions in healthy ways (emotional regulation) is in interaction with another. For example, Matte hugs another toddler (Sienna), whom she likes, just a little too tightly. When Sienna protests with a loud yell and a little shove, Matte releases Sienna and hugs her gently. Matte's desire to continue playing with her friend helps her control her strong urge to squeeze her playmate to show her affection and instead to use a more tender approach. Matte is learning about how to use self-regulation to interact successfully with peers.

CULTURE

When we focus on peers in the early years, we see that through peer experiences children have an opportunity to display and expand their culture.

> It is principally through interacting with others that children find out what the culture is about and how it conceives their view of the world. Unlike any other species, human beings deliberately teach each other in settings outside the ones in which the knowledge being taught will be used. (Bruner, 1996).

What things will they learn that are appropriate to do with peers? Do they hug, kiss, hit, bite, stay physically close, or keep their distance from others? Do they need to ask before they grab, or do they grab before they ask? Young children learn that each peer behaves differently, and yet there are similarities in how others like to be treated. They are learning about their peer culture and the broader cultural ways of others.

A teacher can notice and respect how children from different families and cultures express their social interests. "Often forgotten, however, is the extent to which cultural beliefs and norms play a role in the interpretation of the acceptability of individual characteristics, and the types and the ranges of interactions and relationships that are likely or permissible" (Rubin, 1998, p. 611). Chen et al. (2006) and Rubin (1998) have described how parents in the United States and China view children's shyness very differently, with shyness often as an encouraged trait in China and often as a discouraged trait in the United States. However, as cultures change in both China and the United States, parents' values concerning shyness may change as well, reminding teachers of the importance of becoming familiar with each family's goals for their child and how these goals may play out in peer relationships.

There Can Be a Joy in Peer Relationships—The Prosocial and Gleeful Experiences

In caring settings, peers can immensely enjoy each other's company.

> *While Juanita, Sarah's family child care provider, reads to four children nestled comfortably in her lap, Sarah (18 months old) touches Jacob's (8 months old) nose very gently. He smiles at Sarah and reaches out to touch her face. They both laugh and then turn back to focus on the interesting voice of their caregiver. In a few minutes, they repeat their playful interaction as they enjoy being together and sharing touch.*

Social interest begins early in children's lives. From the beginning, infants stare longer at faces that gaze intently back at them. Infants tune into the sounds of another baby crying and may begin to cry themselves (Hartup, 1970).

A toddler runs excitedly across a room because he sees another person just his size, takes the other child's hand in his, and walks with his height twin to see the world (adults' knees) together from the same level. Young children seem to pay attention to their similar others.

When we "see" infants and toddlers together, we begin to understand how meaningful peer relationships can be to them. Toddlers develop relationships with peers and become friends at younger ages than most have thought possible (Honig & Wittmer, 1996; Howes, 2000; Howes & Farver, 1987; Whaley & Rubenstein, 1994; Wittmer & Honig, 1994).

> **Relationships—"when two people bring out qualities in one another that are neither exhibited nor elicited in their other relationships." (Ross & Lollis, 1989, p. 1083)**

Toddlers enjoy being with a friend, and they hug, kiss, and play in a special way with their friend. Toddler friends help each other, share, and play games that are more complex than games they play with other peers. They work to sustain their relationships and grieve when the relationships end (Whaley & Rubenstein, 1994). For example, when 2-year-old Marta enters her child care room each morning with her mother or father, she looks to see if her friend Tina is there yet. If she is not, Marta looks sad and asks, "Where Tina go?" She enthusiastically greets Tina when she arrives, and they both say good-bye easily to their

1.4 and **1.5.** Two children enjoy being together and sharing touch.
Photo: Mark Herlinger

parents. Tina and Marta are an important part of each other's life. Their affection for each other has grown across the year that they have been together in their child care and development program.

Infants and toddlers are capable of prosocial feelings and behavior (Dunn, 1977; Hay, Castle, Davies, Demetriou, & Stimson, 1999; Hoffman, 1976; Howes & Farver, 1987; Pines, 1979; Zahn-Waxler, Radke-Yarrow, & King, 1979). They learn, in supportive environments, to help, defend, comfort, and cooperate with their peers. A toddler with a pleasant relationship history often looks concerned when another peer is unhappy, and whenever possible, he or she tries to find a way to comfort a tearful peer.

When infants and toddlers laugh, show delight, and experience joy and hilarity with each other, they are demonstrating toddler glee (Lokken, 2000a, 2000b). Children's laughter can echo across the playground when, as in one toddler program, two friends hold hands and twirl so fast around a metal pole that the teacher can only see their smiles.

Chapter 4 shares the many ways in which infants and toddlers delight us with their prosocial behavior and the adult strategies that support young children to experience the joy of being together.

Conflict and Biting—The Need for Proactive Strategies

> [C]onflicts can be quite social affairs . . . . Could experience in peer conflicts aid toddlers in coming to understand distinctions between themselves and others . . . ? (Eckerman & Peterman, 2001, pp. 343–344)

A reason to focus on peers in the early years is to understand the value and challenge of children's conflicts and develop proactive strategies concerning children's learning during times of discordance. Conflicts include times when one person does something and another person objects (Hay, 1984). Conflict is a clash of wills; for example, each child wanting a prized toy (because it looks so attractive in the hands of a peer) or a child resisting a hug from another. Conflict is different from aggression, which occurs when one child intentionally hurts or imposes her will on another.

When infants and toddlers are together, conflict happens and relates to peer competence (Vaughn, 1999). Children are learning about self and other during these inevitable experiences in group programs. Jacobson and Wille (1986) noted that as children engage in conflict, they need to keep in mind the intention of those with whom they are having the conflict. Children learn how to parlay conflicts into play, control strong emotions, and negotiate and cooperate.

In chapter 5, I share a variety of reasons why conflict occurs; why young children may bite, hit, kick, or scratch while learning to negotiate conflict; and the environmental and teacher strategies that help children think of the other.

When Children Are Challenged, They Need Relationship Support

> The timing of early experiences can matter, but, more often than not, the developing child remains *vulnerable* to risks and open to protective influences throughout the early years of life and into adulthood. (National Research Council & Institute of Medicine, 2001, p. 31)

The life challenges that children feel are often made visible with their peers. Peer relationships are a window into the relationship experiences of a child. For example, Twila's experience at home was traumatic, and she was now in a foster home. At 15 months of age in her Early Head Start program, Twila lashed out at her peers and tried to scratch them in the face if they came near her. Sometimes she angrily sought them out only to try to hurt them or push them away. In her short life, she had learned that she must protect herself from others and although she may want to approach another, she cannot trust others—even those who are her size—not to hurt her. She has learned that she must always be ready to defend herself. Her peer behavior tells us how vulnerable Twila feels at an early age.

Children may feel grief and despair, which causes them to withdraw from peers. They may feel fearful, angry, and aggressive with their peers. These children may have no interest in peers, or they may use strategies that are harmful to them and others. Teachers may ask families to remove the child from a program. Families then move the children from program to program while the challenging behaviors become ingrained. These sad, fearful, or angry children are especially challenging to teachers/caregivers, but we must remember that the children themselves are feeling challenged. Adults need sensitive understanding, empathy, and a mountain of strategies to support these challenged and challenging children. Now, in their infant and toddler years, lies the opportunity for adults to make a difference in these children's (and their families') lives that lasts a lifetime (Emde, 2001a).

Chapter 6 explores adults' creative strategies, on the basis of research evidence and individual child sensitivity, to communicate and collaborate with families and community agencies, create a safe environment for children, and promote children's mental health.

Day to Day the Relationship Way—Quality Programs Matter

> A relationship-based program fulfills the needs of children for emotional connections with adults and peers, a sense of belonging, learning, and mastery of their environment.

The last reason to focus on peer relationships in group settings is that the quality of programs profoundly influences how children experience each other, feel about themselves, and learn. Young children deserve a quality day that opens the door to a tomorrow of learning and well-being. Teachers' relationships with families, an important part of a program that focuses on relationships, also provide a framework of support for peer interactions.

Children live in communities in their infant and toddler programs. Lillvist (2005) has emphasized that, "[i]n the curriculum for the preschool [18 months–5 years in Sweden] it is stated that 'the preschool should encourage and strengthen the child's compassion and empathy of others,' and furthermore, that 'all activities should be characterized by care for the individual and aim at developing a sense of empathy and compassion for others.' " When programs focus on strengthening children's compassion for others, we can only imagine how safe and loving such an environment may feel to each child.

Each aspect of a program affects the interactions and relationships that infants and toddlers experience day to day with their peers in an early care and education program. Primary care, continuity of care, and continuity of group are key organizational constructs that build adult–child and peer relationships (Wittmer & Petersen, 2006). The ratios and group size influence how teachers provide nurturing, the curriculum, routines, and the responsive aspects of care that support or challenge peer interactions and relationships. For example, an infant in a crowded room experiences peers very differently than an infant who has room to crawl and space to rest with responsive, affectionate adults who support adult–child and peer relationships. A lack of materials, constant turnover, low pay, and lack of administrative support may hinder a teacher's good intentions.

Public policy decisions influence the quality of programs, which in turn affect peer interactions. The ingredients for external communities that support a caring community within a program include a national value for quality care and education programs, funding, collaboration among community agencies, and adequate teacher salaries to attract quality teachers who know the value of peer relationships.

Often we put peers in untenable situations with too many children and not enough teachers who have an education in early childhood. Teachers experience too little support and too little pay. In low-quality programs, children pay the price with their emotional and social development.

Quality affects children's peer skill and knowledge. Chapter 7 delves into how each aspect of a program and a national value for quality care and education programs influence how infants and toddlers experience their peers in program settings.

Summary

But in the end, the real reason for studying babies and young children is just that they are themselves intrinsically so valuable and interesting. When we look attentively, carefully, and thoughtfully at the things around us, they invariably turn out to be more interesting, more orderly, more complex, more strange, and more wonderful than we would ever have imagined. (Gopnik, Meltzoff, & Kuhl, 1999, p. 207)

Parents and caring teachers know the importance of social and emotional development for infants and toddlers. Young children's social development predicts and is the product of a humane, compassionate community that cares for the quality of life that children experience together. In a responsive program, teacher–parent, teacher–child, and child–child relationships are the key to children's emotional, social, and physical health. The topics introduced in this chapter are discussed in detail in chapters 2 through 7. Let us start with chapter 2, The Power of Relationships on Relationships.

References

Administration for Children and Families. (2007, June). *FFY 2005 CCDF data tables*. Washington, DC: U.S. Department of Health and Human Services, Child Care Bureau. Retrieved August 15, 2007, from www.acf.hhs.gov/programs/ccb/data/ccdf_data/05acf800/table13.htm

Bellagamba, F., Camaioni, L., & Colonnesi, C. (2006). Change in children's understanding of others' intentional actions. *Developmental Science, 9*(2), 182–188.

Blair, C. (2002). School readiness: Integrating cognition and emotion in a neurobiological conceptualization of children's functioning at school entry. *American Psychologist, 57*, 111–127.

Brownell, C. A. (1990). Peer social skills in toddlers: Competencies and constraints illustrated by same-age and mixed-age interaction. *Child Development, 61*, 838–848.

Brownell, C. A., Ramani, G. B., & Zerwas, S. (2006). Becoming a social partner with peers: Cooperation and social understanding in one-and two-year-olds. *Child Development, 77*(4), 803–821.

Bruner, J. (1996). What we have learned about early learning. *European Early Childhood Education Research Journal, 4*(1), 5–16.

Capatides, J., Collins, C. C., & Bennett, L. (1996). *Peer interaction in toddlers: Parallel play revisited.* Paper presented at the conference "Ask the child: Why, when, and how?" Teachers College, Columbia University, New York.

Capizzano, J., & Adams, G. (2000). *The hours that children under five spend in child care.* Washington DC: Urban Institute.

Chen, X., French, D., & Schneider, B. H. (Ed.). (2006). *Peer relationships in cultural context.* Cambridge, England: Cambridge University Press.

Didow, S. M., & Eckerman, C. O. (2001). Toddler peers: From nonverbal coordinated action to verbal discourse. *Social Development, 10*(2), 170–189.

Dunn, J. (1977). *Distress and comfort.* Cambridge, MA: Harvard University Press.

Eckerman, C. O., & Didow, S. M. (2001). *Peer and infant social/communicative development.* Oxford, England: Blackwell Publishers.

Eckerman, C. O., & Peterman, K. (2001). Peers and infant social/communicative development. In G. Bremner & A. Fogel (Eds.), *Blackwell handbook of infant development* (pp. 326–350). Oxford, England: Blackwell Publishers.

Emde, R. N. (1988). The effect of relationships on relationships: A developmental approach to clinical intervention. In R. A. Hinde & J. Stevenson-Hinde (Eds.), *Relation within families* (pp. 334–364). Oxford, England: Clarendon Press.

Emde, R. N. (2001a). A developmental psychiatrist looks at infant mental health challenges for Early Head Start: Understanding context and overcoming avoidance. *Zero to Three, 22*(1), 21–24.

Emde, R. N. (2001b). Foreword. In L. E. Gandini & C. P. Edwards (Eds.), *Bambini: The Italian approach to infant/toddler care* (pp. vii–xv). New York: Teachers College Press.

Emde, R. N., & Clyman, R. B. (1997). "We hold these truths to be self-evident": The origins of moral motives in individual activity and shared experience. In J. D. Noshpitz (Series Ed.), S. Greenspan, S. Weider & J. Osofsky (Vol. Eds.), *Handbook of child and adolescent psychiatry: Vol. I. Infants and preschoolers: Development and syndromes* (pp. 320–339). New York: Wiley.

Fabes, R. A., Hanish, L. D., & Martin, C. (2003). Young children at play: The role of peers in understanding the effects of child care. *Child Development, 74,* 1039–1043.

Farrington, D. P. (1995). The development of offending and antisocial behavior from childhood: Key findings from the Cambridge Study in Delinquent Development. *Journal of Child Psychology and Psychiatry, 36,* 929–964.

Fox, N. A., & Calkins, S. D. (1993). Pathways to aggression and social withdrawal: Interactions among temperament, attachment, and regulation. In K. H. Rubin & J. Asendorpf (Eds.), *Social withdrawal, inhibition, and shyness in childhood* (pp. 81–100). Hillsdale, NJ: Erlbaum.

Galardini, A. & Giovannini, D. (2001). Pistoia: Creating a dynamic, open system to serve children, families, and community. In L.Gandini & C. P. Edwards (Eds.), *Bambini. The Italian approach to infant/toddler care* (pp. 89–105). New York: Teachers College Press.

Gopnik, A., Meltzoff, A. N., & Kuhl, P. K. (1999). *The scientist in the crib. What early learning tells us about the mind*. New York: Harper Perennial.

Hartup, W. W. (1970). Peer interaction and social organization. In P. H. Mussen (Ed.), *Carmichael's manual of child psychology: Vol. 2* (3rd ed., pp. 87–113, 361–457). Baltimore: Brookes.

Hartup, W. W. (1979). Two social worlds: Family relations and peer relations. In M. Rutter (Ed.), *Scientific foundations of developmental psychiatry*. London: Heinmann.

Hartup, W. W. (1996). The company they keep: Friendships and their developmental significance. *Child Development, 67,* 1–13.

Hay, D. F. (1984). Social conflict in early childhood. In G. Whitehurst (Ed.), *Annals of child development* (Vol. 1, pp. 1–44). Greenwich, CT, JAI Press.

Hay, D. F. (2006). Yours and mine: Toddlers' talk about possessions with familiar peers. *The British Psychological Society, 24,* 39–52.

Hay, D. F., Payne, A., & Chadwick, A. (2004). Peer relations in childhood. *Journal of Child Psychology and Psychiatry, 45,* 84–108.

Hay, D. F., Castle, J., Davies, L., Demetriou, H., & Stimson, C. A. (1999). Prosocial action in very early childhood. *Journal of Child Psychology and Psychiatry, 40,* 905–916.

Hinde, R. A. (1979). *Towards understanding relationships*. London: Academic Press.

Hinde, R. A. (1987). *Individuals, relationships and culture*. Cambridge, England: University Press.

Hinde, R. A. (1995). A suggested structure for a science of relationships. *Personal Relationships, 2,* 1–15.

Hinde, R. A., & Stevenson-Hinde, J. (1976). Toward understanding relationships: Dynamic stability. In P. Bateson & R. Hinde (Eds.), *Growing points in ethology* (pp. 451–479). Cambridge, England: Cambridge University Press.

Hoffman, M. L. (1976). Empathy, role-taking, guilt and development of altruistic motives. In T. Lickona (Ed.), *Moral development and behavior* (pp. 124–143). New York: Holt, Rinehart, and Winston.

Honig, A. S. (2002). *Secure relationships: Nurturing infant/toddler attachment in early care settings.* Washington, DC: National Association for the Education of Young Children.

Honig, A., & Thompson, A. (1997). Parent information: Helping toddlers with peer group skills. *Zero to Three, 14* (5), 15–19.

Honig, A. S., & Wittmer, D. S. (1996). Helping children become more prosocial: Part II. Ideas for classrooms, families, schools, and communities. *Young Children, 51*(2), 61–70.

Howes, C. (1988). Peer interaction in young children. *Monographs of the Society for Research in Child Development, 53* (1, Serial No. 217).

Howes, C. (1990). Can the age of entry into child care and the quality of child care predict adjustment in kindergarten? *Developmental Psychology, 26* (2), 292–303.

Howes, C. (2000). *Social development, family, and attachment relationships.* In D. Cryer & T. Harms (Eds.), *Infants and toddlers in out-of-home care* (pp. 87–113). Baltimore: Brookes.

Howes, C., & Farver, J. (1987). Toddlers' responses to the distress of their peers. *Journal of Applied Developmental Psychology, 8,* 441–452.

Howes, C., Hamilton, C. E., & Matheson, C. (1994). Children's relationship with peers: Differential associations with aspects of the teacher–child relationship. *Child Development, 65,* 253–263.

Howes, C., & Phillipsen, L. (1998). Continuity in children's relationships with peers. *Social Development, 7*(3), 340–349.

Jacobson, J., & Wille, D. (1986). The influence of attachment pattern on developmental changes in peer interaction from the toddler to the preschool period. *Child Development, 57,* 338–347.

Katz, J. R. (2004). Building peer relationships in talk: Toddlers' peer conversations in childcare. *Discourse Studies, 6*(3), 329–347.

Lillvist, A. (2005). *Observations of social competence in the preschool—A comparison of children in need of special support and typically developing children.* Unpublished dissertation, Department of Social Sciences Research, Program CHILD, Mälardalen University, Västerås, Sweden. Available from anne.lillvist@mdh.se

Lokken, G. (2000a). The playful quality of the toddling style. *International Journal of Qualitative Education, 13*(5), 531–542.

Lokken, G. (2000b). Tracing the social style of toddler peers. *Scandinavian Journal of Educational Research, 44*(2), 163–176.

Mahler, M. S. (1975). *The psychological birth of the infant.* New York: Basic Books.

Malaguzzi, L. (1993). For an education based on relationships. *Young Children, 49*(1), 9–12.

Maslow, A. H. (1968). *Toward a psychology of being.* New York: Van Nostrand Reinhold.

Max Planck Society. (2006, March 5). Baby's helping hands: First evidence for altruistic behaviours in human infants and chimpanzees. *ScienceDaily.* Retrieved January 17, 2008, from www.sciencedaily.com /releases/2006/03/060303205611.htm

Meltzoff, A. (1995). Understanding the intentions of others: Re-enactment of intended acts by 18-month-old children. *Developmental Psychology, 31,* 838–850.

National Scientific Council on the Developing Child. (2004, Summer). *Young children develop in an environment of relationships* (Working Paper No. 1). Retrieved April 23, 2006, from www.developingchild.net/pubs/wp/Young_Children_Environment_Relationships.pdf

National Research Council & Institute of Medicine. (2000). *From neurons to neighborhoods: The science of early childhood development.* Committee on Integrating the Science of Early Childhood Development. In J. P. Shonkoff & D. A. Phillips (Eds.).Washington, DC: National Academy Press

NICHD Early Child Care Research Network. (2001). Child care and children's peer interaction at 24 and 36 months. *Child Development, 72*(5), 1478–1501.

Park, R. D., & Welsh, M. (1998). Social relationships and academic success. *Thrust for Educational Leadership, 28*(1), 32–34.

Peth-Pierce, R. A. (2001). *A good beginning: Sending America's children to school with the social and emotional competence they need to succeed.* Chapel Hill, NC: The Child Mental Health

Foundation and Agencies Network. Retrieved on August 15, 2007, from http://209.85.165.104/search?q=cache:U2iihzqizvMJ:www.casel.org/downloads/goodbeginning.pdf+America%27s+children+to+school+with+the+social+and+emotional+competence&hl=en&ct=clnk&cd=1&gl=us

Piaget, J. (1953). *The origins of intelligence in the child.* New York: International Universities Press. (Original work published 1936)

Pines, M. (1979, June). Good samaritans at age two? *Psychology Today,* 66–73.

Ross, H. S., & Lollis, S. P. (1989). A social relations analysis of toddler peer relationships. *Child Development, 60*(5), 1082–1092.

Rubenstein, J., & Howes, C. (1983). Social-emotional development in day care: Role of peers and of individual differences. *Advances in Education and Day Care, 3,* 13–45.

Rubin, K. (1998). Social and emotional development from a cultural perspective. *Developmental Psychology, 34,* 611–615.

Rubin, K. (2002). *The friendship factor.* New York: Penguin Books.

Rubin, K. H., & Coplan, R. (2004). Paying attention to and not neglecting social withdrawal and social isolation. *Merrill-Palmer Quarterly, 50*(4), 506–535.

Russell, A., Pettit, G. S., & Mize, J. (1998). Horizontal qualities in parent-child relationships: Parallels with and possible consequences for children's peer relationships. *Developmental Review, 18,* 313–352.

Selby, J. M., & Bradley, B. S. (2003). Infants in groups: A paradigm for the study of early social experience. *Human Development, 46*(4), 197–221.

Shanok, R. S., Wittmer, D., & Capatides, J. (1997, December). *Peer play groups: Enabling individual growth in very young children.* Presented at the ZERO TO THREE National Training Institute, Nashville, TN.

Tremblay, R. E., Nagin, D. S., Se'guin, J. R., Zoccolillo, M., Zelazo, P., Boivin, M., et al. (2004). Physical aggression during early childhood: Trajectories and predictors. *Pediatrics, 114*(1), e43–e50. Available online at www.pediatrics.org/cgi/content/full/114/1/e43

UNICEF. (2002). *United Nations: Convention on the Rights of the Child.* Retrieved November 17, 2007, from www.unicef.org/crc/index_30160.html

Vaughn, B. E. (1999). Power is knowledge (and vice versa): A commentary on "On winning some and losing some: A social relations approach to social dominance in toddlers." *Merrill-Palmer Quarterly, 45*(2), 215.

Verba, M. (1994). The beginnings of collaboration in peer interaction. *Human Development, 37,* 125–139.

Vygotsky, L. S. (1978). *Mind in society: The development of higher psychological processes.* Cambridge, MA: Harvard University Press.

Warneken, F., & Tomasello, M. (2006, March 3). Altruistic helping in human infants and young chimpanzees. *Science, 311*(5765), 1301–1303.

Whaley, K., & Rubenstein, T. (1994). How toddlers "do" friendship: A descriptive analysis of naturally occurring friendships in a group childcare setting. *Journal of Social and Personal Relationships, 11,* 383–400.

Wittmer, D. S., & Honig, A. S. (1994). Encouraging positive social development in young children: Part I. Strategies for teachers. *Young Children, 49*(5), 4–12.

Wittmer, D. L., & Petersen, S. H. (2006). *Infant and toddler development and responsive program planning: A relationship-based approach.* Upper Saddle River, NJ: Prentice Hall.

Women in the Labor Force & U.S. Bureau of Labor Statistics. (2005, May). *Women in the labor force: A data book. Employment status by sex, presence and age of children, race, and Hispanic or Latino ethnicity.* Washington, DC: U.S. Bureau of Labor Statistics.

Zahn-Waxler, C., Radke-Yarrow, M., & King, R. A. (1979). Child rearing and children's prosocial initiations toward victims of distress. *Child Development, 50*(2), 319–330.

2

THE POWER OF RELATIONSHIPS ON RELATIONSHIPS

> **Social and emotional competence is rooted in the relationships that infants and toddlers experience in the early years of life. (Robin Peth-Pierce, 2001, p. vii)**

What is an 18-month-old feeling when he persistently tries to give a ball to a baby on a teacher's lap, even though the baby cannot hold it well and continuously drops it on the ground? What has he learned in other relationships that guide him to understand that the baby's smile means that she is getting pleasure from the activity? What has he learned in previous relationships with adults and peers about reciprocity and mutual enjoyment in give-and-take games?

This chapter attempts to answer these questions by focusing on how the quality of infants and toddlers' relationships with their primary caregivers—parents and teachers—influences children's peer relationships. The third chapter covers the growth of a child's ability to relate to peers—a parallel but different path (Hay, Payne, & Chadwick, 2004).

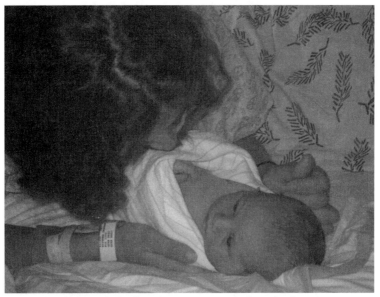

2.1. As they look into each other's eyes, a reciprocal relationship begins.
PHOTO: JOHN CLAUSON

There has been a recognition of the effect of relationships on relationships for many years (Brownell, 1986; Emde, 1988; Hay & Ross, 1982; Hinde & Stevenson-Hinde, 1988; Rubin, Bukowski, & Parker, 1998). Families, teachers, and other professionals influence children's peer relationships by the way they (i.e., the adults) behave and feel in their relationships with the children, both in the moment and over time. Children learn about themselves and others with the significant adults in their lives.

Although children have different experiences with peers than they have with adults, these peer experiences include elements of human communication and connectedness that are similar with all relationships. What children learn in their first and primary relationships with adults about how to relate to others influences how they interact with peers.

Sears and Sears (2003) describe how their 4-month-old baby seems aware of his parents' love, how they are emotionally connected, and how they communicate with each other with expressive eyes and face. The quality of this child's first relationships with caring adults influences his expectations for future relationships.

> **One of the most exciting things about our four-month-old's development is the way he reaches for me with his eyes. He expresses thanks with his eyes. He turns his face and eyes toward me. They are so expressive and adoring. He appears to be fully aware of me as his source of love, nourishment, and well-being. He craves my presence and totally enjoys our togetherness. It's a love affair, full-blown. I recognize the love in his eyes as one more emotion that he's capable of expressing. (Sears & Sears, 2003, p. 480)**

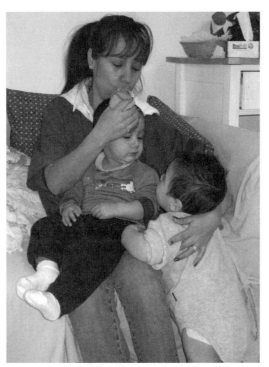

2.2. Infants and toddlers learn how to care for each other as they experience empathy and affection.
PHOTO: ASHANTE BUTCHER

Three Aspects of Adult–Child Relationships to Consider

Sara, just 4 months old, gazed at a toy that her care teacher had in his hand. The puppet danced in the air and Sara smiled. She then turned her gaze to her teacher and she smiled even more. Her care teacher smiled back and Sara felt the warmth from his smile as they connected and communicated across space.

Relationships, such as that between Sara and her care teacher, have many dimensions. As you read this chapter, there are three aspects of adult–child relationships to consider that were introduced briefly in chapter 1. The first is that infants and toddlers have a remarkable capacity to relate to others. The second aspect emphasizes what children bring to the adult–child relationship (transactional theory). A piece of the second aspect is that both children's biological characteristics—including temperament—and their social experiences influence their behavior and attitudes (Hinde, 1992). The third aspect supports a cultural and individual family view of relationships (sociocultural theory; Chen, French, & Schneider, 2006; Rubin, 1998; Vygotsky, 1978). All three of these aspects of relationships influence how we think about the effect of relationships on relationships.

Relationship-Based Theory

As discussed in chapter 1, children are innately sociable and equipped to relate to their primary caregivers, other adults, and their peers in dyads or in groups (Nash & Hay, 2003; Selby & Bradley, 2003). Theorists and researchers seem to agree that babies have "powerful innate emotions of human relating" (Trevarthen, 2001, p. 95) and remarkable relational capacities. In the past, many have thought that babies were only able to interact successfully with adults, but research and observations of infants and toddlers tell us differently. ". . . infants are biologically prepared for social relations with a variety of individuals rather than for only specific attachments" (Nash & Hay, 2003, p. 223). Infants and toddlers' active goal of relating to adults and peers, their ability to read emotional expressions, and their ability to express emotions drive their interactions with both adults and peers.

Another aspect of relationship-based theory is to consider that parent–child and teacher–child relationships are a part of a network of other relationships that influence adults' teaching styles, stress levels, and how they care for their children. Parents' sensitivity or aggressiveness influences a child's behavior; however, the parents' network of relationships influences the parents' ability to parent. For example, the parents' or teachers' past relationship history, the amount and quality of support from other family members, or employment relationships (Bronfenbrenner, 2004) may influence the quality of their parenting. To support peer relationships, we must support families and teachers *and* view young children within a network of relationships.

What infants and toddlers learn about themselves and others in their early relationships with adults sets up their expectations for how others will treat them (Ziv, Oppenheim, & Sagi-Schwartz, 2004) and how they learn to manage their emotions (Trevarthen, 2001). In their first relationships with adults, infants and toddlers learn interaction and communication attitudes and skills that they will use in their peer interactions, and most important, they learn whether they are lovable, enjoy relationships, and are competent persons who can "make things happen" in relationships.

However, although the personality of children becomes more stable as they develop and their first relationships with adults influence their relational capacity—their personality and general approach to relationships—they will not act the same with everyone (Hay & Ross,

1982; Ross, Conant, Cheyne, & Alevizos, 1992; Ross & Lollis, 1989). Peer interactions occur within relationships, and the quality of that relationship influences them. Children (and adults) respond to and converse with their peers differently (Hay & Ross, 1982; Katz, 2004) on the basis of the behavior of those peers and the quality of the relationships with those persons—the duration, past experience, and responsiveness of the other person.

Children, because of their view that others will treat them well, may eagerly approach another toddler. However, if that toddler does not treat him well, then he may ignore that toddler in future interactions. Ross et al. (1992), in their study of Kibbutz toddlers in a group setting in Israel, found that the same toddler might ignore a particular toddler and become fast friends with another. She describes some children as "fighting friends" or "mutually ignoring friends." Perhaps this is because children's primary relational capacity is the ability to read the emotional cues from others and behave accordingly. There may be a relational capacity that results in a child's behaving differently depending on the peer's behavior while he or she maintains a general desire to relate to others.

Transactional View

Transactional theory (Sameroff & Feise, 2000; Sameroff & MacKenzie, 2003) tells us that the influence between adults and children is bidirectional with children's past and present behavior, temperament, and biological characteristics affecting adults' behavior. Children's personality, gender, and age influence how adults interact with them and influence how adult behavior affects them (NICHD Early Child Care Research Network, 2004; Rubin, 2002).

> **Not all difficult infants evidence behavior problems in the preschool years, and there are often complex interactions between child characteristics and aspects of parental behavior that together predict which difficult children will and will not show problem behavior at later ages. (NICHD Early Child Care Research Network, 2004, p. 45)**

A child's effect on adult behavior may occur on one occasion or be a continuing characteristic of an adult and child's relationship. In the immediate sense, a teacher's good mood may dissipate with a child who has an earache and needs immediate attention. However, a child's continuous irritable mood could have an ongoing negative effect on the quality of the teacher's relationship with the child.

Children with different temperaments, for example, require more sensitive adult–child interactions (Ziv & Cassidy, 2002). Irritable babies may need help to gain a sense of control over their emotions, a characteristic that could affect their peer relationships (NICHD Early Child Care Research Network, 2004).

> **Maternal negative affect and intrusiveness in the second and third years of life were more strongly predictive of later behavior problems among irritable than nonirritable toddlers. Toddlers who were more positive in mood were less susceptible to the influence of negative material behavior. (NICHD Early Child Care Research Network, 2004, p. 45)**

Infants rated as having a difficult temperament at 1 and 6 months were significantly less anxious or depressed at ages 2 and 3 years if they had mothers who had been more sensitive (Warren & Simmens, 2005).

In addition, children react differently to parents on the basis of their temperament and other characteristics. For example, mothers' negative guidance strategies (Belsky, Hsieh, &

Crnic, 1998) and mothers' less sensitive and flexible behaviors (Shaw & Vondra, 1995) predict later behavior problems more for children with an irritable temperament than for children with more positive moods.

Not only do the features of the adults' relationships with the children influence the quality of their peer relationships, but also the quality of children's peer relationships affects the adults who interact with them. For example, a peer's relationship history with another peer might influence whether parents or teachers intervene when the two children are in a conflict with each other. Knowing that these two peers often work things out or that they typically end up biting each other determines whether adults observe with care or leap to separate the two.

There is another layer of the effect of relationships on relationships. A child's experience with present and past peers also influences the nature and quality of that child's future peer relationships, both with a particular child or peers in general. This effect of past peer experiences on future peer relationships is explored in chapter 3 of this book.

Cultural and Individual Family View (Sociocultural View)

A cultural style of interacting that has implications for peer behavior emerges in a child's first relationships (sociocultural and ecological theory). Infants and toddlers are part of a family and culture. Vygotsky (1978) discussed how the self is defined within a social context. Infants and toddlers learn language, for example, in a social context first and through language they internalize many of the values expressed in that language.

Cecelia, a 2-year-old, stays near the teacher most of the day, whereas Sylvia eagerly runs to other toddlers to try to entice them to play. There may be temperament differences between these two children; however, culture may also contribute to their approach to peers and adults. Chen, French, and Schneider (2006) in their edited book, *Peer Relationships in a Cultural Context,* described how culture influences the beliefs, values, and practices of young children as related to peer relationships. Infants and toddlers learn, although they certainly cannot articulate, the family's value in helping them become interdependent or independent. These cultural and family values play out in the child's peer interactions. One toddler, who lives in a family that emphasizes more individualistic characteristics, could vigorously express how she has a right to play with a toy as long as she would like without interference from others. Another toddler raised in a more collectivistic society that values interdependence and limited personal privacy might give up a toy easily when another toddler takes it away (Chen et al., 2006).

Family constellations may differ and affect how infants and toddlers interact with their peers. Some children are accustomed to many children and adults around them at all times and, in fact, may sleep with their parents or siblings. They like being close to others and feel most comfortable when they are sitting near other children or on an adult's lap. Other children experience families without other children or relatives nearby, and are used to playing alone. They may become upset when a group of children converges on them, and they may seek out a corner of the room to play alone in their own private space.

There are also cultural differences in how sociable or active children are with peers, how they negotiate conflict, how emotional or expressive they are in relationships, and how certain children are rejected or accepted by peers on the basis of assertiveness or shyness.

Culture may also affect peer relationships by the way that social experiences are organized in a particular country or society. In Sweden, most toddlers enter a preschool after the 15- to 18-month maternal/paternal leave has ended. In the United States, 60% of infants attend some type of child care program, causing them to experience peer interactions with strangers at an earlier age. An institution in one society might organize children in programs by same-age groups, whereas others might emphasize multi-age groups. These structural differences in how social experiences are organized reflect and support different cultural values for social experience.

A cultural view also reminds us to take care when reading research results. Often researchers conduct their studies with children from a particular ethnic group or culture, and we should not generalize the results to children and families of all cultures. In addition, each culture, and each family within that culture, has its unique way of interacting and value for relationships.

What Are Babies Learning in Their First Relationships?

We know that babies need relationships with adults who are more competent than they are to survive. Infants and toddlers need adults who feed them, protect them from danger, and change their diapers. We also know that infants and toddlers need affirmative relationships with parents, family members, teachers, and peers to develop a strong and generally positive sense of themselves and others. Relationships "support a young child's needs for care and affection, shared meaning, and a social place" (Trevarthen et al., 2005, p. 1). However, what *exactly* are infants and toddlers learning in relationships with adults about themselves and others that makes a difference in how they interact with their peers?

Learning About Self With Others and Physical Objects

Distinguishing between self and other is a lifelong task and begins very early in an infant's life. Daniel Stern (2000) emphasizes that infants have a sense of themselves as separate from others from the very beginning of life. Infants and toddlers learn about the self in their relationships with others (Bigelow, 2001), and it is within the context of relationships

2.3. Infants and toddlers need affirmative relationships with adults and peers to develop a strong and generally positive sense of themselves and others.
PHOTO: ASHANTE BUTCHER

that an infant or toddler begins to define who he is (Mintz, 1995). Rochat (2001) empha-sized that infants learn about self, other, and physical objects in their first relationships with adults and peers. It seems that infants and toddlers are busy figuring out "who am I?" (Bullock & Lütekenhaus, 1990) as they relate to others and the world.

Self-confidence is an aspect of self that is developing. Infants and toddlers gain a sense of self-confidence and competence in adult–child relationships that transfer to peer rela-tionships (Sroufe, Egeland, & Carson, 1998). For example, maternal limit-setting patterns affect toddler self-concept and social competence. Children (at 12, 24, and 36 months) of mothers with a teaching style were more socially competent at 3 years of age than children of mothers with an indirect or power-based approach (Houck & LeCuyer-Maus, 2002).

A sense of self-worth develops within adult–child relationships. Jeree Pawl stated that "everyone deserves the experience of existing in someone's mind" (1995, p. 5). Children who positively "exist" in someone's mind feel worthy of care and attention from others. As infants and toddlers look into the eyes of the adults who care for them, their sense of self-worth flourishes if they see admiration, empathy when they are distressed, and the look of love.

Learning About Other in Relationship With Self

Daniel Stern (2000) wrote that the main task of infants is to connect with others. As they grow through infancy, they also learn that others are separate from them. When a parent says, "Ouch" as the infant squeezes a finger too hard, the infant begins to register that the other has feelings. Their use of the words such as "mine," "yours," and "That's Harry's" at around 18 months of age reveals their thinking about others as separate from themselves (Hay, 2006).

One sign that they are beginning to understand that the self is distinct from others and that others may have different feelings from themselves is when they begin to use social referencing. They experience *intersubjectivity*:

> [T] the knowledge that the baby's own thoughts and feelings can be known by others and that they can understand the thoughts and feelings of others. They begin to use the facial expressions and emotional tone of others as a way to interpret the meaning of events in their environment. (Rochat, 2001, p. 94)

At approximately 7 months of age, babies look to their mother or father for cues that the activity they are about to embark on is safe or dangerous. If a parent looks worried, the infant often lays low rather than creep forward. With an adult smile that says, "all is safe," the baby is off and moving. They look to their favorite adult when a stranger appears to see the facial expression of the adult. If it is welcoming to the stranger, the baby usually begins to relax. This ability to socially reference indicates that the infants are beginning to know that others have thoughts and feelings that may be different from their own and that they can understand what those feelings may mean for them.

In addition to experiencing intersubjectivity, they learn that others are intentional and can actually have intentions different from their own.

> Perceiving and understanding others as intentional are critical prerequisites for the social and cognitive development of infants. In particular, this understanding is vital for the emer-gence of language, symbolic functioning, and theories of mind. Without an ability to detect others as intentional, it is hard for us to imagine how children could eventually learn to use conventional signs (language) to communicate and understand that something (a verbal sign) can stand for something else (be a referent). (Rochat, 2001, p. 152)

Young children begin to gain knowledge about other's mental states.

> [C]ognitive advances during infancy permit older infants to come to see people in very different ways from how they view other objects. They learn to see others as *compliant*

agents, beings similar to themselves who behave under their own power and who have the capacity to respond to infants' requests. (Feldman, 2007, p. 183)

Why would they communicate to others—their mothers, for example—to get them "more milk" if they did not see her as separate from themselves, intentional, and even compliant?

Knowledge of self and other, then, are two of the most important things that young children learn in their first relationships with adults that influence how they relate to peers. Of course, they are also learning this in their first peer interactions as well.

How Do Relationships Work Their Magic? Developmental Pathways From Adult–Child Interactions to Peer Interactions

How do adult–child relationships influence peer relationships? How do children learn skills and attitudes in their adult–child relationships that influence peer relationships? We know that infants and toddlers' minds are busy from the moment they are born. They actively process information, constantly problem-solve, and continuously classify information about themselves and others. They learn quickly and remember their experiences through both affective and cognitive schemes (Emde, 1988). They also seem biologically ready to learn from relationships, imitate adults, and develop a sense of self as capable—or not. They learn skills for how to engage in reciprocal interactions, and they develop ideas about what others are like and how they will treat them. Let's look more closely at how relationships work their magic.

"I'm Ready for Relationships"—A Biological Capacity

Some researchers think that there is an initial social impulse in infants that equips infants to interact with both parents and peers (Hay, 1985; Nash & Hay, 2003). As discussed in chapter 1, there seems to be a biological capacity and motivation to interact with others. Babies are ready for relationships, not just with their favorite adults but also with peers (Lewis, 2005). Emde (2001, p. ix) emphasized that "the human infant is active and social from the start." Murphy (1992, p. 3) described this biological capacity in the following way: "I think we have to say that babies are wired to respond prosocially to a prosocial environment." On the other hand, it makes sense that babies may be wired to respond with defensiveness, anger, and hostility in a hostile environment.

"I Internalize"

Murphy (1992) believed that infants internalize experiencing how to be with others.

> The baby learns a great deal, as well, from his mother's response to his distress, as she comforts him when he cries or whimpers. During the early years, the baby or young child may be uncomfortable or distressed when he is hungry, when mother "disappears," when he is bumped accidentally, or during the routines of bathing, shampooing, or dressing. Mother's comforting voice, pats, rubs, and kisses evoke the endorphins in the baby's brain—they actually do make him feel better. Thus, the baby absorbs experiences of helpful response to his distress as a normal part of life and internalizes the experience. In time, he not only empathizes with but also *responds* to the distress of mother, and others. (Murphy, 1992, p. 3)

"I Respond to Your Attention"

Other researchers propose that infants and toddlers learn through adult social contingency or reinforcement of certain behaviors how to be with others (Bigelow, 2001). They learn what behavior to repeat when others respond to their bites with consternation or their hugs with warm cuddles (Nadel, Carchon, Kervella, Marcelli, & Reserbat-Plantey, 1999).

"You Help Me With My Emotions"

Emotional competency is a pathway to social as well as academic competence (Denham et al., 2003; Eisenberg & Fabes, 1992; Eisenberg et al., 1993; Fabes et al., 1999; NICHD Early Child Care Research Network, 2004; Raver, 2003)

> **Emerging research on early schooling suggests that the relationships that children build with peers and teachers are based on children's ability to regulate emotions in prosocial versus antisocial ways and those . . . relationships then serve as a "source of provisions" that either help or hurt children's chances of doing well academically. . . . (Raver, 2003, p. 1)**

One can easily see in the following example how emotional competence led to social competence. A 4-year-old and her 1-year-old sister were taking a bath together. The older sibling, who thought that the younger sibling was being a pest, turned to her mom, who was by the tub. The older sibling exclaimed with intense negative feeling, "Ooh, I just want to hit her." Mom responded with, "You feel like hitting her, but I'm so glad that you told me rather than hit her." The 4-year-old in the example demonstrated emotional competence as she expressed her feelings rather than physically hurting her younger sibling.

EMOTIONAL REGULATION. Emotional regulation involves the ability to express emotions and to control them (Siegel, 1999), and there is strong evidence that children develop emotional competence in their adult–child relationships (Feldman & Klein, 2003; Gergely & Watson, 1996; Kagan & Carter, 1996; NICHD Early Child Care Research Network, 2004; Spinrad, Stifter, Donelan-McCall, & Turner, 2004; Thompson, 1994). Siegel (1999, p. 156) defined self-regulation as "the manner in which the process called the 'self' comes to regulate its own processes." In other words, the self begins to be able to manage both physical movements and emotional reactions. We all need emotional regulation to succeed in our work and social interactions (NICHD Early Child Care Research Network, 2004) and as children develop, their ability to manage difficult emotions influences the quality of their peer relationships.

> **[H]uman emotions constitute the fundamental value system the brain uses to help organize its functioning. The regulation of emotions is thus the essence of self-organization. The communication with and about emotions between parent and infant directly shapes the child's ability to organize the self. (Siegel, 1999, p. 278)**

The following example of a dad with his mobile infant demonstrates how infants and toddlers, in their relationships with adults, learn self-regulation and emotional regulation.

Siri (15 months old) runs across the inviting, wide-open, and long hallway of the health care facility, almost knocking down several adult patients. His dad, following close behind, catches up to him, takes his hand, and gently guides him back to some steps where Siri can practice going up and down, one foot up at a time. With this simple act, the father helps Siri regulate or adjust his behavior to the surroundings. Siri begins to learn that he cannot run pell-mell through a hallway when there are many others present. Left to run without the father's guidance, Siri might quickly get "out of control" and bang into others as his emotions and physical activity escalate. Later, in child care, we can see his attempt to self-regulate. Siri sometimes shows self-regulation as he runs across the room and stops himself as he skids up to another toddler who is unsteady on his feet.

AFFECT DYSREGULATION Those infants and toddlers who have a difficult time with affect dysregulation—managing their strong negative emotions—(NICHD Early Child Care Research Network, 2004) are more likely to have a difficult time with social interactions with peers. One can imagine that a toddler who always has a scowl on his face, feels sad much of the time, or becomes angry easily probably will not have other toddlers approaching him too often.

We can observe children's negative feelings in their interactions with their primary caregivers. "Children's inability to control negative affect in early interactions with their caregivers may forecast continuing difficulties with affective regulation across multiple contexts" (NICHD Early Child Care Research Network, 2004, p. 44). However, don't infants and toddlers often express anger and sadness with their caregivers?

We know that infants and toddlers are just developing their ability to control their emotions and often feel dysregulated. They have a difficult time when they are intent on turning the TV off and on and (from their perspective) an "interfering" adult tries to stop them. They do not have the language to express their emotional needs and feelings. They may feel grouchy, angry, sad, bad tempered, and testy when they are tired. However, if they usually feel these negative feelings and continuously experience affect dysregulation with their primary caregivers, there may be a problem with affect regulation with others in *many* situations.

2.4. These children's positive affect supports successful social interactions.
PHOTO: ASHANTE BUTCHER

HOW TO SUPPORT EMOTIONAL REGULATION   Young children rely on adults to help them control their emotions by comforting, supporting, acknowledging, and scaffolding alternatives (NICHD Early Child Care Research Network, 2004) and by using warm control in a discipline situation (Feldman & Klein, 2003). If adults do not know how to help their children control their emotions, or if they think that comforting children causes them to become demanding, then a cycle of negative emotions between the parents and their children may develop. "Strong or persistent negative affect in the context of the caregiver–child relationship may reflect a lack of mutual cooperation, harmony, or support as toddlers and preschoolers grapple with stage-salient issues such as establishing autonomy and learning to cooperate with others" (NICHD Early Child Care Research Network, 2004, p. 45). Children who experience less than harmonious relationships with significant adults seem to experience less harmonious relationships with peers.

Carson and Parke (1996) also have explained that children count on adults to help them regulate their strong emotions and seem to be particularly sensitive to parents' negative affect. These researchers, in a study of 41 families, found that preschoolers whose fathers respond to their young children's anger or other negative affect with pouting, whining, anger, teasing, mocking, or boredom (defined as negative affect), shared less with their peers in the preschool classroom, were more verbally aggressive, and avoided others. Children who responded to their father's unhelpful, unemotional, excessively emotional, and angry feelings with their own negative affect were described by their teachers as being more physically aggressive. It seems that the preschoolers learned to respond to or escalate another's negativity with negativity of their own. At the same time, during these negative cycles of interaction, the preschools were *not* learning strategies to regulate strong emotions.

"I Do What You Do"—Imitation

An adult places her palm gently on the small baby. The 12-month-old reaches out to pat the baby as well. Another adult gets a bandage for a peer to make an "owie" feel better. The toddlers in the room watch her and soon they are going to the safe cupboard to get a bandage for a friend whenever an "owie" emerges. A parent smacks her 4-year-old across the face when she will not stop crying. The observant toddler in that home smacks her peer when she does not move out of her way.

Infants and toddlers learn how to interact with others by imitating them (Eckerman & Didow, 1996). "Do as they do, not as they say," is the infants' and toddlers' motto. They progress significantly between 9 and 14 months in their ability to imitate adults (Agnetta & Rochat, 2004; Hanna & Meltzoff, 1993; Meltzoff, 1985). Trevarthen (2003) described how imitation is a way of being sociable. When children imitate another, they share an experience together.

Researchers Forman, Aksan, and Kochanska (2004) found that children's willingness and ability to imitate parents is a pathway to preschool-age conscience and thus is an important factor in children's early moral development. Infants who were more likely to imitate their mothers at 14 and 22 months of age were more likely to demonstrate guilt and other behaviors indicative of a conscience as preschoolers. Forman et al. (2004) proposed that mobile infants' willingness to imitate their mothers reflected the children's receptiveness to their parents' guidance.

"I'm Busy Trying to Make Sense of Things"

Infants and toddlers actively organize their experiences (Piaget, 1936/1953). They are sensitive to perceptual information (Rochat, 2001) and organize sensory information constantly. They categorize this information—which adults are nice and which peers touch gently. Emde (1988) discussed how children transform this information into represented relationships in the form of "cognitive schemes, affective themes, and social values" (p. 335). A boy's cognitive scheme that girls don't play with blocks, legitimately developed on the basis of his individual experiences, plays out in peer relationships until some type of dissonance occurs (several girls playing with blocks) that causes him to rethink his ideas.

"I Learn What to Expect from Others"

When infants or toddlers feel that adults understand their communication attempts, reciprocate their affection, and meet their needs for protection, they go forth in the peer world with an expectation for positive interactions with others. Ziv et al. (2004) found that children who felt secure with their mother at 12 months, as opposed to children who did not feel secure, expect that others will treat them well at approximately 7 years of age and are surprised when they do not. "Secure children expected others to be emotionally and instrumentally available to them . . ." (Ziv et al., 2004, p. 327).

"I Do a Dance With You"—A Sense of Reciprocity

Reciprocity is the mutual involvement of two people experiencing each other through give and take communication—each taking turns in a dance of shared and joint interactions. One responds to the other, and the other responds in turn. Two people experience being in tune with each other. Infants and toddlers learn about reciprocity in their experiences with their favorite adults and later they experience it with their peers; for example, when one child rolls a ball and the other child rolls it back. In the following vignette (Forman & Hall, 2005b), a sense of reciprocity is established as a 12-month-old (Sarah) and her teacher (Leah) experience a nonverbal conversation through their drumming activity.

Together, sharing a space with a drum between them, the infant taps the drum with her fingertips. Leah responds by using her fingertips to drum lightly.

> Excited by Leah's acknowledgement of her initial hits on the drum, Sarah swings her body in a playful manner. Realizing that Leah is "listening" to her, Sarah hits the drum twice to "answer." Leah returns Sarah's two hits with two of her own. Leah wonders, "If I hit the drum twice, just like Sarah did, will she understand that I am copying her? And, if Sarah understands that I am copying her, will she respond by copying me in return?" Seemingly processing the conversation thus far, Sarah gazes at Leah and ponders her next action. Sarah decides to hit the drum twice. (Forman & Hall, 2005b, p. 2)

When reading the vignette one can think about how, if infants and toddlers feel the satisfaction of reciprocal interactions with adults, they may strive for the same feeling of satisfaction with peers.

> **The experience of a satisfying, reciprocal relationship that meets the child's needs for comfort and security leads the child to value the relationship and become more amenable to socialization efforts. (NICHD Early Child Care Research Network, 2004, p. 46)**

"I Learn How to Communicate"

Infants and toddlers learn to communicate within their important adult–child relationships. Hay (2006) emphasized that toddlers' and 2-year-olds' growing conversational ability promotes social development.

"You Help Me Learn"—Scaffolding Social Interactions

In the following vignette (Forman & Hall, 2005a, p. 1), the adult (George) supports two toddlers as they play with cars to become more purposeful and cooperative in their play.

Yellow and White, each about 2 years old, are playing with small toy cars on a raised platform. George, a visiting adult, enters the game. Throughout this episode George looks for opportunities to increase the complexity of the children's play. He is careful not to voice the details of his own actions, but instead he adds descriptions of effects, thus providing the children with the opportunity to invent their own strategies. By the end of the episode, the children's play with cars becomes more purposive . . . the shape of the game changes from parallel-play (with both children rolling cars at once) to role-play (where the tasks are differentiated: one rolls three cars at a time; the other catches and puts them in a basket).

By supporting or scaffolding the play "just enough" and not too much, George helped these 2-year-olds cooperate with each other rather than compete. The children had fun and learned about themselves as cooperative partners in play.

Summary of the Magic of Relationships

In summary, there are many developmental pathways from the adult–child (dyadic) and family–child (triadic or more) relationship to children's success with peers. Infants' and toddlers' attachment relationships with the special adults in their lives also play a part.

Attachment Relationships

Many researchers who study attachment have concluded that children develop a "working model of relationships" with their primary caregivers in their first relationships that influence the quality of the subsequent caregiver–child relationship as well as their peer relationships (NICHD Early Child Care Research Network, 2006). According to Bowlby (1988), infants and toddlers develop expectations and beliefs about relationships in their first relationships with parents. In their first attachment relationships, they learn about their own worth, whether they can trust others, reciprocity and negotiation strategies, and feelings of safety to explore their world. These expectations for relationships influence their social attitudes and skills with peers (Rubin, 2002).

Description of Attachment

Studies on attachment have focused on the behavior of infants or toddlers as they attempt to elicit caregiving and protection from, seek proximity to, and stay in contact with an adult or adults who care for them (Ainsworth, Blehar, Waters, & Wall, 1978; Bowlby, 1969/1982, 1988; Main & Solomon, 1990). On the basis of research and theory, Edwards (2002) defined the attachment relationship as follows:

> Bowlby (1979) and Ainsworth et al. (1978) defined attachment as a special type of affectional bond between individuals. An affectional bond: (1) is persistent; (2) involves a specific person who is not interchangeable with anyone else; (3) is emotionally significant; (4) produces a desire to maintain proximity; and (5) results in distress from involuntary separation. An attachment bond involves all five of these criteria, and involves seeking security and comfort in the relationship with that person. (Edwards, 2002 p. 390)

Another important aspect of the attachment relationship is the child's ability to explore his or her environment while feeling safe in the presence of the attachment figure (Bowlby, 1979). The quality of the child's attachment is generally observed with the mother in a protocol called the Strange Situation but has also been observed with fathers and care teachers in child care programs. Through a series of observations of the young child responding to the stress of a parent leaving the room, a stranger entering, and the parent returning, researchers have observed how the child responds to separation and reunion with the parent. Researchers describe the attachment relationship as secure or insecure: anxious–resistant, avoidant, or disorganized.

SECURELY ATTACHED   These children seem to feel secure and protected with their parents, seek the parent after separation, are comforted by the parent, feel safe to explore as a toddler, and are more socially competent as preschoolers (Braungart-Rieker, Garwood, Powers, & Wang, 2001; McElwain, Cox, Burchinal, & Macfie, 2003). They know what it is like to feel genuine affection for another and enjoy human interaction. They learn to self-regulate with caring adults and expect that others can be trusted

> **Their [securely attached children] openness to their own emotions and to the overtures of others is thought to help them regulate their emotions and emotional responsiveness and adapt creatively and successfully to changing circumstances and new challenges. (NICHD Early Child Care Research Network, 2004, p. 38–39)**

Parents of securely attached children encourage reciprocity and cooperativeness (Russell, Pettit, & Mize, 1998), are more sensitive (Braungart-Rieker et al., 2001), help infants manage difficult feelings (NICHD Early Child Care Research Network, 2004), read their children's communication cues and respond accordingly (Emde & Robinson, 2000; McElwain et al., 2003), are more emotionally available (Aviezar, Sagi, Joels, & Ziv, 1999), and are more empathic (Weil, 1992). "Mothers of secure infants have been observed to be more reliable, consistent, sensitive, and accepting of their infants than mothers of insecurely attached infants" (Braungart-Rieker et al., p. 252).

INSECURELY ATTACHED: ANXIOUS–RESISTANT   Children who are identified as ambivalent or resistant increase their efforts to stay close to their caregiver because of the inconsistency of the adult's response to the child's distress. Harel and Scher (2003) wrote about insufficient responsiveness of the adult with ambivalently attached children.

The children feel ambivalent about the relationship, wanting to be near the adult but unable to feel satisfied in the relationship (NICHD Early Child Care Research Network, 2006). They stay close to the adult to feel protected, and "as a result of the infant's heightened vigilance of the caregiver's whereabouts, exploration of the environment may become limited" (McElwain et al., 2003, p. 139). The child's competence is compromised if parents of children who are resistantly attached are intrusive, interfere with the child's explorations, and are negatively controlling (Rubin, 2002). Children may also feel incompetent because caregivers tend to interfere with the infants' explorations (McElwain et al., 2003, p. 139).

Mothers of ambivalently attached children, however, seem to be feeling stressed as well. Scher and Mayseless (2000) found that mothers of ambivalent infants have higher separation anxiety and stress than do mothers of children classified as securely attached.

INSECURELY ATTACHED: AVOIDANT   Children identified as avoidantly attached experience "a chronic failure of communication" (Edwards, 2002, p. 391). In an attempt to defend themselves and to self-regulate, they avoid the adult (e.g., tune out, look away, arch their backs) and turn to the environment rather than to others as a source of interest and comfort. They have been found to be able to persist with toys better than other children, but at a cost to relationship building. They see their caregivers as unavailable, and they learn to suppress their negative emotions of distress and anger (NICHD Early Child Care Research

Network, 2006). They may demonstrate these feelings inappropriately with other adults and peers (Carlson & Sroufe, 1995).

Mothers of avoidantly attached children have been found to be particularly sensitive to distress, however, they then withdraw from the child rather than take "effective emotional action" (Mills-Koonce et al., 2007).

INSECURELY ATTACHED: DISORGANIZED–DISORIENTED Researchers have classified children who seem dazed and confused when they are with their primary caregiver as having disorganized attachments. This can be a result of abuse and mistreatment or of a parent's experience of emotional abuse as a child. For example, a foster caregiver's experience of childhood trauma relates to children's disorganized–disoriented attachment (Cole, 2005).

Relationship Between Attachment Types and Peer Relationships

What is the most important thing that infants and toddlers learn in secure attachment relationships? They are learning that relationships are satisfying and valuable and that they can manage negative affect (NICHD Early Child Care Research Network, 2004). They are "affiliative" (warm, eager to socialize; LaFreniere & Sroufe, 1985).

Pairs of securely attached children are more harmonious, less controlling, and more responsive than pairs of children with insecure attachments (Park & Waters, 1989). Securely attached toddlers (ages 20–23 months) observed in a 30-minute play session with their mothers present were more sociable than insecurely attached toddlers (Pastor, 1981). Toddlers (18–24 months old), observed at home with their parents at 18 months of age and in peer playgroups, received more positive reactions and fewer negative reactions from peers than did insecurely attached children (Fagot, 1997). Jacobson and Wille found that "[t]ypical toddlers with good relationship history were seen as 'attractive interactive partners' by their peers. . . . They had greater confidence and effectiveness in dealing with objects and people. They were more interesting and other children sought them out as playmates" (1986, p. 338).

Anxious-resistant children were found to be lowest in peer status and less affiliative (LaFrenier & Sroufe, 1985), less self-assertive among friends (McElwain et al., 2003), more stressed by peer situations and ignoring of other peers' offers (Pastor, 1981), and received fewer positive reactions from peers and more negative reactions (Fagot, 1997). Children who are anxious-resistant tend to withdraw from social interaction with others and are more dependent on adults (McElwain et al., 2003; Rubin, 2002). Thus, they both give and receive fewer positive responses.

Avoidantly attached children have challenges with peer interactions in the early years. Avoidantly attached children were more aggressive with peers (McElwain et al., 2003) and more negative (Pastor, 1981) than securely attached children. Rubin (2002), in his longitudinal study, found that avoidant children expect to be frustrated in interactions with others, view other kids as potentially hostile, and tend to strike out proactively and aggressively. Toddlers who were avoidantly attached received more negative reactions from their peers in playgroups than did securely attached children (Fagot, 1997).

A disorganized–disoriented attachment is related to child aggression (Gauthier, 2003).

McElwain et al. (2003) summarized research demonstrating that children draw out or bring out behavior in other children that is consistent with the attachment interactions they have experienced.

Attachment and Temperament

Because attachment relationships are co-constructed, the influence of the child's temperament on the nature of the parents' responses must be considered (Zeanah & Fox, 2004). It can be challenging for parents and care teachers to remain sensitive with children who are extremely irritable and fussy; however, caregiver sensitivity does seem to be the key to temperament success. In their research on infants at 1 and 6 months with difficult temperaments, Warren and Simmens (2005) found that caregiver sensitivity, measured when children were 6 and 15 months, reduced anxiety and depressive symptoms in children by 2 years of age. Caregivers may need additional support from family members and programs to remain sensitive and involved with temperamentally challenging children.

Children Become Attached to Teachers, Too

Attachment relationships, as well as their influence on peer relationships, apply to teachers and children as well as parents and children. Howes, Hamilton, and Matheson (1994) found that toddlers' security with teachers was negatively associated with hostile aggression and positively associated with complex peer play and gregarious behaviors.

Attachment to Different Caregivers

A child may have a secure attachment to his father and to his mother because infants seem to have a relational capacity to interact and attach to more than one person (Selby & Bradley, 2003). However, what are infants and toddlers learning about relationships when they are securely attached to the father, for example, but insecurely attached to the mother? Even adults described as securely attached identify at least one person with whom they had a negative relationship experience (Roisman, Bahadur, & Oster, 2000). Additional research is needed to delineate how these differing attachment relationships influence the child's approach to relationships with new adults and peers.

Caregivers can act as a security buffer. Pelaez-Nogueras, Field, Cigales, Gonzales, and Clasky (1994) found that infants of depressed mothers show less depressed behavior with their nursery teachers.

Continuity of Quality of Caregiving

What if the quality of the parents' or teachers' behavior changes over time? Does the attachment classification change as well? How does changing adult behavior toward the child influence the child's peer relationships? What is the process for how early attachment influences later child behaviors? These are questions that arise when considering how attachment influences children's peer relationships. There is evidence for both the idea of children having a working model of relationships with continuing influence on peer behavior *and* evidence for change in peer behavior based on the increasing or decreasing quality of parent–child relationships.

Internal working models of relationships developed in a child's first adult–child relationships may influence a child's personality and attitudes about subsequent relationships. In the recent NICHD Early Child Care Research Network (2006) analysis of data on over 1,000 children, their parents, and their teachers, children who were securely attached at 15 months of age exhibited fewer externalizing problem behaviors than other children did, even if the quality of their parenting decreased. It was hypothesized that securely attached children learn how to express their emotions openly and know how to engage others in a positive way (NICHD Early Child Care Research Network, 2006). They interpret changing parent quality in a way that does not reflect on their own self-worth.

However, we also know that attachment classifications can change when life circumstances and family stress changes (Belsky & Fearon, 2002; Howes & Hamilton, 1993; NICHD Early Child Care Research Network, 2006). Although there may be a personality disposition that develops early within first attachment relationships, the specific behaviors of children can change based on their present experience. This is considered a relational view of attachment rather than a personality view (Kobak, 1994).

Children's behavior may become more aggressive if they lose a favorite teacher or change from a secure to an insecure relationship with a teacher. Howes and Hamilton (1993), in their study of how changes in teachers influence children's social competence with peers, found that when 24-month-olds (average age) changed primary teachers, they were more aggressive with other children. At 30, 36, and 42 months of age, the children's experiences of changes in their primary teacher "were most aggressive if they also changed from a secure to an insecure teacher–child relationship" (Howes & Hamilton, 1993, p. 26).

Young children's behavior can also improve if they change from an insecurely attached relationship to a secure one. Belsky and Fearon (2002) found that infants who were insecurely attached at 15 months had better social, behavior, and language outcomes at 36 months of age if they subsequently experienced high-sensitive mothering. "Insecurely-attached children who subsequently experienced high-sensitive mothering significantly outperformed secure children who subsequently experienced low-sensitive mothering" (Belsky & Fearon, 2002, p. 361).

Research that is more recent also supports the notion that, as the child's relationship with the parent improves, so does his or her social competence, especially for children who are insecurely attached (NICHD Early Child Care Research Network, 2006). However, children with insecure attachment histories who continue to experience low and declining parental quality are especially at risk for social challenges.

There is a positive message in this research: If the quality of parenting and teaching improves, children's peer relationships can improve (NICHD Early Child Care Research Network, 2006). There is another message—adults must pay close attention to the relationship environment that the child is experiencing *now*, not just past attachment history.

Attachment and Culture

Culture also plays a part in the attachment process; however, children's perception of emotional availability of adults is the foundation of the attachment relationships. Thus, *how* parents or teachers are sensitive to the child's distress may differ, but if the child perceives the adult as meeting his or her emotional needs, then the child is likely to be securely attached and have a working model of self and others that is positive.

Relationship-Based Strategies That Support Peer Competencies

Martin wriggled on his back with excitement as he lay on a blanket on the floor. His care teacher, Carolee, had just caught his gaze and smiled. Carolee responded warmly by touching Martin's tummy and saying, "Ooh, you want to play." She leaned over him and smiled again. Martin reached out with a big smile on his face and touched her nose as if to say, "I like you. Play with me some more."

Martin is learning about human relationships from this positive and emotionally available care teacher.

As discussed earlier, the type of relationships that children experience in the present influences their peer behaviors. Parents and care teachers can use many specific strategies to help infants and toddlers develop a sense of self and others that positively influences their peer development. Adults can think about how they want infants and toddlers to be with each other—interested, warm, and sympathetic—and be that way with the children.

You know that infants and toddlers cannot always be this way because they are still developing social skills (Tremblay & Nagin, 2005); however, adults can help infants and toddlers feel safe to explore, interested in others, motivated to communicate, and as they grow, sympathetic and caring with others. Observing and documenting, warm ways of interacting, and environment designs are powerful ways to support adult–child relationships that then influence peer relationships.

Opening the Window of Understanding—Observation and Documentation

When adults observe, they open a window into understanding infant and toddler behavior. Teachers are always observing—who is crying, who is making hunger noises, or who is showing interest in an experience. Teachers also document children's behavior while trying to capture the meaning of the behavior. *Documentation* is a term used in the Reggio Emilia approach to indicate observing, capturing, and then interpreting adult and child behavior through photographs, panels, videotapes, memory books, portfolios, and other visual methods. Documentation is a tool for reflection and responsive planning for infants and toddlers (Gandini & Goldhaber, 2001; Lally, 2001). Observing and documenting implies a belief in the importance of "listening" to children, and that they have something important to show us about their intentions, strategies, and theories (Gandini & Goldhaber, 2001). Adults, then, can reflect on documentation to understand development and plan enriched personal and physical environments for children. Each photo is a window into understanding infant and toddler peer behavior.

In this series of photos, we see a very young boy try to comfort his crying peer. We can ask, What is he learning in his relationships with adults that generalizes to peers? Is he imitating the adult or creating a new strategy that he has not seen the adult use? Does he feel empathy toward the crying child as he listens to the adult comfort the child who has been hurt? Often, documentation inspires more questions that require further observation to truly understand children's and adult's behavior, motivating a new or renewed interest in the beginnings of peer relationships.

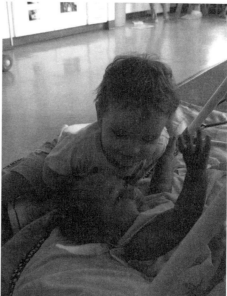

2.5 and **2.6.** A toddler tries to comfort a peer who is feeling sad.
PHOTO: ASHANTE BUTCHER

The Adult Interactions That Count for Peer Relationships

As discussed previously in this chapter, babies come into this world ready to relate to other humans. They are ready to communicate and to connect emotionally with those who care for them. We want them to learn that human touch is kind, that intimacy is safe, and that trusting is good. We would like them to wriggle with excitement when they see another, anticipating warmth, loving caregiving, or fun. We want them to learn the give and take of communication, the self-regulation that comes with being comforted, that they do not have to literally fall apart to be heard, to read the emotional cues of others, and to share emotions. We hope they learn to be sociable, friendly, and responsive with others (Howes, 1988). Although infants and toddlers also learn social behavior with their peers (Williams, Ontai, & Mastergeorge, 2007), we know that they learn sociable attitudes within the supportive arms of caring adults at home and in the programs they attend.

Although children who are securely attached to their mothers or fathers bring a more positive attitude to subsequent relationships, they respond to caregivers differently on the basis of the caregiver's behavior (Zimmerman & Fassler, 2003). It is important, then, that teachers in child care and education programs continuously use techniques that promote a child's sociability. Both family members and care teachers can use the following specific behaviors to promote a child's disposition to be social.

HOW YOU ARE IS AS IMPORTANT AS WHAT YOU DO Jeree Pawl and Marie St. John (1998) wrote a book titled *How You Are Is as Important as What You Do*. Do children sense that you are the kind of person who is emotionally available and who really cares about them?

BE SENSITIVE TO TEMPERAMENT Children with more irritable or negative temperaments show higher levels of stress hormones as the quality of their care decreases (Gunnar & Cheatham, 2003). These children with temperamental vulnerability (Warren & Simmens, 2005) need individualized care. Difficult infants need more synchrony to develop self-control at age 2 (Feldman, Greenbaum, & Yirmiya, 1999). Children who are dysregulated and with a frequent negative mood need predictable and comforting care (NICHD Early Child Care Research Network, 2004) to become more regulated.

Children who have difficulty organizing themselves may contribute to anxiety in adults (Als, Tronick, Adamson, & Brazelton, 1976). If adults find themselves becoming anxious with children with irritable or negative temperaments, they should seek assistance to provide responsive care.

LISTEN TO BABIES Babies can tell you when they have had enough interaction and need to take a break by turning or moving away. Most likely, if the adult is patient and responsive, the child returns for more eye gazing or interactions. Infants are quite capable of playing a role in staying in tune with the adults. "It is argued that infants can play an active role in face-to-face communication, regulating their actions and feelings in accordance with the actions and feelings of the mother even before the age of 2 months" (Lavelli & Fogel, 2002, p. 289).

BE AFFECTIONATE Warmth, affection, and smiles are related to infants' and toddlers' desire to interact with you. Parental warmth is related to children's social competence (Brook, Zheng, Whiteman, & Brook, 2001). Infants and toddlers need to feel that the stable adults in their lives like them, and in fact, children need "someone who is just crazy about them" (Bronfenbrenner & Weiss, 1983, p. 398).

USE POSITIVE AFFECT AND AFFECT MIRRORING   Affect mirroring requires adult sensitivity to children's moods and facial expressions. When a teacher, holding an infant in her arms, responds to a baby's furrowed brow by saying, "I know, you are feeling upset" with an empathetic tone, the baby develops emotional awareness and self-control (Gergely & Watson, 1996). When adults share positive affect and empathize with negative affect, they create the glue that holds a relationship together. Sharing joy and delight tells a child that life can be fun and that you really like spending time with the child.

COMFORT CHILDREN IN DISTRESS   Stay calm in the face of a young child's whining, crying, anger, and negativity. When parents responded to their preschoolers' negativity with unconstructive responses, children were more likely to be aggressive with peers or avoid their peers in preschool (Carson & Parke, 1996). Infants who cry and toddlers who run to adults in fear need reassuring, soothing, and understanding responses. Ziv and Cassidy noted that "consistent parental sensitive responsiveness to the infants' distress signals is particularly important for the infant's well being" (2002, p. 16).

Stay aware of your own emotional responses. Mills-Koonce et al. (2007) found that most mothers became less sensitive at high levels of infant negative affect. If parents and teachers find themselves avoiding distressed children or are unable to comfort them, they will want to seek support from family members, teachers, or a mental health professional.

BE EMOTIONALLY AVAILABLE   Infants crawl and toddlers run away, but they need to be able to come back to a sensitive adult who understands that young children need a secure base from which to explore (Honig, 2002, 2003). Adults provide this base by letting children sit in their laps, lean against them, run up and look into their faces, pull their arm to get their attention, or sit next to them with thumbs in their mouths. The providing of this base, a home base, is called *emotional availability* and is associated with secure infant attachment (Mahler, Pine, & Bergman, 1975; Ziv et al., 2000). Adults provide *quiet supportiveness* for autonomous play (Mahler et al., 1975; Ziv et al., 2000), which means they stay near so that infants and toddlers feel their safe presence and absorb emotional energy to explore and learn, or they follow children's lead in play.

Emotional availability also promotes a child's self-regulation (Kagan & Carter, 1996) and compliance (Lehman, Steier, Guidash, & Wanna, 2002).

When infants and toddlers are comforted when they are hungry, in pain, or afraid, they learn how, in the arms of caring adults, to become calm again and to tune in to others' feelings as well as their own.

BE EMPATHIC—USE NURTURING CARE   Do not be afraid of spoiling, but rather be concerned of not enough loving, holding, and positive regard with children. When a child feels emotionally connected with you, trust between you grows, and as the child develops, he learns to wait and listen, wants to please you more, and shows empathy toward you and others (Zahn-Waxler, 1992).

USE GENTLE TOUCH, HOLD, AND ENFOLD   Carlson (2005) found that touch lowers levels of the stress hormone cortisol in the brain: "Children who sustain chronically high cortisol levels demonstrate cognitive, social, and motor delays in greater numbers than children with more normal levels of cortisol" (p. 79).

Teachers of infants and toddlers can make touch a part of a responsive curriculum. It can be a curriculum goal, along with nurturing language interactions. The role of therapeutic touch—for example, infant massage—for abused children or children who are sensitive to touch is important to try (Barnard & Brazelton, 1990; Carlson, 2005). A program can develop appropriate policies for touch and education for families and staff members on "what constitutes appropriate touch versus sexually abusive touch" (Carlson, 2006, p. 63).

To enfold a child means to surround the child with care, figuratively and literally. Children can do brave things, such as touch a worm or give a toy to another child, when they feel embraced by adults they trust.

ENGAGE IN EYE CONTACT AND FACE-TO-FACE RESPONSIVE INTERACTIONS A "transformation in neural functions that occurs toward the end of the 2nd month has recently been shown to indicate a radical turn in the way infants interact with social partners and express themselves" (Lavelli & Fogel, 2002, p. 288). Long, mutual gazes into each other's eyes seem especially important in establishing an infant's sense of "making things happen" and in establishing that human relationships are pleasant and important. Eye contact has been found to be related to attachment security (Lohaus, Keller, & Voelker, 2001). "Eye-contact regulation at about three months of age can therefore be regarded as a first developmental result of relationship formation" (Lohaus et al., 2001, p. 542).

Eye contact in the first 3 months is related not to fewer crying episodes, but shorter bouts of crying (Lohaus et al., 2001). On the other hand, adults' unresponsiveness to infants' attempts to interact leads to infant fussing and gaze aversion (Anisfeld, Casper, Nozyce, & Cunningham, 1990, p. 1625).

ENGAGE IN RECIPROCAL INTERACTIONS Reciprocity involves a give-and-take with infants and toddlers in play, language, physical movements, and gestures. It implies that there are shared responses, with each partner in an interaction taking equal turns. As a teacher or parent sits on the floor with their infant or toddler, she can initiate a game or conversation, imitate the child, or follow the child's lead in play. In reciprocal interactions, there is no power assertion or intrusion, doing for a child, or directing the play. Reciprocal interactions may require that the adult be high on "empathetic perspective taking." Kochanska (1997, p. 94), in a study of children observed at 26 and 41 months of age, found that mothers who were more empathetic established "a system of reciprocity" with their children. There was cooperation between mother and child, and they had "shared positive affect." Moreover, all of this adult turn-taking with young children has a positive effect with peers. Infants with extensive turn-taking practice with attuned adults engage in more extensive turn-taking with peers (Vandell & Wilson, 1987).

BE RESPONSIVE—READ CUES A baby yawns and a caregiver responds by saying, "Are you telling me you're tired?" in a soothing voice. A toddler pulls on a care teacher's pant leg and the teacher, reading the tired toddler's cues, picks him up. It is within this context of adult responsiveness to their body language, gestures, and communication efforts that infants and toddlers learn that they are capable of communicating, that adults care, that they are effective at relationships, and that they are worthy of attention. Positive, responsive caregiver behavior was the feature of child care most consistently associated with positive, skilled peer interaction at 24 and 36 months (NICHD Early Child Care Research Network, 2001).

BE SENSITIVE Sensitivity includes the ability to be attentive, compassionate, caring, warm, understanding, engaged, and respectful of the fact that young children's nonverbal and verbal communication has meaning. When child care teachers become more sensitive through training programs, young children in both center and family child care homes became more secure with their teachers.

Sensitivity of the mother helped 2- and 3-year-olds with difficult temperaments to become less anxious or depressed (Warren & Simmens, 2005). Maternal sensitivity is related to more compliance in the second year of life (Feldman & Klein, 2003; van der Mark, van IJzendoorn, & Bakermans-Kranenburg, 2002).

USE ATTACHMENT PARENTING AND TEACHING STRATEGIES   Sears and Sears (2003) have recommended attachment parenting and caregiving. They have recommended "baby wearing" in a sling and "baby reading" of cues. Research supports their recommendations. Teenagers who were given front carriers had children who were more securely attached than teens who were given baby carriages (Anisfeld et al., 1990).

To prevent and calm fussiness, parents and teachers can try baby carrying. A teacher might worry that infants will always want to be carried. Rather, trust that as infants and toddlers feel secure, they will want to explore the environment near an adult rather than be continuously in their arms. Toddlers may come for a hug or to be picked up for a while, and then they are usually off again to play. If not, they may need an extra snuggle to gain emotional energy for the difficult task of being a toddler.

USE KIND, TEACHING GUIDANCE   Infants and toddlers need safe boundaries to bounce against and help them feel safe (Koplow, 1996; Lieberman, 1993). As adults set appropriate limits so that children do not harm themselves, others, or the environment, children gain a sense of morality (Emde, 1990); and as adults teach children what to do, children develop social competence (Houck & Le Cuyer-Maus, 2002).

PROMOTE A SENSE OF MASTERY   Securely attached children feel freer to explore their environment. Try not to be intrusive (Ispa et al., 2004), as this predicted negativity in four cultural groups when infants were 15 months of age. Rather, follow the child's lead when you are playing. Provide toys and ample time for children to explore them with you nearby. Children will awe you with their pursuit of "figuring out" how things work and the many strategies they attempt.

ENCOURAGE SELF-REGULATION   As discussed earlier in this chapter, self-regulation is a pathway to social competence (Fabes et al., 1999). Irritable children need adults to use all of their resources to calm, comfort, and soothe them.

2.7. Carrying babies in slings helps them feel secure and builds attachment.
PHOTO: DONNA WITTMER

SUPPORT FAMILIES Family support in the form of home visiting or responsive interactions in center or family child care makes a difference to families' sense of well-being. Families are feeling stressed with both employment and family life and this can affect their relationships with their infants and toddlers. In fact, "Stress, whether in the form of daily hassles, chronic life stressors, or stressful life events, has consistently been shown to impact the quality of the parent–child relationship" (McKelvey, Fitzgerald, Schiffman, & Von Eye, 2002, p. 164).

Families who experience less stress are more likely to be able to be responsive to their children. The authors of a study on the effects of maternal stress reported that

> . . . mothers who report fewer stressors are observed to have more positive interactions with their infants, namely they are more sensitive to infant cues, more responsive to distress signals, and foster social and emotional growth (McKelvey et al., 2002, p. 174).

Teachers' support for families who are feeling challenged will not only help to relieve the families' levels of stress, but is also likely to improve the parent–child relationships.

Family-centered practices in a program can make a difference for children who are ambivalently attached. As a parent becomes more sensitive to the child's needs and the quality of interactions change, children who have experienced ambivalent attachment can change, too, as they begin to trust in others, feel that their needs are met, and develop a sense of self-worth. *Any* change in adults' behaviors and attitudes toward becoming more sensitive makes a difference for insecurely attached children (NICHD Early Child Care Research Network, 2006)!

Set Up a Nurturing Environment

A responsive and relationship-based environment supports young children's affectionate and emotionally regulating relationships with adults.

Cozy corners with soft furnishings allow adults and children to spend leisurely moments together. Mirrors placed low on the wall in strategic places encourage teacher and child to play "look at my face" games. Comfortable chairs on the floor for adults allow them to be emotionally available and present in the moment. Look at the environment with an eye toward children's relationship building with adults and peers.

Summary

Babies from birth to 3 years of age learn about "self" with others and learn how to be with others through their primary relationships. They have a biological capacity to relate to adults as they are primed to communicate and engage in reciprocal interactions when they are born. Adults can support the social disposition of young children through their responsive interactions with children. In these first relationships, children learn how to regulate their strong emotions, communicate, and engage in positive ways with others. They learn what to expect from relationships.

Children's relationships with their primary caregivers influence how they interact with their peers. There are many relationship-based strategies that family members and teachers can use to support young children's social dispositions, knowledge, and skills that then influence how they interact with peers.

References

Agnetta, B., & Rochat, P. (2004). Imitative games by 9-, 14-, and 18-month-old infants. *Infancy, 6,* 1–36.

Ainsworth, M. D. S., Blehar, M. C., Waters, E., & Wall, S. (1978). *Patterns of attachment: A psychological study of the strange situation.* Hillsdale, NJ: Erlbaum.

Als, H., Tronick, E., Adamson, L., & Brazelton T. B. (1976). The behavior of the full-term yet underweight newborn infants. *Developmental Medicine and Child Neurology, 18*(5), 590–603.

Anisfeld, E., Casper, V., Nozyce, M., & Cunningham, N. (1990). Does infant carrying promote attachment? An experimental study of the effects of increased physical contact on the development of attachment. *Child Development, 61,* 1617–1627.

Aviezar, O., Sagi, A., Joels, T., & Ziv, Y. (1999). Emotional availability and attachment representations in kibbutz infants and their mothers. *Developmental Psychology, 35,* 811–821.

Barnard, K. E., & Brazelton, T. B. (1990). *Touch: The foundation of experience.* Madison, CT: International Universities Press.

Belsky, J., & Fearon, R. M. P. (2002). Early attachment security, subsequent maternal sensitivity, and later child development: Does continuity in development depend upon continuity of caregiving? *Attachment and Human Development, 4,* 361–387

Belsky, J., Hsieh, K., & Crnic, K. (1998). Mothering, fathering and infant negativity as antecedents of boys' externalizing problems and inhibition at age 3: Differential susceptibility to rearing influence? *Development and Psychopathology, 10,* 301–319.

Bigelow, A. E. (2001). Discovering self through other: Infants' preference for social contingency. *Bulletin Menninger Clinic, 65*(3), 335–346.

Bowlby, J. (1979). *The making and breaking of affectional bonds.* London: Tavistock.

Bowlby, J. (1982). *Attachment and loss (Vol. 1: Attachment).* London: The Hogarth Press. (Original work published 1969 by Basic Books.)

Bowlby, J. (1988). *Attachment and loss (Vol. 3: Loss—Sadness and depression).* London: Random House.

Braungart-Rieker, J. M., Garwood, M. M., Powers, B. P., & Wang, X. (2001). Parental sensitivity, infant affect, and affect regulation: Predictors of later attachment. *Child Development, 72,* 252–270.

Bronfenbrenner, U. (2004). *Making human beings human: Bioecological perspectives on human development.* London: Sage.

Bronfenbrenner, U., & Weiss, H. B. (1983). Beyond policies without people: An ecological perspective on child and family policy. In E. F. Zigler, S. Kagan, & E. Klugman (Eds.), *Children, families and government: Perspectives on American social policy,* (pp. 393–414). New York: Cambridge University Press.

Brook, J. S., Zheng, L., Whiteman, M., & Brook, D. (2001). Aggression in toddlers: Associations with parenting and marital relations. *Journal of Genetic Psychology, 162,* 228–241.

Brownell, C. (1986). Convergent developments: Cognitive developmental correlates of growth in the infant/toddler peer skills. *Child Development, 57,* 275–286.

Bullock, M., & Lütekenhaus, P. (1990). Who am I? Self-understanding in toddlers. *Merrill-Palmer Quarterly, 36,* 217–238.

Carlson, F. M. (2005). The significance of touch in young children's lives. *Young Children, 60,* 4, 79–85.

Carlson, F. (2006). *Essential touch: Meeting the needs of young children.* Washington, DC: NAEYC.

Carlson, E. A., & Sroufe, L. A. (1995). Contribution of attachment theory to developmental psychopathology. In D. Cicchetti & D. Cohen (Eds.), *Developmental psychopathology: Vol. 1. Theory and methods* (pp. 581–617). Oxford, England: Wiley.

Carson, J., & Parke, R. D. (1996). Reciprocal negative affect in parent–child interactions and children's peer competency. *Child Development, 67,* 2217–2226.

Chen, X., French, D., & Schneider, B. H. (Ed.). (2006). *Peer relationships in cultural context.* Cambridge, England: Cambridge University Press.

Cole, S. A. (2005). Infants in foster care: Relational and environmental factors affecting attachment. *Journal of Reproductive and Infant Psychology, 23*(1), 43–61.

Denham, S., Balir, K. A., DeMulder, E., Levitas, J., Sawyer, K., Auerbach-Major, S., & Queenan, P. (2003). Preschool emotional competence: Pathway to social competence? *Child Development, 74*(1), 238–257.

Eckerman, C. O., & Didow, S. M. (1996). Nonverbal imitation and toddlers' mastery of verbal means of achieving coordinated action. *Developmental Psychology, 32,* 141–152.

Edwards, M. E. (2002). Attachment, mastery, and interdependence: A model of parenting processes. *Family Process, 41*(3), 389–404.

Eisenberg, N., & Fabes, R. A. (1992). Emotion, regulation and the development of social competence. In M. S. Clark (Ed.), *Review of personality and social psychology: Vol. 14. Emotion and social behavior* (pp. 119–150). Newbury Park, CA: Sage.

Eisenberg, N., Fabes, R. A, Bernzweig, J., Karbon, M., Poulin, R., & Hanish, L. (1993). The relations of emotionality and regulation to preschoolers' social skills and sociometric status. *Child Development, 64,* 1418–1438.

Emde, R. N. (1988). The effect of relationships on relationships: A developmental approach to clinical intervention. In R. A. Hinde & J. Stevenson-Hinde (Eds.), *Relation within families* (pp. 334–364). Oxford, England: Clarendon Press.

Emde, R. N. (1990). Presidential address: Lessons from infancy: New beginnings in a changing world and a morality for health. *Infant Mental Health Journal, 11*(3), 196–212.

Emde, R. N. (2001). Foreword. In L. E. Gandini, & C. P. Edwards (Eds.), *Bambini: The Italian approach to infant/toddler care* (pp. vii–xiv). New York: Teachers College Press.

Emde, R. N., & Robinson, J. (2000). Guiding principles for a theory of early intervention: A developmental-psychoanalytic perspective. In J. Shonkoff & S. Meisels (Eds.), *Handbook of early childhood intervention* (2nd ed., pp. 160–178). Cambridge, England: Cambridge University Press.

Fabes, R. A., Eisenberg, N., Jones, S., Smith, M., Guthrie, I., Poulin, R., Shepard, S., & Friedman, J. (1999). Regulation, emotionality, and preschoolers' socially competent peer interactions. *Child Development, 70*(2), 432–442.

Fagot, B. I. (1997). Attachment, parenting, and peer interactions of toddler children. *Developmental Psychology, 33*(3), 489–499.

Feldman, R. S. (2007). *Child development* (4th ed.). Upper Saddle River, NJ: Prentice Hall.

Feldman, R., & Klein, P. S. (2003). Toddler's self-regulated compliance to mothers, caregivers, and fathers: Implications for theories of socialization. *Developmental Psychology, 39,* 680–692.

Feldman, R., Greenbaum, C. S., & Yirmiya, N. (1999). Mother–infant affect synchrony as an antecedent of emergence of self-control. *Developmental Psychology, 35,* 223–231.

Forman, D. R., Aksan, N., & Kochanska, G. (2004). Toddlers' responsive imitation predicts preschool-age conscience. *Psychological Science, 15*(10), 699–704.

Forman, G., & Hall, E. (2005a). *Emphasizing effects.* Retrieved September 10, 2007, from www.videatives.com/content-new/store/product_info.php?products_id=34

Forman, G., & Hall, E. (2005b). *Talking with drums.* Retrieved September 15, 2007, from www.videatives.com/content-new/store/product_info.php?products_id=78

Gandini, L., & Goldhaber, J. (2001). Two reflections about documentation. In L. Gandini & C. P. Edwards (Eds.), *Bambini: The Italian approach to infant/toddler care* (pp. 124–145). New York: Teachers College Press.

Gauthier, Y. (2003). Infant mental health as we enter the third millennium: Can we prevent aggression? *Infant Mental Health Journal, 24*(3), 296–308.

Gergely, G., & Watson, J. S. (1996). The social biofeedback theory of parental affect-mirroring: The development of emotional self-awareness and self-control in infancy. *International Journal of Psycho-Analysis, 77*(6), 1181–1212.

Gunnar, M., & Cheatham, C. L. (2003). Brain and behavior interface: Stress and the developing brain. *Infant Mental Health Journal, 24*(3), 195–211.

Hanna, E., & Meltzoff, A. (1993). Peer imitation by toddlers in laboratory, home, and day-care contexts: Implications for social learning and memory. *Developmental Psychology, 29*, 701–711.

Harel, J., & Scher, A. (2003). Insufficient responsiveness in ambivalent mother-infant relationships: Contextual and affective aspects. *Infant Behavior and Development, 26*(3), 371–383.

Hay, D. F. (1985). Learning to form relationships in infancy: Parallel attainments with parents and peers. *Developmental Review, 5*(2), 122–161.

Hay, D. F. (2006). Yours and mine: Toddlers' talk about possessions with familiar peers. *British Journal of Developmental Psychology, 24*, 39–52.

Hay, D. F., Payne, A., & Chadwick, A. (2004). Peer relations in childhood. *Journal of Child Psychology and Psychiatry, 45*, 84–108.

Hay, D. F., & Ross, H. S. (1982). The social nature of early conflict. *Child Development, 53*(1), 105–113.

Hinde, R. A. (1992). Ethological and relationship approaches. In R. Vasta (Ed.), *Six theories of child development* (pp. 251–285). London: JKP Press.

Hinde, R. A., & Stevenson-Hinde, J. (Ed.). (1988). *Relationships within families*. Oxford, England: Clarendon Press.

Honig, A. S. (2002). *Secure relationships: Nurturing infant/toddler attachment in early care settings*. Washington, DC: National Association for the Education of Young Children.

Honig, A. S. (2003, September). Infants & toddlers/development: Helping babies feel secure. *Scholastic Early Childhood Today*, 27–29. Available online from http://content.scholastic.com/browse/article.jsp?id=3747141

Houck, G. M., & LeCuyer-Maus, E. A. (2002). Maternal limit-setting patterns and toddler development of self-concept and social competence. *Issues in Comprehensive Pediatric Nursing, 25*(1), 21–41.

Howes, C. (1988). Peer interaction in young children. *Monographs of the Society for Research in Child Development, 53* (1, Serial No. 217).

Howes, C., & Hamilton, C. E. (1993). The changing experience of childcare: Changes in teacher and in teacher-child relationships and children's social competence with peers. *Early Childhood Research Quarterly, 8,* 15–30.

Howes, C., Hamilton, C. E., & Matheson, C. (1994). Children's relationship with peers: Differential associations with aspects of the teacher–child relationship. *Child Development, 65,* 253–263.

Ispa, J. M., Fine, M. A., Halgunseth, L. C., Harper, S., Robinson, J., Boyce, L., et al. (2004). Maternal intrusiveness, maternal warmth, and mother–toddler relationship outcomes: Variations across low-income ethnic and acculturation groups. *Child Development, 75*(6), 1613–1631.

Jacobson, J., & Wille, D. (1986). The influence of attachment pattern on developmental changes in peer interaction from the toddler to the preschool period. *Child Development, 57,* 338–347.

Kagan, N., & Carter, A. S. (1996). Mother-infant reengagement following still-face: The role of maternal emotional availability in infant affect regulation. *Infant Behavior and Development, 19,* 359–370.

Katz, J. R. (2004). Building peer relationships in talk: Toddlers' peer conversations in childcare. *Discourse Studies, 6*(3), 329–347.

Kobak, R. (1994). Adult attachment: A personality or relationship construct? *Psychological Inquiry, 5*(1), 42–44.

Kochanska, G. (1997). Mutually responsive orientation between mothers and their young children: Implications for early socialization. *Child Development, 68,* 94–112.

Koplow, L. (1996). *Unsmiling faces. How preschools can heal.* New York: Teachers College Press.

LaFreniere, P. J., & Sroufe, L. A. (1985). Profiles of peer competence in the preschool: Interrelations between measures, influence of social ecology, and relation to attachment history. *Developmental Psychology, 21*(1), 56–69.

Lally, R. J. (2001). Infant care in the United States and how the Italian experience can help. In L. Gandini & C. P. Edwards (Eds.), *Bambini: The Italian approach to infant/toddler care* (pp. 15–22). New York: Teachers College Press.

Lavelli, M., & Fogel, A. (2002). Developmental changes in mother–infant face-to-face communication: Birth to 3 months. *Developmental Psychology, 38*(2), 288–305.

Lehman, E. B., Steier, A. J., Guidash, K. M., & Wanna, S. Y. (2002). Predictors of compliance in toddlers: Child temperament, maternal personality and emotional availability. *Early Child Development and Care, 172,* 301–310.

Lewis, M. (2005). The child and its family: The social network model. *Human Development, 48,* 8–27.

Lieberman, A. F. (1993). *The emotional life of the toddler.* New York: Free Press.

Lohaus, A., Keller, H., & Voelker, S. (2001). Relationships between eye contact, maternal sensitivity, and infant crying. *International Journal of Behavioral Development, 25*(6), 542–548.

Mahler, M., Pine, F., & Bergman, A. (1975). *The psychological birth of the human infant.* New York: Basic Books.

Main, M., & Solomon, J. (1990). In M. T. Greenberg, D. Cicchetti, & M. Cummings (Eds.), *Attachment in the preschool years: Theory, research, and intervention* (pp. 121–160). Chicago: The University of Chicago Press.

McElwain, N. L., Cox, M. J., Burchinal, M. R., & Macfie, J. (2003). Differentiating among insecure mother-infant attachment classifications: A focus on child-friend interaction and exploration during solitary play at 36 months. *Attachment and Human Development, 5*(2), 136–164.

McKelvey, L., Fitzgerald, H., Schiffman, R., & Von Eye, A. (2002). Family stress and parent-infant interaction: The mediating role of coping. *Infant Mental Health Journal, 23*(1–2), 164–181.

Meltzoff, A. (1985). Immediate and deferred imitation in fourteen- and twenty-four-month-old infants. *Child Development, 56,* 62–72.

Mills-Koonce, W., Roger, W., Jean-Louis, G., Propper, C., Sutton, K., Calkins, S., et al. (2007). Infant and parent factors associated with early maternal sensitivity: A caregiver-attachment systems approach. *Infant Behavior & Development, 30*(1), 114–126.

Mintz, J. (1995). Self in relation to other: Preschoolers' verbal social comparisons within narrative discourse. *New Directions for Child Development, 69,* 61–73.

Murphy, L. B. (1992). Sympathetic behavior in very young children. *Zero to Three, 12*(4), 1–5.

Nadel, J., Carchon, I., Kervella, C., Marcelli, D., & Reserbat-Plantey, D. (1999). Expectancies for social contingency in 2-month-olds. *Developmental Science, 2*(2), 164–173.

Nash, A., & Hay, D. F. (2003). Social relations in infancy: Origins and evidence. *Human Development, 46,* 222–232.

NICHD Early Child Care Research Network. (2004). Affect dysregulation in the mother-child relationship in the toddler years: Antecedents and consequences. *Development and Psychopathology, 16,* 43–68.

NICHD Early Child Care Research Network. (2006). Infant–mother attachment classification: Risk and protection to changing maternal caregiving quality. *Developmental Psychology, 42*(1), 38–58.

Park, K. A., & Waters, E. (1989). Security of attachment and preschool friendships. *Child Development, 60*(5), 1076–1081.

Pastor, D. L. (1981). The quality of mother–infant attachment and its relationship to toddlers' initial sociability with peers. *Developmental Psychology, 17*(3), 326–335.

Pawl, J. (1995). The therapeutic relationship as human connectedness: Being held in another's mind. *ZERO TO THREE, 15*(4), 1, 3–5.

Pawl, J., & St. John, M. (1998). *How you are is as important as what you do.* Washington, DC: ZERO TO THREE.

Pelaez-Nogueras, M., Field, R., Cigales, M., Gonzales, A., & Clasky, S. (1994). Infants of depressed mothers show less depressed behavior with their nursery teachers. *Infant Mental Health Journal, 15*(4), 358–367.

Peth-Pierce, R. A (2001). *A good beginning: Sending America's children to school with the social and emotional competence they need to succeed.* Chapel Hill, NC: The Child Mental Health Foundation and Agencies Network. Retrieved on August 15, 2007, from www.casel.org/downloads/goodbeginning.pdf

Piaget, J. (1953). *The origins of intelligence in the child.* New York: International Universities Press. (Original work published 1936)

Raver, C. C. (2003). *Young children's emotional development and school readiness.* Champaign, IL: ERIC Clearinghouse on Elementary and Early Childhood Education. (ERIC Document Reproduction Service No. ED477641) Retrieved January 15, 2008, from http://ceep.crc.uiuc.edu/eecearchive/digests/2003/raver03.pdf

Rochat, P. (2001). *The infant's world.* Boston: Harvard University Press.

Roisman, G., Bahadur, M., & Oster, H. (2000). Infant attachment security as a discriminant predictor of career development in late adolescence. *Journal of Adolescent Research, 15*(5), 531–545.

Ross, H. S., Conant, C., Cheyne, A., & Alevizos, E. (1992). Relationships and alliances in the social interactions of kibbutz toddlers. *Social Development, 1*(1), 1–17.

Ross, H. S., & Lollis, S. P. (1989). A social relations analysis of toddler peer relationships. *Child Development, 60*(5), 1082–1092.

Rubin, K. (1998). Social and emotional development from a cultural perspective. *Developmental Psychology, 34*, 611–615.

Rubin, K. (2002). *The friendship factor.* New York: Penguin Books.

Rubin, K. H., Bukowski, W., & Parker, J. G. (1998). Peer interactions, relationships, and groups. In N. Eisenberg (Ed.), *Handbook of child psychology, Volume 3: Social, emotional, and personality development* (5th ed., pp. 619–700). New York: Wiley.

Russell, A., Pettit, G. S., & Mize, J. (1998). Horizontal qualities in parent-child relationships: Parallels with and possible consequences for children's peer relationships. *Developmental Review, 18*, 313–352.

Sameroff, A. J., & Feise, B. H. (2000). Transactional regulation: The development ecology of early intervention. In J. P. Shonkoff & S. J. Meisels (Eds.), *Handbook of early childhood intervention* (2nd ed., pp. 135–159). New York: Cambridge University Press.

Sameroff, A. J., & MacKenzie, M. J. (2003). A quarter-century of the transactional model: How have things changed? *Zero to Three, 24*(1), 14–22.

Scher, A., & Mayseless, O. (2000). Mothers of anxious/ambivalent infants: Maternal characteristics and child-care context. *Child Development, 71*(6), 1629–1639.

Sears, W., & Sears, M. (2003). *The baby book.* New York: Little, Brown.

Selby, J. M., & Bradley, B. S. (2003). Infants in groups: A paradigm for the study of early social experience. *Human Development, 46*(4), 197–221.

Shaw, D. S., & Vondra, J. I. (1995). Infant attachment security and maternal predictors of early behavior problems: A longitudinal study of low-income families. *Journal of Abnormal Child Psychology, 23*(3), 335–357.

Siegel, D. J. (1999). *The developing mind: How relationships and the brain interact to shape who we are.* New York: Guilford Press.

Spinrad, T. L., Stifter, C. A., Donelan-McCall, N., & Turner, L. (2004). Mothers' regulation strategies in response to toddlers' affect: Links to later emotion self-regulation. *Social Development, 13*(1), 40–55.

Sroufe, L. A., Egeland, B., & Carlson, E. A. (1998). One social world: The integrated development of child-parent and peer relationships. In A. C. B. Laursen (Eds.), *Relationship as developmental contexts* (pp. 241–261). Hillsdale, NJ: Erlbaum.

Stern, D. (2000). *The interpersonal world of the infant*. New York: Basic Books.

Thompson, R. A. (1994). Emotional regulation: A theme in search of a definition. *Monographs of the Society for Research in Child Development, 59*(Serial No. 240), 25–52.

Tremblay, R. E., & Nagin, D. S. (2005). The developmental origins of physical aggression in humans. In R. E. Tremblay, W. W. Hartup, & J. Archer (Eds.), *Developmental origins of aggression* (pp. 83–106). New York: Guilford Press.

Trevarthen, C. (2001). Intrinsic motives for companionship in understanding: Their origin, development, and significance for infant mental health. *Infant Mental Health Journal, 22*(1–2), 95–131.

Trevarthen, C. (2003). Infant psychology is an evolving culture [Review of the article "Infants in Groups: A Paradigm for the Study of Early Social Experience," *Human Development, 46,* 197–221]. *Human Development, 46,* 233–246.

Trevarthen, C., Barr, I., Dunlop, A. W., Gjersoe, N., Marwick, H., & Stephen, C. (2005). *Supporting a child's needs for care and affection, shared meaning and a social place. Review of childcare and the development of children aged 0–3: Research, evidence and implications for out-of-home provision.* Edinburgh, Scotland: The Scottish Executive. Retrieved January 29, 2008, from www.scottishexecutive.gov.uk/Topics/Research/Research/14478/9218

Vandell, D., & Wilson, K. (1987). Infants' interactions with mother, sibling, and peer: Contrasts and relations between interaction systems. *Child Development, 58,* 176–186.

Van der Mark, I., Van IJzendoorn, M. H., & Bakermans-Kranenburg, M. J. (2002). Development of empathy in girls during the second year of life: Associations with parenting, attachment, and temperament. *Social Development, 11*(4), 451–469.

Vygotsky, L. S. (1978). *Mind in society: The development of higher psychological processes.* Cambridge, MA: Harvard University Press.

Warren, S. L., & Simmens, S. J. (2005). Predicting toddler anxiety/depressive symptoms: Effects of caregiver sensitivity on temperamentally vulnerable children. *Infant Mental Health Journal, 26*(1), 40–55.

Weil, J. L. (1992). *Early deprivation of empathic care.* Madison, CT: International University Press.

Williams, S. T., Ontai, L. L., & Mastergeorge, A. M. (2007). Reformulating infant and toddler social competence with peers. *Infant Behavior and Development, 30,* 353–365.

Zahn-Waxler, C. (1992). Development of concern for others. *Developmental Psychology, 28,* 126–136.

Zeanah, C. H., & Fox, N. A. (2004). Temperament and attachment disorders. *Journal of Clinical Child and Adolescent Psychology, 33*(1), 32–41.

Zimmerman, L., & Fassler, I. (2003). The dynamics of emotional availability in childcare. How infants involve and respond to their teen mothers and childcare teachers. *Infants and Young Children, 3,* 258–269.

Ziv, Y., Aviezer, O., Gini, M., Sagi, A., & Koren-Karie, N. (2000). Emotional availability in the mother-infant dyad as related to the quality of infant-mother attachment relationship. *Attachment & Human Development, 2*(2), 149–169.

Ziv, Y., & Cassidy, J. (2002). Maternal responsiveness and infant irritability: The contributions of Crockenberg and Smith's "Antecedents of mother-infant interaction and infant irritability in the first three months of life." *Infant Behavior and Development, 25*(1), 16–20.

Ziv, Y., Oppenheim, D., & Sagi-Schwartz, A. (2004). Children's social information processing in middle childhood related to the quality of attachment with mother at 12 months. *Attachment & Human Development, 6*(3), 327–349.

3

SO MUCH MORE THAN
PARALLEL PLAY

PHOTO: ASHANTE BUTCHER

This chapter focuses on infants' and toddlers' development of peer awareness and appreciation. Because so many peers are spending time together in programs and family playgroups, we can ensure that infants and toddlers spend their days in satisfying peer ways. We want them to grow each day to become more socially competent, not socially adverse, protective, and fearful.

In the past, researchers described peer interactions in the early years as solitary or parallel (Parten, 1932). In solitary play, each child plays alone, and in parallel play, children play side by side with other children but do not seem to be aware of each other: "The children play beside, but not with, each other" (Johnson, Christie, & Yawkey, 1987, p. 49).

If we think of infants and toddlers as capable of only solitary or parallel play, we miss "seeing" peer interest, learning, capabilities, possibilities, and peer joy. We may see parallel play (playing side by side) among infants and toddlers, but their interactions are much more interesting and complex than the term *parallel play* implies.

Infants and toddlers demonstrate remarkable growth in their ability to interact, develop relationships, and function in a group setting (Brownell & Kopp, 2007; Brownell, Ramani, & Zerwas, 2006; Eckerman & Didow, 1996, 2001; Hay, 2006; Rubin, Bukowski, & Parker, 1998). Infants and toddlers develop in perception, memory, mobility, and mastery, which in turn influence their peer abilities. Their volitional abilities, which both enhance and interfere with peer interactions, grow each day. They begin imitating each other quite early. They explore cause-and-effect relationships with a poke or a squeal to make a peer cry out or laugh.

Their peer capabilities grow as they develop schemas, both with objects (balls roll) and with people (other babies cry when I crawl over their heads). They develop from having eyes only for the adult to being able to enjoy their peers. There is unexpected "reciprocity of exchange in toddler sharing behavior" (Levitt, 1985, p. 122). If one toddler shared with a second toddler then the second toddler was more likely to share with the first one when given an opportunity to do so. Toddlers can even adjust their social behavior to the age or ability of their peer partner (Brownell, 1990). For example, toddlers interacted with another toddler with cerebral palsy, who had a difficult time moving but who could make interesting sounds, by imitating him and getting him to laugh.

As sounds, gestures, words, sentences, and sign language develop, so do the complexity of children's peer interactions. They begin to understand possession (e.g., "That's mine"), cooperate, play follow-and-lead games, and become friends with peers as long as caring and emotionally available adults are present.

As they develop emotionally, they can begin to share happy, frustrated, and angry feelings with peers. As their ability to distinguish self, others, and objects develops, they begin to understand that they have an effect on others and that others can feel and want things differently that they do (intersubjectivity).

In a social–constructivist model, infants and toddlers are learning in these first peer relationships. They construct ideas about how peers work, how to communicate, and how to make a friend. Infants' and toddlers' remarkable growth in peer abilities results in a blossoming of peer relationships when caring adults and the environment are encouraging of peer interactions and compassionate with the challenges that occur as children develop.

In a relationship-based model, we see how children's behavior differs with their peers on the basis of their relationship with them and that children develop strong and positive relationships with certain peers.

This chapter focuses on infants' and toddlers' development of self-awareness, identity, peer awareness, appreciation, and ability to interact with each other. If we look closely and are open to learning from infants and toddlers, we can understand their goals, strategies, and their thinking about themselves and others—specifically, their peers. First, we think about the concepts that relate to children's peer interactions such as interest, imitation, and shared meaning across the infant and toddler age period. Then, the stages of development that infants and toddlers experience as they progress in peer capabilities are explored. At the end of the chapter is a multitude of ideas to use to encourage and support peer abilities and interests.

Children Are Active Learners With Peer Goals and Strategies

Infants and toddlers are motivated and active in their learning. They set goals and try out many strategies to attain their goals. As they try out these strategies, they develop ideas about how objects and people work. They do not always know how to achieve their goals (e.g., how to get the attention of another child), and sometimes their goals aren't obvious, but we can see them if we watch carefully. Sometimes they achieve what they want, and at other times, they have to try, try again. Still, at other times, they need our help!

Sara crawled over to Sam, reached out, and pulled his hair. What were her goals? What was she trying to achieve? Through observation, an adult might guess that Sara saw something interesting about Sam's hair and wanted to see what it was. Depending on her age, she may have been trying a strategy to get Sam's attention. An astute parent or teacher shows Sara other ways that might be more successful in gaining Sam's agreeable attention.

Infants and toddlers are volitional (Bullock & Lütkenhaus, 1988). As infants develop into toddlers, they become increasingly task oriented and want to "make something happen" or "make something work." When Bullock and Lütkenhaus observed children between 15 and 35 months of age during a series of play and clean-up tasks, they increasingly observed that the toddlers and 2-year-olds corrected and controlled their own activities, and children increasingly reacted to their outcomes with happiness and satisfaction, as if to say, "I did it."

Jennings (2004) also found that between the ages of 1 and 3 years old, the ability to organize actions toward achieving goals increases greatly.

> At 12 months, most actions are carried out with the intention of attaining a goal; however, goals are quite fluid, changing almost moment to moment as attention is drawn to different objects or events in the immediate environment. By the age of 3 years, children are able to maintain a goal over a considerable period and to organize a series of disparate actions to accomplish the goal. In addition, children become invested in reaching the goal through their own actions without help, and they show pride when they meet the goal. (p. 319)

As infants and toddlers become more goal directed, they also have goals with peers and try out different strategies to communicate with and engage them—or avoid them.

3.2 and **3.3.** Two infants reach out to touch each other.
PHOTO: ASHANTE BUTCHER

"I Understand What You Are Trying to Do!"

Brownell et al. (2006) discussed evidence that 9- to 12-month-olds can understand other's goals and use this awareness to govern their own behavior. For example, an infant will interpret a peer's sitting at the bottom of a short slide as the child's intent to climb the slide. The infant may then pull back and wait to see what the peer will do.

Peers Are Fascinating

Infants show great interest in their peers, and in some settings toddlers prefer to play with their peers rather than with the adults.

THEY PREFER TO LOOK AT EACH OTHER   An infant sees another infant just his size, and his face brightens with interest. Infants and toddlers seem attracted to other infants and toddlers.

Research conducted over 30 years ago in 1976 (Brooks & Lewis, 1976) found that infants as young as 7 months of age showed more interest in peer strangers than in adult strangers. Infants smiled at their peers but frowned or looked away from adult strangers. Brooks and Lewis concluded that infants seemed to be determining whether the other person was "like me" or "unlike me."

Interesting and innovative research conducted more recently (Sanefuji, Ohgami, & Hashiya, 2006) confirmed that infants, 6-month-olds, and 9-month-olds preferred to look at babies of their same age. The researchers asked whether babies preferred babyish characteristics or babies who were similar to themselves. Just as adults seem drawn to the eyes and movements of infants, perhaps infants are as well. Six-month-old infants banged their arms, smiled, vocalized, and looked to show their preference for still photos of babies their own age rather than those of 9- or 12-month-olds. On the basis of these findings with

3.4. Langston waits before going farther down the slide as if to see what Matt will do.
PHOTO: ASHANTE BUTCHER

3.5. Infants (7-month-old and 4-month-old) look at each other with great interest and delight.
PHOTO: DONNA WITTMER

6-month-olds, the researchers still did not know whether babies preferred same age or babyish characteristics. However, after further study they found that 9-month-olds showed their preference for still photos *and* movies of babies their own age rather than of 6- or 12-month-olds. They seemed to prefer babies who looked like them, rather than younger babies with characteristics that are more babyish.

These infants, many of whom were not yet walking, could recognize infants that were similar to themselves. Could this mean that they know how they, themselves, look? Has gazing in a mirror influenced them? On the other hand, Sanefuji et al. (2006) ask, are the infants selecting others whose movements they can imitate? Research and astute observers of infant behavior will need to answer these questions.

Infants 10 to 14 months old even preferred to look at other infants of their own gender, leading the authors of this study (Kujawski & Bower, 1993) to conclude that babies had a capacity to represent self and others; that they understood that the other babies of the same gender looked and moved like themselves.

SPENDING TIME WITH EACH OTHER Do infants and toddlers prefer to spend time with peers more than with caregivers? We've known from previous research (Eckerman, Whatley, & Kutz, 1975) that unfamiliar pairs of children ages 10–12, 16–18, and 22–24 months of age who were observed in an unfamiliar play setting with their mothers smiled, vocalized, and imitated each other, with limited contact with their mothers. Eckerman et al. (1975) concluded, "[r]esults suggest that children generalize to peers' behaviors developed through child–adult interaction, but that peers provide stimulation differing from that of familiar adults" (p. 42).

In child care centers of moderate quality in the Netherlands, however, 15-month-olds had twice as many interactions with their caregivers than with peers (Deynoot-Schaub & Riksen-Walraven, 2006). Time with peers increased from 15 to 23 months of age, but children still spent significantly more time with caregivers than peers at 23 months. The quality of the setting, children with parents versus caregivers, and the number of other children who are prosocial or aggressive may make a difference in how safe toddlers feel to venture out with peers.

"I Know What You Mean"—The Concept of Shared Meaning

Behavior has meaning to infants and toddlers that adults may not immediately understand. Hitting among 2-year-olds provides an example of shared meaning (Brownlee & Bakeman, 1981). From an adult perspective, it is unacceptable for a child to hit another child.

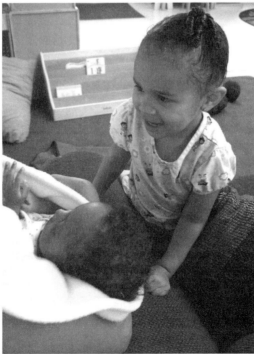

3.6 and **3.7.** A toddler is enthralled with a baby who was brought by a mother into the room of her Early Head Start program.
PHOTO: ASHANTE BUTCHER

Table 3.1.   Types of Hits and Their Typical Results

Types of hits	Results of the hits with peers
(a) An open-hit; a low-intensity hit or swipe at the torso or limb (which seems to mean "Hey, leave me alone")	No further interaction
(b) Hitting with an object in the hand, such as a stuffed toy; a low-intensity hit or swipe to any part of the body (which seems to mean "Hey, wanna play?")	Positive or neutral interaction
(c) A hard hit or any hit to the head (which seems to mean "*Bam*, I don't like that")	Negative interaction

Note. Data from "Hitting in Toddler–Peer Interaction," by J. Brownlee and R. Bakeman, 1981, *Child Development, 52,* pp. 1076–1077.

However, within a group of toddlers, different types of hits had different meanings—shared meanings. The toddlers systematically interpreted the unique hits and responded to them differently. Table 3.1 lists the types of hits and their typical results.

Toddlers who experience "shared meaning" are seeing behavior as having meaning beyond the specific behavior (a representation). Two-year-olds seem to understand these nonverbal meanings better than 1-year-olds and 3-year-olds. Three-year-olds may respond better to language than gestures. The authors of the "hitting study" concluded that the meanings of gestures may change as children become more verbal.

Most adults respond negatively to peers hitting each other, but they can look more closely to see how the toddlers interpret other toddlers' behavior—their shared meaning. A "kiss is just a kiss" and "a hit is just a hit" does not hold true for toddlers (or for adults). Adults can respect the meaning of hits to the children while helping the toddlers to learn the words "Do you want to play?" or "I don't like that!" rather than hitting.

What other meanings can toddlers share? Six toddler boys ranging in age from 12 months to 18 months, observed in pairs in playgroups for over 1,200 minutes, were able to share 12 themes (shared themes) that both of the children in the interaction understood in their play with each other. The following list describes these themes or shared meanings.

1. **Vocal prosocial.** The children talk with each other, even though their messages may not be composed of words.

2. **Positive affect as a meaning sharer.** The children use laughter to indicate understanding of each other's actions. They encourage each other to repeat their performances by laughing and/or smiling.

3. **Vocal copy.** The children copy each other's vocalizations.

4. **Motor copy.** The children copy each other's specific motor action(s).

5. **Curtain running.** The children are engaged in mutual curtain running, where each child both (a) runs in turn through the curtain and (b) acknowledges the other's runs by stopping and watching and/or by positive affect.

6. **Run-chase (or run-follow).** The children run after one another. They both indicate that this is an enjoyable (and social) interaction by laughing, screeching happily, or looking back over the shoulder.

7. **Peek-a-boo.** The children are engaged in peek-a-boo, where one child hides and appears suddenly, and the other acknowledges this by smiling or laughing. The acknowledging child may or may not himself hide.

8. **Object exchange.** The children exchange an object, utilizing the behaviors of "offer" and "receive."

9. **Object possession struggle.** The children struggle over possession of an object. This is recognized both by the attempts of each to get or keep the object and by their acknowledgment that the other wants it (e.g., mad face, vocal protest).

10. **Aggression.** The children fight with each other and seek to do harm to each other, using such behaviors as hit, kick, hit with object.

11. **Rough-and-tumble.** The children are engaged in rough-and-tumble play, with acts like tickle, back into, and push away . . . They *both* acknowledge the play with smiles and shrieks.

12. **Shared reference.** The children name or label an object or set of objects as indicated by mutual pointing and vocalizing. (List from Brenner & Mueller, 1982, pp. 384–385)

Another shared meaning that I have observed among toddlers is "affection." Infants and toddlers will touch noses, pat each other, and smile warmly at another child.

Sharing a dance, a game of peek-a-boo, or running through a curtain may at first glance seem to be dancing, peeking, and running, but toddlers are engaged in much more: relationship building through shared meaning.

Imitation—The Sincerest Form of Relating

One infant claps and another does as well. One throws a ball and the other throws one, too. One tries to sit in the teacher's lap and another is right there to try it, too. Imitation is a powerful way in which infants and toddlers learn from adults and from each other.

Imitation is communication (Trevarthen & Aitken, 2001). An emotional connection, an affiliate feeling, develops among peers as they imitate each other's actions. Laughter erupts as a toddler chases a fly in the room and another toddler takes off after him, even repeating the first child's words, "Fly away, fly." "Imitative responses occur at a moment in the stream of interaction where they can act as affirmations, acceptances, or commentaries with respect to accentuated displays of the other person" (Trevarthen & Aitken, 2001, p. 7).

Fascinating research on mobile infants (14–18 months of age) shows that not only do infants imitate peers, but also they can imitate three-step sequences, they imitate peers more than adults (in the laboratory setting), and they can remember the actions after a delay in time.

- Mobile infants imitated peers at a higher rate than the infants imitated adults. Fourteen- to 18-month-olds imitated peer models in performing a three-step sequence (put teddy to bed) both immediately and 1 week later (Ryalls, Gul, & Gyalls, 2000).

- Mobile infants could use deferred imitation (imitating after a delay in time). Fourteen- to 18-month-olds could imitate peers both 5 minutes and 48 hours after they observed the peer (who had been taught particular actions with toys). The infants who imitated 48 hours after the observation did not have an opportunity to try the actions at 5 minutes (Hanna & Meltzoff, 1993).

- Mobile infants imitate peers, even if they are only given a chance to imitate in a different setting—home, in the laboratory, and day care centers—and not in the original setting where the behavior was observed (Hanna & Meltzoff, 1993).

As you observe infants, try to notice how early they are imitating each other. Also, notice how they are building and reinforcing relationships through imitation. "[T]his deceptively simple way of behaving—doing what another has just done—may have great power and effectiveness" (Eckerman & Peterman, 2001, p. 331).

Through imitation, young children are learning important lessons about the difference between self and other. They can see themselves in others as others imitate them, and they see others in themselves as they imitate the others.

3.8 and **3.9.** Imitation is a powerful way that toddlers learn from each other.
PHOTO: ASHANTE BUTCHER

Play and the Stages of Play

A primary way in which infants and toddlers relate to others is through play. Play is an activity that the child is not required to do and that engages them.

There are cognitive theorists such as Vygotsky (1978) who believed that play contributes to a child being able to understand symbols. Bruner emphasized the creative aspect of play.

> **Jerome Bruner (1972) pointed out that in play, the means are more important than the ends. When playing, children do not worry about accomplishing goals, so they can experiment with new and unusual combinations of behavior they never would have tried if they were under pressure to achieve a goal. Once children have explored these new behavioral combinations in play, they can use these to solve real-life problems (Johnson, Christie, & Yawkey, 1999, p. 11).**

The purposes of play are many—to master the environment, to practice skills, to rid oneself of negative feelings, to learn new skills, and to create—but one of the most important purposes of social play is to relate.

Infants need time on the floor to move and grasp, shake, rattle, and roll toys. As infants grow toward 1 year of age, they need play time to sit, crawl, and experiment with toys. Toddlers and 2-year-olds need play time to select materials and toys from choices attractively displayed in the room. Young children do not benefit from being herded together from one activity to another, never having the opportunity to choose among an appetizing array of materials. When young children are not involved in routines, they are playing by themselves, with adults, or with peers. Given this leisurely time to play, social interactions occur.

Parten (1932) identified the following social stages of play in infants and toddlers (see Table 3.2).

Table 3.2.   Parten's Play Stages

Play stage	Age	Description
Solitary play	2–2½ years	Plays alone
Parallel play	2½–3½ years	Plays beside children but not with them
Associate play	3½–4½ years	Plays with others; converses about common activity. Child primarily follows own interest
Cooperative play	4½ years	Plays with others; activity is organized, with different children playing unique roles that complement each other

Note. Adapted from *Play and Early Childhood Development* (2nd ed., p. 61), by J. E. Johnson, J. F. Christie, & T. D. Yawkey, 1999, New York: Longman. Copyright 1999 by Longman Press.

Subsequent researchers, however, discovered that although infants and toddlers may engage in solitary and parallel play during the first 3 years of life, they are capable of much more. Brenner and Mueller (1982) identified three roles that toddlers play with each other.

> **[They used] role considerations in classifying toddler games into three categories—imitative, complementary, and reciprocal. In complementary games one child somehow completes an action begun by another. They give the lovely example of one child playfully sticking a block in her mouth and allowing her age mate to remove it. Reciprocal games add to complementarity the ability to switch or reverse roles. The child who stuck the block in her mouth now becomes the one to take it out of the other child's mouth (Brenner & Mueller, 1982, p. 380, reporting on Goldman & Ross, 1978).**

Howes and Matheson used a system of observation that captured how the play behavior of children becomes more complex during the early years.

Howes's Stages of Play

1. Parallel play—children engage in a similar activity to the peer but without eye contact or social behaviors.

2. Parallel aware play—children engage in a similar activity to the peer with eye contact.

3. Simple social play—children engage in the same or similar activity and talk, smile, offer and receive toys, or otherwise engage in social interaction.

4. Complementary and reciprocal play—children demonstrate action-based role reversals in social games, such as run and chase or peek-a-boo displays.

5. Cooperative social pretend play—children enact complementary roles within social pretend play.

6. Complex social pretend play—children demonstrate both social pretend play and metacommunication about the play. The metacommunication included naming the roles, explicitly assigning roles, leaving a role to modify the play script, proposing a play script, and prompting the other child. (List adapted from Howes, Matheson, & Hamilton, 1992)

In this research conducted about 15 years ago, the authors identified the percentage of children from ages 10 months to 3 years old who participated in each level of play (see Table 3.3).

Howes et al. (1992) found that infants progress from primarily parallel play from 10–12 months of age (67%) to primarily complementary and reciprocal play at 30–36 months of age (64%); however, some children at each age group played at higher levels. Except at 10–12 months, the majority of children were playing at levels higher than parallel or parallel aware play.

At the simple social level and above, children are enjoying each other; making efforts to relate and communicate; and growing in emotional, social, cognitive, and language development.

Examples of play are provided in the next major section on development, and as you will see, even parallel play takes on a different meaning when we consider how infants communicate with each other.

Peer Interactions Are Relational and Reciprocal

Peer interactions have a relational component to them. Although children may be more or less sociable with peers, there seems to be changes in how children relate to peers based on the experiences and relationship that children have with the others. Reciprocity, as discussed in chapter 2, involves a give-and-take and a sense of equal turns on the part of partners. The opposite of reciprocity is onesidedness, or one person in a pair of children

Table 3.3. Highest Level on Peer Play Scale

Age group (in months)	Number of children	Percentage of children in play stage					
		Parallel	Parallel aware	Simple social	Complementary and reciprocal	Cooperative social–pretend	Complex social–pretend
0–12	27	67	7	19	7	0	0
13–15	11	33	16	24	27	0	0
16–18	13	7	12	26	50	5	0
19–23	16	2	15	21	56	6	0
24–29	27	2	2	30	57	9	0
30–35	28	0	0	5	64	25	6

Note. Adapted with permission from "Sequences in the Development of Competent Play With Peers: Social and Social-Pretend Play," by C. Howes & C. Matheson, 1992, *Developmental Psychology, 28,* p. 972. Copyright 1992 by American Psychological Association.

involved in all of the action. This sense of reciprocity may affect peer relationships in interesting ways. Levitt (1985), in a study of the reciprocity of exchange in toddler sharing behavior, observed pairs of toddlers by using an innovative strategy. A barrier separated the two toddlers. One child had toys, and the other had no toys. The researcher then reversed the situation so that the other child had the toys. At this young age, the toddlers behaved as if they expected the other child to share. If a toddler did not share, then, when it was the other toddler's turn to have the toys, that toddler was less likely to share. Levitt suggested that the toddlers were operating on the basis of a principle of reciprocal exchange—do unto others as others do unto you.

Experience Makes a Difference

Parents and teachers may ask, "Does experience make a difference in children's social skills?" Eckerman, Whatley, and McGehee (1979) proposed that "social skill may arise in large measure from social experience" (p. 593). Another research study conducted 30 years ago agreed: Becker (1977) found that 32 pairs of 9-month-olds, observed in their own homes during 10 play sessions, increased both the complexity and degree of their peer behavior, whereas a control group of children who did not participate in playgroups did not.

In more recent work (National Institute of Child Health and Human Development [NICHD], 2001), the authors emphasized that social experience makes a difference in children's social skills.

> From the perspective of social learning theory (Bandura, 1989; Charlesworth & Hartup, 1967), children who have had more positive experience with age-mates or near age-mates would be expected to be more familiar and comfortable with peers, and hence, more sociable and engaged, more playful, and more affectively positive with other children.
>
> Likewise, from a social-cognitive perspective . . . children who are more often engaged with age-mates in either positive or negative exchanges would have the opportunity to acquire greater social and emotional knowledge, more effective communication skills and greater skill in compromise, negotiation, and reciprocity. . . . (NICHD, 2001, p. 1478)

However, Brownell (1986) emphasized, on the basis of her extensive research on peer interactions, that there are age constraints that experience can not override or overcome. Development plays its part as well!

Development

The next section covers development from birth to 3 years old. Communication, cognition, coordination, and cooperation skills develop incrementally from birth to age 3.

Infants From Birth to 4 Months

> *Two infants, placed close together, resting on their Boppies [ring-shaped pillows] with their bodies at a slant accidentally touch hands across the space between them. One turns her head to what her hand has touched. The other cannot turn to see where her body ends and the other begins.*

An infant of this age experiences another child who might lie beside her on a blanket through all of her senses. She can see the peer and feel her. She might try to taste her, if she is close enough. She hears her peer cry and might begin to become distressed herself. She is just learning how her own body works, but is still aware of the other child.

Infants 4–8 Months

A baby on her tummy placed on a Boppy with her head and arms peeking over could view the child slightly below her on the floor. She reached out to touch the baby boy, sensing a person separate from herself. She laughed when the baby boy laughed and frowned when she couldn't quite reach the other infant just her size.

This child was aware that there was another child below her. At other times, it is as if infants do not notice that the toy in the other child's hand is held by another person. The toy and the hand seem to be a part of the landscape.

With interest, they watch the faces and movements of other children. For example, one infant sat on the edge of a large piece of paper, kicked her feet, and with great attention watched another infant paint.

They initiate (Selby & Bradley, 2003) and coo to each other (Porter, 2003). Creepers (on belly) and crawlers (on hands and knees) often use creative ways to move across a space toward a peer. A child might use a peer for his or her own means—for example, turning over—by grabbing the other child's clothes.

Infants 8–12 Months

The ability to enjoy each other grows during this age period. Porter (2003), who observed different infants and toddlers in a child care program for 5 years, tells a wonderful story about Peter (8 months old) and Nathan (11 months old).

Peter sat and laughed at the antics of Nathan. Soon both boys were responding to each other with joyful belly laughs. These infants were clearly delighting in each other.

Can infants this age interact with more than one infant at a time? Selby and Bradley (2003), studying babies' relational capacity by asking whether they could interact in groups, brought babies from 6 to 10 months into a room in triads, with the three children facing each other while sitting in strollers. Mothers left the room and returned if their babies became upset. These babies were able to interact with two other babies at the same time; for example, toe touching with both simultaneously. A baby might squeal and then look to one baby and then the other as if to include them both. They found ways to keep one another's attention by smiling and by using gestures including pointing at each other, frequent vocalizing, and playing "footsie." One child, Mona, definitely preferred interacting with Joe rather than Ann. After a bout of toe touching with Mona, who withdrew her foot from Ann, Joe turned and smiled at Ann. Mona began to cry while watching Joe "deserting" her (Selby & Bradley, 2003, p. 216). Another child, who looked often to the door to see where her mother had gone, held her own toe, seemingly in an effort to hold herself together. She spent more time looking at the other children when she was holding her own toe than when she was not. The researchers concluded that there were many ways in which the babies communicated with each other (both to engage and withdraw from others) and that there were powerful feelings circulating in the group. These babies definitely showed that they have the capacity to engage with more than one person at a time.

As discussed previously, infants from 9 to 12 months old seem to be able to determine the goal of another child, especially while that child is in the act of the goal-oriented behavior—toddling to a ball or on the way up some steps (Brownell et al., 2006).

Infants can communicate in an astonishing number of ways, as shown in the following list of ways in which infants, toddlers, and 2-year-olds communicate through gestures and other physical actions.

Pines (1984), a science writer and contributing editor of *Psychology Today,* wrote an article describing the work of Montagner (1978), an ethologist, observing infants' ability to communicate with each other. He discovered five major styles of nonverbal communication among children that begin as early as 9 to 12 months of age.

1. Actions that pacify others or produce attachment: offering another child toys or candy, lightly touching or caressing the other child, jumping in place, clapping one's hands, smiling, extending one's hand as if begging, taking the other child's chin in one hand, cocking one's head over one's shoulder, leaning sideways, rocking from left to right, or vocalizing in a non-threatening way.

2. Threatening actions that generally produce fear, flight, or tears in the target child: loud vocalizations, frowning, showing clenched teeth, opening one's mouth wide, pointing one's index finger toward the other child, clenching one's fist, raising one's arm, learning one's head forward, leaning one's whole trunk forward, or shadow boxing.

3. Aggressive actions: hitting with hands or feet, scratching, pinching, biting, pulling the other child's hair or clothes, shaking the other child, knocking the other child down, grabbing something that belongs to the other child, or throwing something at the other child.

4. Gestures of fear and retreat: widening one's eyes, blinking, protecting one's face with bent arms, moving one's head backward, moving one's trunk or one's whole body backward, running away or crying after an encounter with another child.

5. Actions that produce isolation: thumb-sucking, tugging at one's hair or ear, sucking on a toy or a blanket, standing or sitting somewhat apart from the other children, lying down, lying curled into the fetal position, or crying alone (List from Pines; 1984, p. 63).

Pines (1984), continuing to describe Montagner's (Restoin et al., 1984) work, reported that young children differed greatly in the combinations of gestures that they used with their peers. The secret to children's peer success—in fact, becoming a leader among peers—seems to be the children's use of as many of the pacifying gestures as possible, the use of affection and power, and defending themselves with threatening behaviors only when necessary. Children learn to "read" other children's behavior quickly, avoiding children who use frequent aggressive strategies. As we focus on young children's nonverbal cues to each other, we begin to understand their remarkable ability to communicate their fears, desires, and goals.

Infants 12–18 Months

In this stage, the child develops a more complex notion of object permanence and person permanence—understanding that objects and people still exist when out of sight. Crawling fast and pulling to stand and then walking, running, and pulling toys contribute to much more interaction with peers. Children view the world from their upright stance and see peers in a different way.

DO TOUCH THE TOY Eckerman et al. (1979) studied 11- to 13-month-olds approaching and contacting the object that a peer manipulates. "[B]y 1 year of age, the infant systematically goes to objects that a potential social partner manipulates and manipulates them in a similar fashion" (Eckerman et al., 1979, p. 585).

Some adults might try to stop the approach of one infant toward another; however, Eckerman et al. (1979) discussed the positive aspects of a 1-year-old touching the object that a peer holds. Rather than stopping the infant approach, think about how:

(a) Going to another's object brings the two potential interactors into close physical proximity, a state that may increase the chances of each attending to the other, directing behaviors toward the other, and responding to the other's overtures.

(b) Going to another's object may increase the likelihood of the infant's sharing that person's focus of attention (the object), and hence, understanding the person's communications.

(c) Acting on the same object as another allows the infant to engage in behaviors effective in initiating or maintaining social interaction.

(d) [C]ontacting the same object as another and performing similar actions may enhance the infant's awareness of his or her similarity to others and increase interest in them (List from Eckerman et al., 1979, p. 586).

Eckerman et al. (1979) further emphasized the following:

[A]pproaching and contacting the object another manipulates is a basic interactive skill of the 1-year-old. The term *interactive skill* denotes a way of behaving in social encounters that functions to facilitate the generation of social interaction with another . . . . The infant may show or offer that object to the partner, imitate the partner's action on the object, vocalize or gesture about the object, or transform almost any act on the object into a socially directed behavior by accompanying it with shouts, laughter, or visual inspection of the partner. (pp. 591–592)

This view of object touching again reminds us to think about the children's possible intentions—from the children's perspective.

Viewing going to another's object as an interactive skill that facilitates the establishment of a topic for interaction between two individuals brings a different perspective to bear on the often emphasized parallel play of young peers (Parten, 1932).

Playing with the same play material side by side while exchanging glances, vocalizations, and perhaps smiles and laughter might better be considered a joint social enterprise than a precursor to social participation (Eckerman et al., 1979, p. 592).

Interesting toys are important to provide at this age. Johnson et al. (1999, p. 61) refer to toys as "social butter" for infants moving into toddlerhood peer interactions.

GAMES, ROUTINES, AND SOCIAL SEQUENCES Toddlers at this age "make 'music' together, playfully composing a 'We' through frolicking moods . . ." (Lokken, 2000a, p. 541).

A peer "conversation" may be a series of glances, a kinesthetic dance (Capatides, Collins, & Bennett, 1996), or peer talk (Katz, 2004). Toddlers have a "toddling style" (Lokken, 2000b, p. 173)—a social style that includes "running, jumping, trampling, twisting, bouncing, romping, shouting, falling ostentatiously, and laughing ostentatiously." Play emerges as interest and joins children together in cooperative and collaborative play by the end of the second year.

Furthermore, these stylish ways had the roles of constructing games, rituals, or routines, enhancing peer culture, peer relations, and peer community. At this age, the art of head shaking . . . appear[s] as meaningful ways of children celebrating and/or utilizing being in a (public) toddler group. Toddlers communicate using their bodies—this is their "social style" (Lokken, 2000b, p. 173).

Children in this age group begin to play out social play sequences and routines of, for example, exchanging materials with each person, changing the game just a bit each time an exchange happens. They may even participate in a game of "lick the table" (Eckerman,

1993). One toddler may lick the table, another toddler follows suit, and soon the game of "lick the table" is played each day for a while.

Lokken (2000b, p. 169) shared an example of shared meaning in 14-month-olds' peer play based on Stambeck and Verba's (1986) research.

> Sylvie licks the piece of paper and makes clear her intention of having Aurelien do the same. Aurelien takes the hint and shares in the game right away. Both of them, in turn, repeat the action of licking the piece of paper at Sylvie's initative. As a result of these repetitions, Aurelien introduces the idea of offering the piece of paper directly to Sylvie without licking it himself. However, his partner does not approve of this idea . . . (Stambeck & Verba, 1986, p. 238).

Sylvia finally responded to Aurelien by offering him a paper. Then Aurelien changed the game again by introducing a combination of the paper licking-and-offering game, by licking the paper before offering it to Sylvie. Lokken emphasized that "the children's actions showed that they tried to understand and adapt to each other's actions" (2000b, p. 169). Becoming friends does not always require licking a piece of paper, but in this case it certainly enhanced the relationship.

PEER OBSERVATIONS BY PORTER   Porter (2003) captured some delightful examples of the peer interaction among infants from 8 to 18 months of age in child care. She wrote the following:

1. They can point and words begin to emerge, however primarily kinesthetic conversations occur.

2. An 8-month-old shares joyful belly laughs with an 11-month-old.

3. By 12 months, infants interact in play, initiating games and instigating the action.

4. When walking, hands become free and the infants offer each other toys and food. They even try to feed bottles to younger ones. Their increased mobility and helpfulness further enhances socialization.

5. A 13-month-old girl assumes the role of leader with a group of 8-, 11-, and 13-month-old children. She offers toys and food to the boys.

6. A 14-month-old child plays peek-a-boo under the double-decker combination playpen/maze. She entices other children to play with her. She taught several of the younger babies how to use this piece of equipment, and they now get others to join them there in their play.

7. One often sees infants caring for each other. One child puts pacifiers into the mouths of younger, fussing infants. Other babies offer favorite blankets or transition objects to their owners in order to soothe their crying.

USING THEIR WORDS   Children also begin to use their words to enhance social interaction. Forman and Hall (2005), describing eight 15-month-old toddlers playing with clay, emphasized that:

> "The children have a growing understanding of how words work:
>
> **To ask someone to move an intact object from one place to another:** Andy used the word 'ball' to ask the teacher to pass her the clay ball.
>
> **To ask someone to reshape an object:** Kaitlyn used the word 'ball' to ask the teacher to make her clay into a ball.
>
> **To describe the quality of an object:** John used the word 'big' to describe the size of his clay ball.

To develop a pretend play script: John used the word, 'yummy' as part of pretend script to support cooperative play with Andy.

To explain the significance of an object: Sophia said 'cooking' in an effort to tell Nicholas that the metal can was an important part of her pretend play.

To foster a sense of membership in a social group: John's talk about his 'big ball' encouraged Kaitlyn to join in the conversation by naming the material 'clay.'

The children strengthened their experience of group togetherness and fostered an early sense of friendship by echoing each other's talk and sound effects" (Forman & Hall, 2005, pp. 14–15).

Toddlers: 18–24 Months

Toddlers gain language and cognitive skills that result in increased ability to interact and develop relationships with their peers. It is important to try to think like they do to understand their intentions and social style.

IMITATION—"I KNOW WHAT YOU ARE TRYING TO DO!" Eighteen-month-olds can imitate what an adult intended to do, even when the adult tried but failed to perform certain acts (Meltzoff, 1995).

Two toddlers and an infant play with a ball outside at their family child care home. One toddler tries to make a basket but ends up throwing the ball into the air, away from the basket. The other toddler takes the ball, moves closer to the basket, and tries to make a basket as well.

Did the second toddler just want to make a basket, or did she understand the intention of the first toddler and then try to imitate her in a more successful way? It is difficult toknow, but the second toddler seemed to understand the game they were beginning to play.

By 18 months of age, toddlers are also watching where adults look when they are talking. Although the ball in the toddler example went flying into the air, the first toddler's eyes may have glanced at the basket.

"IT'S MINE, AND I'M NOT SHARING" It is challenging to peers and also to adults when children say "mine" and grasp tightly to a beloved object that they have owned since birth (e.g., their "blankies") or have possessed for just a few minutes. Children's understanding of ownership and possession, however, relates to their social competence. Children who understand ownership demonstrate knowledge that they and the object of possession existed in the past, and they remember that the object belongs to them. The memory of ownership is an important part of self-knowledge, self-concept, and awareness of the self as "continuous in time" (Fasig, 2000, p. 370). Fasig studied children 18 to 28 months old and found the following:

- Children 24 to 28 months old, and some children as young as 18 months, understand the difference between *ownership* and *possession*.

- Toys become a way of children defining boundaries between themselves and others.

When young children say "mine" and "yours," they are demonstrating a knowledge of self and other—an important social competence skill. Dale Hay (2006), a researcher from the United Kingdom, studies how the verbal abilities of young children reduce aggression

United Kingdom, studies how the verbal abilities of young children reduce aggression among toddlers and 2-year-olds. He studied how 66 British toddlers at home with familiar peers talked about possessions. Children began saying "mine" between 18 and 24 months of age. Children who said "mine" were more likely to say "yours" and share at 24 months. Hay pointed out that when a child says "yours," that child is aware that "different people are entitled to different things" (Hay, 2006, p. 41).

DISTRIBUTING TOYS   Toddlers may distribute toys rather than give them away and think they should have the toys back when *they* want them. This misunderstanding between *distributing* and *giving* can contribute to peer conflict (Porter, 2003).

Two-Year-Olds: 24–36 Months

Two-year-olds become true social partners with peers. The majority of children are engaged in complementary and reciprocal play (e.g., reversing roles as they play follow the leader through the sandbox). From 24 to 30 months old, a few children begin cooperative social pretend play, and by 30 to 36 months, a few children are naming roles during social pretend play and proposing a play script (Howes, Matheson, & Hamilton 1992).

> **During the 3rd year, children's cooperative play becomes more responsive to their peer's actions and desires, and they actively influence one another's behavior and goals (Brownell et al., 2006, pp. 803–804).**

TRUE SOCIAL PARTNERS   Brownell et al. (2006) conducted research on the ability of 1-year-olds and 2-year-olds to cooperate. They concluded that 2-year-olds are becoming true social partners. A toy that could be activated by two children pulling handles at the same time or in a sequence was used to assess 19-, 23-, and 27-month-old children's ability to cooperate. The researchers strategically placed the handles so that one child could not activate the toy alone. Adults modeled the strategies for the children. Despite adults demonstrating the task and reminding the children of the common goal, only a few of the 1-year-olds (19- and 23-month-olds) were successful on both versions of the handle-pulling cooperative task. Nearly all of the 2-year-olds (27-month-olds) were successful.

The researchers asked whether the simultaneous and sequential handle pulling was an accident or whether the young children understood their partner's goal and shared it. The answer was that the 19-month-olds were more than twice as likely to pull the handle individually rather than cooperatively, the 23-month-olds equally pulled individually and cooperatively, and the 27-month-olds were almost twice as likely to pull their handles cooperatively as individually. Cooperating did not seem to be an accident but rather a shared goal of the older 2-year-olds.

To cooperate, Brownell et al. (2006) emphasized, young children have to be able to "reason about their own and others' intentions and put their understanding to use in an interaction" (p. 816). Adults can observe to see how their children cooperate on a task, such as carrying a heavy bucket of sand that requires two children. Do they each yank on the handle, or do they coordinate their movements to accomplish the goal together?

TEACHING ANOTHER   Guided action occurs when one child manages the interaction by guiding the activities of another child through prompting, demonstration, and affective signals in relation to a goal (Eckerman & Didow, 2001, discussing Verba's [1994] work). One toddler becomes the guide in learning and informs or leads the other child in exploration. In the following example, Bridger (25 months old) seems to be teaching the other children about shadows.

"There's your shadow" he says to the other children, guiding them to notice their shadows on this sunny day. Another boy asks Bridger, "Where you find your shadow?" Bridger answers, "Under your feet," pointing down to his own feet, guiding him to look down. "You're standing on it."

Individual and Group Differences

One infant wants to stay near a teacher and not venture out with peers. It is as if this infant needs to soak up love and confidence before moving out and exploring with others his size. Another infant crawls away but checks back often by creeping quickly back and burying her head in the teacher's lap. Another beginning walker leaves the caring teacher's side for long periods of time, catching the teacher's eye as she careens back by and swings around the room.

Gender

Toddlers may also begin to act differently from each other based on their gender. By age 3, when given a choice of who to play with, both boys and girls show a preference for play with same-sex peers (Fabes, Martin, & Hanish, 2004). Martin and Fabes (2001) suggested that young children were influenced by the opportunities that they have to experience other-sex peer play, which leads to the importance of adults providing opportunities for boys and girls to play together. Young children may also be influenced by their own temperament. Moller and Serbin (1996) reported that girls who liked to play with girls at 35 months of age were more socially sensitive while boys who generally liked to play with only boys were more active and disruptive. Much more research is needed to untangle the complexities of the issue. Astute teachers and parents can observe their infants and toddlers to determine whether children show a preference for play with same-sex peers, and if so, why (Serbin, Moller, Gulko, Powlishta, & Colbourne, 1994).

3.10. Each child brings his or her individual characteristics to peer interactions. One of these twins likes to get dirty while painting and the other does not.
PHOTO: JODY BERG

Peers With Disabilities

Children with identified special needs are often included in programs for children without disabilities. Both the children with and without special needs benefit from interactions with each other. The motivation to learn from a peer is great (Wittmer & Petersen, 1992)!

Children with special needs may require extra support and a positive attitude from teachers to engage in peer interactions. There are strategies that teachers can use to encourage peer interactions and relationships. Place nonmobile children with their peers. Use adaptive equipment to support children's participation with others. Find ways for a child with disabilities to communicate to peers using sign language, communication boards, or words. Support a child with disabilities to start a game of "pat the table" or "give and give back" with her peers. Toys that are attractive, in the hands of a child with disabilities, may entice another child to touch the object and initiate an interaction.

Encourage children who are typically developing to talk or walk with children with disabilities. Comment on how children are alike rather than different: Say, for example, "Look, Sarah's eyes are blue, just like yours." Provide opportunities for toddlers to interact with each other. For example, one child could pull another child in a wagon.

Children with autism spectrum disorders will experience challenges with joint attention, communication, and emotion sharing with adults and peers (Wetherby & Woods, 2006). Children with these challenges should receive early intervention services that support parents' and teachers' responsive interactions to improve children's ability to communicate and play with peers both at home and, if attending an inclusive program, in the child care and education center.

With thoughtful planning, teachers can support all children's "togetherness and diversity" (Janson, 2001, p. 135). All of the strategies described in the next section will also enhance peer relationships.

Strategies That Make the Difference

Infants and toddlers are trying to figure out how to interact with their peers. They try different strategies to see what works and what does not. Observing children's interests, goals, and strategies is a way to begin to "see" what children know and do with their peers. When teachers and parents really see and support positive peer interactions and relationships based on the children's interests and development, they are building children's relationship skills, joys, and opportunities to learn. The thoughtful focus on relationships will create a community of caring.

Observation and Documentation

Observe and document peer shared meaning, imitation, games, play, and cooperative strategies. Ask the following questions as you observe infants and toddlers.

- **Observe Infants, Toddlers, and 2-Year-Olds**
  - What are the goals that the child is are trying to achieve with their peers?
  - What strategies is a child using to interact with other children?
  - Does the child seem to prefer particular children? How does the child change his behavior with different peers?

- **Observe Infants**

  - Does the child show any interest in his/her peers? If so, how is the child showing interest?

  - Does the child touch others' toys? Does this seem to be an attempt to interact with the other child?

  - When near another child, does the child try to touch the other child?

  - How do infants communicate with each other?

- **Observe Toddlers and 2-Year-Olds**

  - Is there a leader who emerges among the children?

  - How do they demonstrate that they understand possession and ownership?

  - Are any children saying "mine" and "yours"?

  - How does a child demonstrate that she knows the difference between herself and others?

  - Which children are friends? How do they show they are friends?

  - What are the words that they are using with each other? What seems to be the function of the words?

  - What routines, games, and shared themes emerge?

  - What contributes to toddler glee?

To answer these questions, teachers observe, take photographs, or use a video camera. Share them with families and discuss children's intentions. Ask families to share similar behaviors they have seen at home. Discuss the answers to the questions with team members. Create a portfolio for each child with examples of peer interest and behavior.

Adult–Child Interactions

Adults can use their understanding of infants' interest in each other and toddlers' and 2-year-olds' need for movement, imitation, repetition, routines, and shared themes.

ASSUME GOOD INTENTIONS   When teachers assume children's good intentions with peers they are supporting children's positive peer interactions. Forman and Hall (2005) share an example of a videative called "It takes to give."

> *A walking infant (Carrie) stood crying with a pacifier in her mouth. As a teacher soothed her, a peer (Lana) approached and patted the crying child on the head. As Lana's hand smoothed Carrie's hair, her hand circled around to the pacifier in Carrie's mouth. She pulled it out and immediately put it back in Carrie's mouth. The wise teacher instantly recognized that Lana's goal was not to upset Carrie by taking her pacifier but rather to console Carrie by giving her the pacifier. However, Lana had to take to give. The astute teacher applauded Lana by saying "Oh, thank you, Lana" and clapping her hands. Lana began to clap, too, feeling good about how she had helped.*

The teacher could easily have assumed that Lana was trying to upset Carrie but rather assumed that Carrie was trying to help. Lana learned that helping feels great!

USE RICH DESCRIPTIVE AND EMOTIONAL LANGUAGE   Use descriptive language to describe peer interactions, peer intentions, and peer feelings. As a toddler touches another toddler's toy, seemingly with the intent to interact, comment on these intentions. Use words for a variety of feelings expressed by children. Point out to a peer how another child feels; for example, say to a peer, "Lamont is crying . . . he feels sad." As children learn the names of feelings they will be better able to express them with each other.

ENCOURAGE TODDLERS AND 2-YEAR-OLDS TO USE LANGUAGE WITH PEERS   Encourage toddlers and 2-year-olds to talk or sign to communicate with their peers. When a toddler is crying, help him say to his peer who just stepped on him, "Please, stop," or "That hurt me."

ENCOURAGE PEER INTERACTIONS   Adults who sit on the floor and make their laps available promote peer interaction as they talk or sing with several infants on the floor. Mobile infants and toddlers come and go as they refuel emotionally by touching or plopping backwards with great trust on the caregiver's lap, and then they are off to explore the hinterlands found a few feet from the caregiver.

SCAFFOLD SOCIAL COMPETENCE   A toddler stands outside the dramatic play area watching but not entering. Honig and Thompson (1997) described strategies to help young children enter play with other children. Two-year-olds who successfully enter a dramatic play scene join in the play scenario rather than try to disrupt or change the scene. Sit or kneel by a 2-year-old who wants to enter a group of other children washing rocks. Find a rock for that child to show the group as he enters, or find a small tub of water near but not intruding on the other children's play. Alternatively, ask the children whether Sam, who wants to enter the play, can dry the rocks with a special cloth you've found that is just right for "making rocks sparkle." If a teacher watches the play with the entering child, then there usually is a way for a child to be with, and not against, the other children.

Set up experiences that require two toddlers to cooperate, such as moving a pumpkin from outdoors to indoors or carrying water from the sink to a plant. Attach two safe markers to an easel to encourage cooperative circle drawing. Think about how to support children's cooperative tendencies, rather than their competitive actions.

READ MANY BOOKS ABOUT SOCIAL INTERACTIONS   Find cloth and nondestructable cardboard books for infants and books with large pictures for toddlers and 2-year-olds. Look for books that emphasize babies with others as well as by themselves. There is no need for formal groups where all of the young children are required to sit in a circle. These required circle times often discourage children's love of books because of the teacher strategies needed to keep a large group of toddlers and 2-year-olds together—all sitting and listening. Rather, read books to one child or several snuggled on a couch or the floor together (Honig, 1998). Place books around the room and in a cozy corner with a comfortable space for teachers and children. Display books so that children can see the cover. A small couch for the children encourages children to sit together with a book. Provide a large couch for a teacher and one child or a group who has gathered together to hear an enthusiastic teacher read. From the time they are very young, children can be read to many times a day.

PROVIDE PHOTOGRAPH BOOKS   Small photograph books just right for little hands can be filled with photos of the children in the family child care center or room in a center. This helps children learn to associate the name of a child with his photo. Make these photograph books available so that infants, toddlers, and 2-year-olds can pick

3.11. Toddlers gather informally around a teacher to see an interesting book and hear the teacher read.

PHOTO: ASHANTE BUTCHER

them up, carry them around, and bring them to a teacher to look at together. A photograph book filled with photos of a child from birth to age 3 also helps that child gain a sense of self.

Fill photograph books with photos of the children playing or just being together during different parts of the day. As children look at these by themselves, with others, or with the teacher, they delight in seeing themselves, and the memory of social interactions grows as the teacher says, "Remember when. . . ." Create a book with the children's pictures based on *Brown Bear, Brown Bear* (Martin, 2008).

USE CHILDREN'S NAMES AND SING NAME SONGS OFTEN   Most people love at least some types of music, and babies are no exception. They perk up and listen when a care teacher sings a lively tune such as, "Where is Thumbkin?" They relax to a soothing song such as, "Lullabye and Good Night." They also join with their peers when a teacher sits on the floor and brings out her mitten with the props of "The Little Old Lady Who Swallowed a Fly." There is no need to require toddlers and 2-year-olds to sit. If not forced, they come toddling from across the room to join the small informal group—if they are not too busy with other tasks.

Name games are perfect for infants and toddlers. Sing "Where is Rakaia? Where is Rakaia? Here he is (pointing to him with a surprised or pleased look)." Laminate large photos of each child, and hold them up to an informal group of children who are standing or sitting near you. Ask, "Who is this?" If no one can guess (including the child whose photo it is), tell them and hold the photo near the subject's face.

Use the names of the children often to point out to one child what another child is doing. As a care teacher sits with a small group of toddlers and 2-year-olds to eat at a table, she can say each child's name to greet them. When a child says good-bye for the day, encourage the other children to say good-bye to the child by name.

Using children's names and singing songs with names encourages children to notice each other and learn their peer's names—an important step toward positive social relationships.

Environments

Long periods of time to explore in an organized environment with a selection of materials that are age- and stage-appropriate encourage peer interactions.

The Right to Move in an Enriched Environment

Lokken (2000b) argued that it may be a *right* of toddlers to move freely with their peers. She emphasized that "play supported mainly by the toddler body may be argued to be more *socially* meaningful to the children than play with small toys" and that "the cultivation of peer relations at this age seems to be more bodily joyful than toyful . . ." (p. 174).

Toddlers need space, time, and an understanding teacher to use their bodies to communicate with each other. *Containerizing* (Porter, 2003) is a barrier to social interactions. When a child is wrapped in the hard plastic of a car seat, a stationary entertainer, or a swing, that child is hindered from experience, including peer experience.

EQUIPMENT AND COZY CORNERS THAT ENCOURAGE PEER INTERACTIONS Place infants in a "nest" together, with a caring adult close by to support peer watching and touching. A safety mirror attached to the wall with a mat in front of it entices infants and toddlers to play with their images, imitating each other in their reflections. Comfortable child- and adult-size couches allow older infants and toddlers to sit close to each other, look at books, and share hugs with teachers and their peers.

For toddlers and 2-year-olds, larger equipment, structures, or play elements lead to fewer conflicts and aggression (DeStefano & Mueller, 1982). On the basis of her study of toddlers in programs in Norway, Lokken (2000b) made the following interesting point:

> One might argue that an adjacent meaning constructed by toddlers playing with small toys seems to be "this toy is for me to play with," while a corresponding adjacent meaning emerging in toddler play around a large element may be more like "this thing is for us to play with." (p. 170)

Create cozy corners for two or a small center that is just right for several children. Rocks in a shallow container of water set on a short table invites four children to stand around the table, splash the water, feel the rocks, and laugh with each other. Place the table against the wall, hang a safe mirror on it, supervise closely, and the children have a new peer experience.

TOYS AND MATERIALS Freedom and space to move is important; however, thoughtful offerings of toys and materials contribute to peer interactions and relationships. Creative and sensory materials lead to peer imitation and cooperation. Dramatic play clothes, scarves, and housekeeping materials promote peer discoveries and social play.

Summary

Infants and toddlers are active learners. They set goals for themselves and use a variety of strategies to accomplish their goals, which include interacting with peers. They show interest in other peers at an early age, preferring to watch peers their own age. They share meaning with other children, imitate them, and begin to share reciprocal and synchronous interactions. They develop remarkable new skills at each stage of development on their way to becoming adept at understanding and interacting with their peers.

3.12. Toddlers cooperate together to make a card for a teacher who is leaving the program.
PHOTO: ASHANTE BUTCHER

Adults can scaffold social competence by using language to talk about what peers are doing, encouraging toddlers and 2-year-olds to use language with their peers, and staying close to support peer interactions. Interesting environments with cozy areas for infants and toddlers spark children's interest in each other.

References

Becker, J. M. (1977). A learning analysis of the development of peer-oriented behavior in nine-month-old infants. *Developmental Psychology, 13*, 481–491.

Brenner, J., & Mueller, E. (1982). Shared meaning in boy toddlers' peer relations. *Child Development, 53*, 380–391.

Brooks, J., & Lewis, M. (1976). Infants' responses to strangers: Midget, adult, and child. *Child Development, 47*, 323–332.

Brownell, C. (1986). Convergent developments: Cognitive developmental correlates of growth in the infant/toddler peer skills. *Child Development, 57,* 275–286.

Brownell, C. A. (1990). Peer social skills in toddlers: Competencies and constraints illustrated by same-age and mixed-age interaction. *Child Development, 61*, 838–848.

Brownell, C. A., & Kopp, C. B. (Eds.) (2007). *Socioemotional development in the toddler years. Transitions and transformations.* New York: Guilford.

Brownell, C. A., Ramani, G. B., & Zerwas, S. (2006). Becoming a social partner with peers: Cooperation and social understanding in one- and two-year-olds. *Child Development, 77*(4), 803–821.

Brownlee, J., & Bakeman, R. (1981). Hitting in toddler-peer interaction. *Child Development, 52*(3), 1076–1080.

Bruner, J. (1996). What we have learned about early learning. *European Early Childhood Education Research Journal, 4*(1), 5–16.

Bullock, M., & Lütkenhaus, P. (1988). The development of volitional behavior in the toddler years. *Child Development, 59*(3), 664–674.

Capatides, J., Collins, C. C., & Bennett, L. (1996). *Peer interaction in toddlers: Parallel play revisited.* Paper presented at the conference "Ask the Child: Why, When, and How?" Teachers College, Columbia University.

DeStefano, C. T., & Mueller, E. (1982). Environmental determinants of peer social activity in 18-month-old males. *Infant Behavior & Development, 5*, 175–183.

Deynoot-Schaub, M. G., & Riksen-Walraven, M. (2006). Peer interaction in child care centres at 15 and 23 months: Stability and links with children's socio-emotional adjustment. *Infant Behavior and Development, 29*(2), 276–288.

Eckerman, C. (1993). Imitation and toddlers' achievement of co-ordinated action with others. In J. Nadel & L. Camaioni (Eds.), *New perspectives in early communicative development* (pp. 116–138). London: Routledge.

Eckerman, C. O., & Didow, S. M. (1996). Nonverbal imitation and toddlers' mastery of verbal means of achieving coordinated action. *Developmental Psychology, 32*, 141–152.

Eckerman, C. O., & Didow, S. M. (2001). *Peer and infant social/communicative development.* Oxford, England: Blackwell Publishers.

Eckerman, C. O., & Peterman, K. (2001). Peers and infant social/communicative development. In G. Bremner & A. Fogel (Eds.), *Blackwell handbook of infant development* (pp. 326–350). Oxford, England: Blackwell Publishers.

Eckerman, C. O., Whatley, J. L., & Kutz, S. L. (1975). Growth of social play with peers during the second year of life. *Developmental Psychology, 11*, 42–49.

Eckerman, C. O., Whatley, J. L., & McGehee, L. J. (1979). Approaching and contacting the object another manipulates: A social skill of the 1-year-old. *Developmental Psychology, 15*, 585–593.

Fabes, R. A., Martin, C. L., & Hanish, L. D. (2004). The next 50 years: Considering gender as a context for understanding young children's peer relationships. *Merrill-Palmer Quarterly, 50*(3), 260–274.

Fasig, L. G. (2000). Toddlers' understanding of ownership: Implications for self-concept development. *Social Development, 9*, 370–382.

Forman, G., & Hall, E. (2005). *Social clay.* Retrieved September 15, 2007, from www.videatives.com/content-new/store/product_info.php?products_id=77

Hanna, E., & Meltzoff, A. (1993). Peer imitation by toddlers in laboratory, home, and day-care contexts: Implications for social learning and memory. *Developmental Psychology, 29*, 701–711.

Hay, D. F. (2006). Yours and mine: Toddlers' talk about possessions with familiar peers. *The British Journal of Developmental Psychology, 24*, 39–52.

Honig, A. S. (1998, October/November). Babyroom & toddler time. Bring on the books. *Scholastic Parent and Child, 28,* 30.

Honig, A. S. (2002). *Secure relationships: Nurturing infant/toddler attachment in early care settings.* Washington, DC: National Association for the Education of Young Children.

Honig, A. S. (2003, September). Infants & toddlers/development: Helping babies feel secure. *Scholastic Early Childhood Today,* 27–29. Available online from http://content.scholastic.com/browse/article.jsp?id=3747141

Honig, A. S., & Thompson, A. (1997). Parent information: Helping toddlers with peer group skills. *Zero to Three, 14*(5), 15–19.

Howes, C. (1988). Peer interaction in young children. *Monographs of the Society for Research in Child Development (Serial No. 217), 53*(1), 1–78.

Howes, C., Matheson, C., & Hamilton, C. E. (1992). Sequences in the development of competent play with peers: Social and social-pretend play. *Developmental Psychology, 28*, 961–974.

Janson, U. (2001). Togetherness and diversity in preschool play. *International Journal for Early Years Education, 9*, 135–143.

Jennings, K. D. (2004). Development of goal-directed behaviour and related self-processes in toddlers. *International Journal of Behavioral Development, 28*(4), 319–327.

Johnson, J. E., Christie, J. F., & Yawkey, T. D. (1987). *Play and early childhood development.* Glenview, IL: Scott, Foresman and Company.

Johnson, J. E., Christie, J. F., & Yawkey, T. D. (1999). *Play and early childhood development* (2nd ed.). New York: Longman.

Katz, J. R. (2004). Building peer relationships in talk: Toddlers' peer conversations in childcare. *Discourse Studies, 6*(3), 329–347.

Kujawski, J. H., & Bower, T. G. R. (2003). Same-sex preferential looking during infancy as a function of abstract representation. *British Journal of Developmental Psychology 11*(2), 201–209.

Levitt, M. (1985). Reciprocity of exchange in toddler sharing behavior. *Developmental Psychology, 21*, 122–123.

Lokken, G. (2000a). The playful quality of the toddling style. *International Journal of Qualitative Education, 13*(5), 531–542.

Lokken, G. (2000b). Tracing the social style of toddler peers. *Scandinavian Journal of Educational Research, 44*(2), 163–176.

Martin, C. L., & Fabes, R. A. (2001). The stability and consequences of young children's same-sex peer interactions. *Developmental Psychology, 37*, 431–446.

Martin, B. (2008). *Brown bear, brown bear ,what do you see?* (paperback edition). New York: Henry Holt.

Meltzoff, A. (1995). Understanding the intentions of others: Re-enactment of intended acts by 18-month-old children. *Developmental Psychology, 31*, 838–850.

Moller, L. C., & Serbin, L. A. (1996). Antecendents of toddler gender segregation: Cognitive consonance, gender-typed toy preferences and behavior compatibility. *Sex Roles, 35*, 7–8, 445–460.

Montagner, H. (1978). *L'Enfant et la communication.* Paris: Stock.

NICHD Early Child Care Research Network. (2001). Child care and children's peer interaction at 24 and 36 months. *Child Development, 72*(5), 1478–1501.

Parten, M. B. (1932). Social participation among preschool children. *Journal of Abnormal and Social Psychology, 27*, 243–269.

Pawl, J. (1995). The therapeutic relationship as human connectedness: Being held in another's mind. *Zero to Three, 15*(4), 1, 3–5.

Pines, M. (1984, December). Children's winning ways. *Psychology Today,* 59–65.

Porter, P. (2003). *Social relationships of infants in daycare.* Bloomington, MN: Educarer. Retrieved June 27, 2005, from www.educarer.com/current-article-relationships.htm

Rubin, K. H., Bukowski, W., & Parker, J. G. (1998). Peer interactions, relationships, and groups. In N. Eisenberg (Ed.), *Handbook of child psychology, Volume 3: Social, emotional, and personality development* (5th ed., pp. 619–700). New York: Wiley.

Ryalls, B. O., Gul, R. E., & Ryalls, K. R. (2000). Infant imitation of peer and adult models: Evidence for a peer model advantage. *Merrill-Palmer Quarterly, 46*(1), 188–202.

Sanefuji, W., Ohgami, H., & Hashiya, K. (2006). Preference for peers in infancy. *Infant Behavior and Development, 29*(4), 584–593.

Selby, J. M., & Bradley, B. S. (2003). Infants in groups: A paradigm for the study of early social experience. *Human Development, 46*(4), 197–221.

Serbin, L. A., Moller, L. C., Gulko, J., Powlishta, K. K., & Colbourne, K. A. (1994). The emergence of gender segregation in toddler groups. In C. Leaper (Ed.), *Childhood gender segregation: Causes and consequences* (New Directions for Child Development, No. 65, pp. 7–18). San Francisco: Jossey-Bass.

Stamback, M., & Verba, M. (1986). Organization of social play among toddlers: An ecological approach. In E. C. Mueller & C. R. Cooper (Eds.), *Process and outcomes in peer relationships* (pp. 229–247). Orlando, FL: Academic Press.

Trevarthen, C., & Aitken, K. J. (2001). Infant intersubjectivity: Research, theory, and clinical applications. *Journal of Child Psychology and Psychiatry, 42*, 3–48.

Vygotsky, L. S. (1978). *Mind in society: The development of higher psychological processes.* Cambridge, MA: Harvard University Press.

Wittmer, D., & Petersen, S. (1992). Social development and interaction: Facilitating the prosocial development of typical and exceptional infants and toddlers in group settings. *Zero to Three, 12*, 14–20.

Wetherby, A., & Woods, J. J. (2006). Early social interaction project for children with autism spectrum disorders beginning in the second year of life: A preliminary study. *Topics in Early Childhood Special Education, 26*(2), 67–82.

4

BECOMING PROSOCIAL, MAKING FRIENDS, AND EXPERIENCING "GLEE"—THE JOY OF RELATIONSHIPS

> **Lois Barclay Murphy . . . reminds us, adults often fail to recognize the caring impulses and capacities of infants and toddlers. (Murphy, 1992, p. 3)**

This chapter turns the lens, allowing adults to "see" children learning how to be prosocial (kind, empathetic, comforting), how familiarity with peers enhances positive interactions, how important friendships develop between toddlers, and how they, with trusting abandon, experience glee with a peer. Adults hold the key to promoting and supporting children's prosocial attitudes and behavior (Howes, 2000; Zahn-Waxler, 1992).

Prosocial Behavior

After Maria gets hurt, she grabs her bunny tightly around his neck and cries a few tears. Santiago (who is sitting near her looking concerned) comments, "She sad," as he gently reaches out to touch Maria's head. "Are you OK?" asks Timmy, as he touches her arm while seemingly aware that Maria may need space. He looks concerned as he asks her, "What's wrong?" Santiago goes to get a sticker after commenting to the others, "Maybe she'd like a sticker." Ella moves in closer and touches Maria gently on the head.

This example is remarkable not only for what the boys and Ella do, but for what they don't do. They don't move in too closely, and they don't compete with each other for Maria's attention. They seem to have her "in mind."

Prosocial behaviors involve children beginning to think of the other and include "voluntary behavior intended to benefit another, such as helping, sharing, and comforting behaviors" (Eisenberg, 1992, p. 3). Prosocial behaviors include being accommodating to others; showing warmth and affection; sharing space, adults, and objects; cooperating; and showing empathy, compassion, and understanding of others.

As shown in the example above, there is also evidence of thinking of the other in Zack's behavior described in the following example:

Zack (25 months old) is bringing Tamara's (27 months old) baby doll and blanket back to her in their homeroom. Tamara had been playing with them at the end of the hallway, started crying, and ran back to her homeroom, leaving behind her blanket and doll. Zack, with a look of determination, marches the doll and blanket up the hallway and into the homeroom to Tamara. He doesn't seem to value the doll himself (he hangs onto it by its toes), but he behaves as if he thinks it is of value to Tamara. He strides in the homeroom and gives them immediately to Tamara. Zack seems to have Tamara in his thoughts as he intentionally delivers Tamara's prized possessions to her. He seems to have "another in his mind."

Our focus on increasing young children's prosocial behavior is a key to their present and future peer success (Denham, McKinley, Couchoud, & Holt, 1990; Hay, 2006). As we focus, we begin to understand the intricacies of when, how, and why children become prosocial.

Comforting Others in Distress

In 1936, Lois Murphy (1936, 1992) was told that very young children were incapable of sympathetic behavior—comforting peer behavior. Instead of believing this, she studied 2-year-olds attending a nursery school. After many observations Murphy (1936) wrote examples of sympathy, such as the following one of Heinrich:

Heinrich was on the Kiddie car. Wallis was on the bicycle nearby. Wallis fell off the bicycle, pulled it over on himself. He wiggled and struggled to get out. Heinrich left the Kiddie car, pulled the bike so that Wallis could get out. He rode off as soon as Wallis jumped up. (Murphy, 1937, p. 102; quoted in Murphy, 1992, p. 1)

Murphy found that toddlers:

- Comfort other children with pats, hugs, kisses, and solicitous expressions such as, "That hurts, doesn't it?";

- Attempt to remove the cause of another's distress (e.g., remove a tricycle from a fallen child);

- Help a child out of physical distress (e.g., pick a child up after a fall);

- Protect another child (e.g., catching a child as she falls);

- Warn another child by saying, for example, "you might fall"; and

- Suggest solutions (e.g., tell an adult to keep a child out of danger).

Instead of not being capable of sympathy, 2-year-olds had a repertoire of sympathetic behaviors. These young children did not respond to bruises, swellings, or a person's use of crutches, but rather to physical dilemmas such as accidents, falls, and bandages.

The Capacity to Care

In the late 1970s, other researchers also discovered that *both* infants and toddlers are capable of comforting others in distress and other prosocial behavior. Researchers studied the

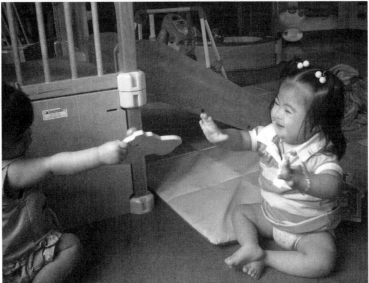

4.3 and **4.4.** Very young children are capable of being prosocial. Shana is delighted with Therese's gift.

PHOTO: CARLA MESTAS

"capacity to care" in children from 10 months to 2½ years old (Zahn-Waxler, Radke-Yarrow, & King, 1979, p. 109). The researchers studied children in three age groups—10 months, 15 months, and 20 months old. For 9 months, mothers reported on their children's responses to others' anger, fear, sorrow, pain, or fatigue (or any other negative emotion), as well as others' positive emotions, such as affection and pleasure. Researchers read the parents' detailed journals that they kept for 9 months and also analyzed simulated emotional incidents set up by the researcher every third week in the home (e.g., mother bumped her foot against an object and verbalized, "Ouch, my foot"). This groundbreaking study revealed very interesting information about the development of infants' and toddlers' prosocial behaviors.

Zahn-Waxler et al. (1979) analyzed both the *content* of children's behavior and how the responses to another person's distress *changed* through the early years. The young children of all three age groups showed a variety of reactions to others' distress, including no response, orients to emotion, distress cries, seeks caregiver, positive affect, aggression, imitation, and prosocial intervention. Children responded to 80%–90% of the distress situations by looking, laughing, crying, running to their caregiver, copying another baby's cry or their father's cough, hitting, or helping. Young children's responses developed from primarily self-distress as a response to "more focused efforts to interact positively with victims in distress" (Zahn-Waxler et al., 1979, p. 120).

Prosocial behavior increased with the age of the children and took many forms. Incredibly, 11% of the 10- to 15-month-old children's responses were prosocial (usually touching, patting, or presenting objects), whereas 33% of the older age group's responses were prosocial. In the 15-month and 20-month age groups, 87% of the children showed verbal sympathy, reassurance, and concern, saying things such as, "That's okay," or "You're OK now, you'll be happy." Many asked questions of others ("What's the matter?") or rubbed a hurt foot of another. Many (87%) egocentrically tried to lovingly help the victim by providing something that would help comfort themselves; for example, a child offered her own bottle to her mother, lay down with her, and then proceeded to drink her own bottle. We can recognize that, although the mother probably did not want to drink the bottle, the toddler offered her something that was very precious to herself—her own bottle.

Toddlers were, however, capable of thinking about what the other might need (decentering). Eighty-one percent used instrumental help; for example, one child brought a sweater to a chilly grandmother or another toddler fetched toilet paper to clean another child's injury. In these distress situations, the toddlers figured out what was needed, and in other cases (62% of the children) they had the great idea of enlisting the help of a third party—usually their mother. Almost all (94%) of the children in the oldest of the three age groups shared at some time during the study.

Although most of the children were capable of behaving prosocially, it is important for parents and professionals to know that most toddlers (81%) also could be ambivalent at times in their responses demonstrated by alternating prosocial and aggressive behaviors. They need ongoing support from adults on how to handle their own feelings of distress when they see others in distress, how to understand what the other person needs, and how to help in a way that is actually helpful to the other. Also, a few children deliberately hurt others and, although seemingly aware of the other child's distress, continued to inflict pain and distress. Box 4.1 summarizes the techniques that parents in Zahn-Waxler et al.'s (1979) study used to help their children become prosocial.

Responses to Peers' Cries

How do young children respond to other children's crying? Do they notice and if they notice, do they cry, too? A classic study conducted in a child care center examined the responses to the distress of peers in a sample of toddlers attending community-based child care and examined individual differences in responses to the distress of peers (Howes & Farver, 1987, p. 442).

BOX 4.1

They gave a clear, intense message that their child must not hurt others. A parent might say to the child, "Look what you did. You must never poke anyone's eyes" (said with feeling). The message was given to the child in a serious voice, but these parents did not slap or hurt their child in any way. They knew that they would model inappropriate behavior if they slapped or spanked their child when the child hurt a peer.

■ They helped their children with perspective taking—to see the connection between what they did and how it affected the other child. For instance, "You poked him. That hurt him" (said dramatically).

■ They gave reasons and explanations for why the child should or should not behave in a particular way. They didn't just say "No" or "Stop."

■ They taught their children what to do instead of biting, hitting, etc. A parent might say, "You can say 'Stop,' " or "Pat gently—it feels good when you pat gently."

■ They were kind and loving toward their own children. They gave hugs and kisses, soothing words, Band-Aids, and tissues for gently wiping runny noses. The children imitated their parents and used the same prosocial behaviors with their peers.

■ They helped others when they saw that they were in distress.

(From Infant and Toddler Development and Responsive Program Planning: A Relationship-Based Approach by D. L. Wittmer & S. H. Petersen, 2006, p. 123, Upper Saddle River, NJ: Prentice Hall. Copyright 2006 by Prentice Hall. Adapted with permission. Based on Pines, 1979.)

Forty-three children (aged 16–33 months) were observed as they interacted with their peers in child care centers. Each child was observed for sixteen 5-minute periods. If a child cried, researchers recorded the response of the peer and the teacher. Teachers independently identified peer friendships. Toddlers responded to other children's cries 24% of the time. When they responded, 93% of their peer responses to cries were prosocial in nature.

Empathy

A toddler looks concerned when a peer across the room beings to cry. Another toddler brings a grumpy peer some toys. A child goes to get a sticker for a friend who has hurt herself and is crying while holding her stuffed bunny tightly. These are examples of empathy. Empathy can be a look in a child's eyes that tells us that she is responding to the feelings of another child. Roth-Hanania, Busch-Rossnagel, and Higgins-D'Alessandro (2000, p. 7) emphasized that "empathy does not equal prosocial behavior. Empathy can be observed in infants long before any capacity for prosocial behavior occurs." Empathy, then, according to Roth-Hanania et al. (2000), is a feeling that doesn't require action.

Empathy, however, is also defined as "the capacity to observe the feelings of and to respond with care and concern . . ." (Quann & Wien, 2006). Using this definition, Quann and Wien studied "The Visible Empathy of Infants and Toddlers." These researchers documented 13 episodes of empathy during nine 3-hour observations and concluded that "the young children seemed fine-tuned to one another's feelings and able to put themselves in the position of others long before researchers in moral reasoning expect to observe empathy" (2006).

4.5, 4.6, and **4.7.** A toddler looks concerned that her peer is crying and tries to comfort her by handing her a toy.

PHOTO: MARK HERLINGER

Three types of empathy emerged from the observations. The first type was *proximal empathy*. A child did not cause another child to be hurt or upset but still responded with care and concern to the other child's distress. The example of proximal empathy includes Destiny (23 months) and Pratha (20 months).

> *Destiny and Pratha play in the creative area, attempting to use scissors to cut paper. Destiny, who has not had much experience using scissors, struggles to hold them. As she struggles her index finger bends backward and she begins to cry. Pratha says, "Ouch," and touches Destiny's hand. Pratha then looks up, presumably for a teacher. Teacher Leona comes over with ice and comforts Destiny. Pratha stands near with a concerned look on her face* (Quann & Wien, 2006).

A second type of empathy was *altruistic empathy*. A child is further away from the distressed child but stops what he or she is doing to try to comfort the upset child. The child goes out of his or her way to help another child. Quann and Wien (2006) have provided the following example of altruistic empathy.

> *Matthew (22 months) is out of sorts today, crying at the gate of the classroom door, wanting to leave (presumably to go after his mother, who left about an hour earlier). Two teachers have tried to comfort and distract him, but he remains upset. Amanda (17 months) brings him several trains; everyone knows they are his favorite toy. He throws them over the gate. One teacher successfully redirects him to a puzzle. Later, the other teacher picks up the trains and returns them to their bin. Amanda peers into the bins. She looks around the room, and when she sees Matthew, her face lights up. She brings the trains over and silently puts them on the table beside him. Colin (17 months) walks by the table, picks up the trains, and walks away. Matthew cries out and begins to chase Colin. He moves to a corner, crying loudly, and throws several toys. He has a large bell in his hand as Amanda approaches with another train she has found; she offers it to him. He puts the bell down, takes the train, and sits on the carpet, holding it. Amanda returns to reading books with Emma and a student teacher. Matthew puts down the train, goes to a bookshelf, picks out a book, and joins them. He is much happier for the rest of the morning* (Quann & Wien, 2006).

In this example, Amanda is persistent about helping Matthew, and as Quann and Wien (2006) pointed out, Amanda's solution is more fine tuned than the teacher's ideas.

Quann and Wien (2006) called the third type of empathy *self-corrective empathy*. This type occurs when a child causes another child's distress and then tries to remedy it.

Young children's responses to others' distress have received special attention in the prosocial research literature. We often see very young children show empathy and sympathy in their concern for another and their heartfelt attempts to comfort others when they are distressed. Toddlers and 2-year-olds seem to understand that others can feel sad and that they can express it with tears, sad faces, and slumping bodies. They "feel with" other children (Quann & Wien, 2006).

EMPATHY—KNOWING THE DIFFERENCE BETWEEN SELF AND OTHER Toddlers and 2-year-olds do seem to be able to think of the other:

> [M]ost of the prosocial behaviors studied reflect some level of understanding of the other person's experiences, and of what would provide help or comfort to the victim in that particular situation. (Zahn-Waxler & Radke-Yarrow, 1982, p. 125)

Empathy, then, seems to require knowledge of the difference between self and other. Van der Mark, van IJzendoorn, & Bakermans-Kranenburg (2002, p. 452) highlighted how empathy is related to a child's knowledge of self and other.

A prerequisite for empathic concern in the moral sense might be that children know the difference between themselves and the other person, and are able to take the perspective of the other (Hoffman, 1984). Otherwise, empathy would just be a passive reflection of distress and lead to self-comforting behavior, and not predispose to supportive moral behavior. (Van der Mark et al., 2002, p. 452)

If they did not know the difference between themselves and others they would comfort themselves in face of another child's distress rather than comforting the other child, which many of the younger children in the Zahn-Waxler et al. (1979) study did. However, as the children developed in the second year of life they were much more inclined to respond prosocially to the other. As infants develop into toddlers they are less likely to confuse their own emotions with the emotions of others.

In addition to knowing the difference between self and other, affection between two toddlers increases their empathic responses. Children who like each other seem to understand each other's emotions and reactions (Howes & Farver, 1987). These authors noted that although peers between 16 and 33 months old may perceive that another child is distressed, they may not respond unless the child is a friend.

Accommodation

Can young children change their behavior in response to other children's behavior? "One important aspect of social competence is the ability to accommodate social behavior to different contexts . . ." (Brownell, 1990, p. 838). Toddlers in the following example could adapt their language and style of playing when interacting with Sammy.

> *Sammy has cerebral palsy and can make clucking noises with his tongue. Without a teacher telling them to, two toddlers go to where he is lying on a couch. They begin to make clucking noises to him while standing beside the couch looking over him at his face. He makes the noises, they imitate it, and Sammy breaks out in laughter. They are accommodating their language to the sounds that he can make. Rather than using language that Sammy could not use to communicate, they accommodate their language to his. They speak his language.*

Warmth and Affection

Do infants and toddlers snuggle, nestle, huddle, or cuddle together? How do they show another child affection? When a younger infant started to cry, a toddler in the room ran over and kissed her on the head. Toddlers and 2-year-olds will pat each other as they have been gently patted when they are distressed.

Familiarity

> **They [peers] are more likely to initiate play, direct positive affect to, and engage in complex interactions with familiar than with unfamiliar playmates. (Howes, 1988, cited in National Research Council & Institute of Medicine, 2000, p. 167)**

If professionals want to build peer relationships, they increase the familiarity among children in a group. Contrary to the notion that familiarity breeds contempt, very young children find it easier to play with familiar peers.

Friendship

> **[At 15 months of age, a child] was very excited to see his "friend" after being separated for 4 months. They squealed with recognition, tentatively touched each other, and then hugged and kissed each other. (Porter, 2003)**

Toddlers look to the door to see if their "friend" has arrived for the day. They enjoy being with a friend and hug, kiss, and play in a special way with their friend. Toddler friends help each other, share, and play more complex games than they do with other peers.

What Is a Toddler Friendship?

Relationships are different from interactions, although relationships involve, as Rubin, Bukowski, and Parker noted, "a succession of interactions between individuals known to each other. . . . In a close relationship, influence is frequent, diverse, strong, and enduring" (1998, p. 625). In friendship, there is reciprocity—affirmed and recognized by both parties. They have a genuine affection for each other. They want to spend more time with each other, and they even miss each other when apart.

Can toddlers behave differently with different children? Ross and Lollis (1989) used a social relations analysis of toddler peer relationships to examine whether young children form different relationships with specific peers. They found that toddlers did behave differently in how they initiated and how they engaged in conflict with different partners. Ross and Lollis found that toddlers do not have one set of behaviors that they use consistently with all children; rather, they can behave differently depending on the children they are with and can develop friendships with certain children while not being friends with others.

Infants and toddlers can make a friend, be a friend, and have a friend. Howes (2000) found that over half of toddlers and 2-year-olds in her study of children in child care had friendships that lasted over the year in which they were studied and that they appeared some time after children's first birthdays.

In their article, "How Toddlers 'Do' Friendship," Whaley and Rubenstein (1994) considered two toddlers or 2-year-olds (aged 22–36 months) as friends when

- The toddlers and 2-year-olds have opportunities in their daily lives for regular play interactions with a particular partner;

- The toddler and 2-year-old partners are sufficiently well acquainted to have constructed scripted social interactions; and

- Companionship, intimacy, and affection can be inferred from these interactions.

Whaley and Rubenstein (1994) also identified friendships when these young children experienced time together, continuity, and mutual preference. They emphasized a social constructivist view of children's ability to make friends.

> The social constructivist view of development in friendship, then, would indicate that through activities and interactions with friends, children become aware of how friendship is accomplished, as well as the function of these relationships in their lives. (Whaley & Rubenstein, 1994, p. 386)

Zack and Maria, for example, are 2-year-olds who are friends. They have been together in the same class since they were infants. They spend a great deal of time together when they are in their school. They have opportunities in their daily lives for regular play interactions; they are sufficiently well acquainted to have constructed scripted social interactions; and they are affectionate with each other.

Zack and Maria prefer to be together, selecting each other as partners over others in the group. These two children gain pleasure in being together. They tell each other, "I love you." Because they have been together in the program since they were infants, they have had time together and continuity of group.

Dimensions of Toddler Friendships

Whaley and Rubenstein (1994) identified six dimensions that were present in the 2-year-olds' friendships that they observed. These dimensions included the following:

■ Helping

■ Intimacy

■ Loyalty

■ Sharing

■ Similarity

■ Ritual activity

HELPING   Toddlers help each other during play. The researchers saw two types of helping among 2-year-olds in Whaley and Rubenstein's (1994) observations of children—one involved helping a child during an activity and another included helping a friend who had

4.8. Young children teach their peers. Joshua teaches Geneva how to hang up the doll clothes.
PHOTO: ASHANTE BUTCHER

been hurt or was sad. The following is an example of the second type of helping—the more empathic type.

> Carly is playing near the toy shelf when Tommy runs by, accidentally stepping on her fingers. She begins to cry. Orly stands by briefly and watches as a teacher comes and picks Carly up into her lap. Orly turns, walks to the cubbies and gets Carly's bottle and "blankie." Orly takes this to Carly, hands it to her and stands briefly until Carly stops crying so hard. Orly then returns to the book she was reading. (Whaley & Rubenstein, 1994, p. 390)

INTIMACY   Whaley and Rubenstein (1994) identified intimacy as another dimension of toddler friendship. Two-year-olds nonverbally expressed intimacy through excluding others from their activity, staying in close physical contact, and experiencing "companionable silence." They may even ignore others as in the following example.

> Jed and Beth are sitting side by side on the child size couch, both drinking their bottles. Jed puts his bottle end to end with Beth's. They both drink and then laugh. Jed holds his bottle up and Beth does the same. Orly approaches them, jiggling a set of bells right next to their heads. Both ignore her and hold their bottles up again. Orly approaches again, this time putting her bells on Beth's head. Beth brushes the bells off but does not look at Orly. Jed puts his bottle on his foot and Beth does the same. Orly walks away as Jed and Beth continue their play. (Whaley & Rubenstein, 1994, pp. 390–391) [Note: Now it is not recommended by state licensing regulations nor is it recommended practice that children carry their bottles around and feed themselves.]

LOYALTY   Children supported their friend in the presence of other children. Through mostly nonverbal means, they defended their own objects as well as their friends.

> Beth and Jed have been playing with the balls for about 15 minutes when a teacher interrupts to take Jed for a diaper change. While he is in the bathroom, Harry walks across the room and picks up the red ball Jed has been using. Beth watches this, then turns and runs to the back of the room. She reaches into the basket holding the balls and gets a yellow ball out. Beth takes the yellow ball to Harry and reaches for the red one saying "Jed's ball." Beth hands the yellow ball to Harry, who continues to play using this ball. Beth walks toward the bathroom, both her ball and Jed's in her arms. (Whaley & Rubenstein, 1994, p. 392)

SHARING   Two-year-olds will give something that belongs to them to a friend.

> Jed and Beth are sitting in cube chairs with upside-down cube chairs in front of each of them serving as tables. Each has a cup from dramatic play. Beth looks in her cup, and puts in some Cheerios from a bag she has brought from home. Beth looks at Jed and says, "Do you have some?" Jed looks in his cup and shakes his head no. Beth reaches into her bag and fills his cup. They continue to eat. (Whaley & Rubenstein, 1994, p. 392)

Sharing was not frequently observed and usually came from one partner in the friendship pair. However, in the setting where observations were taken, resources were abundant, and children could usually get an identical toy to the one their partner had.

SIMILARITY   The 2-year-olds imitated each other, and in this way they seemed to be creating "similarity"—and a "we're together" feeling.

> Carly and Orly have been playing together, imitating one another for 35 minutes when Orly begins running around the large table in the room, singing "Ring Around the Rosie" at the top of her lungs. Carly follows and runs behind Orly, singing along. Orly is wearing blue jeans that are slightly too big and Carly has on a one piece jump suit. While running, Orly's pants begin to fall down so she reaches behind her and grabs a hold of her pants

with her right hand to keep them up while running. Almost immediately, Carly reaches back with her right hand, grabs the back of her jumpsuit in the same place, and continues to run with Orly. (Whaley & Rubenstein, 1994, p. 393)

These experiences give 2-year-olds a sense of emotional and physical connection to each other. Before two children are able to use language, nonverbal imitation binds them together almost as one.

The feature of imitation that distinguished imitation between friends from imitation between children who were not friends was its exactness. Between friends, imitation led to a synchrony. Even when this synchrony was disrupted by a teacher, the 2-year-olds would return to imitations so closely matched that it was often difficult to determine which child started the interaction (see Figure 4.1 and Figure 4.2).

When children do not mutually prefer each other, they seem to be out of synchrony (see Figure 4.3). The children represented in Figure 4.3 start in rhythm but quickly move out of rhythm.

RITUALS   Games such as playing babies, bears, and monsters were just a few rituals that were observed among toddler friends. Two toddlers developed these games with their friend, played them only with their friend, and seemed to look forward to playing them.

GRIEVING   Toddlers can be more committed to their friendships, and their relationships were more complex than had previously been reported in the literature. These children "worked to sustain their relationships and grieved when the relationships ended in some way" (Whaley & Rubenstein, 1994, p. 396). A toddler teacher at Boulder Journey School in Boulder, Colorado, captured how a child in her room seemed to remember and grieve for her friend who had to move to another room in the school.

FIGURE 4.1
Interaction chart — friendship dyad

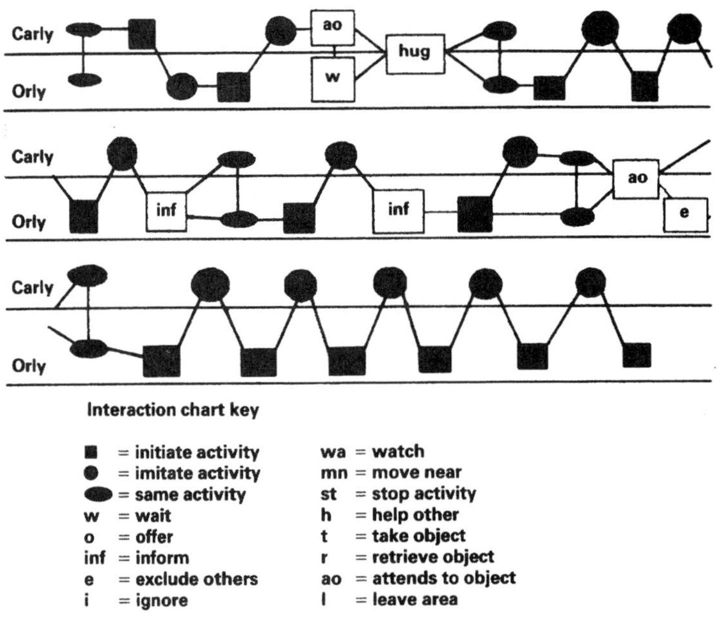

Interaction chart key

■ = initiate activity   wa = watch
● = imitate activity   mn = move near
⬭ = same activity   st = stop activity
w = wait   h = help other
o = offer   t = take object
inf = inform   r = retrieve object
e = exclude others   ao = attends to object
i = ignore   l = leave area

Source: Reprinted with permission from K. Whaley & T. Rubenstein (©1994), How toddlers "do" friendship: A descriptive analysis of naturally occurring friendship in a group care setting. *Journal of Social and Personal Relationships, 11,* 383–400, by permission of Sage Publications Ltd.

FIGURE 4.2
Interaction chart — friendship dyad

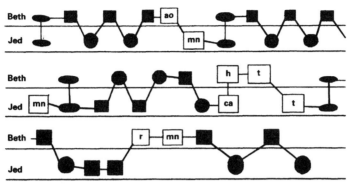

Note. See Figure 4.1 for key.

Source: Reprinted with permission from K. Whaley & T. Rubenstein (©1994), How toddlers "do" friendship: A descriptive analysis of naturally occurring friendship in a group care setting. *Journal of Social and Personal Relationships, 11,* 383–400, by permission of Sage Publications Ltd.

FIGURE 4.3
Interaction chart — non-friend dyad

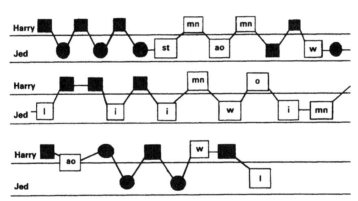

Note. See Figure 4.1 for key.

Source: Reprinted with permission from K. Whaley & T. Rubenstein (©1994), How toddlers "do" friendship: A descriptive analysis of naturally occurring friendship in a group care setting. *Journal of Social and Personal Relationships, 11,* 383–400, by permission of Sage Publications Ltd.

> Maria, a toddler girl, looks at an "All About Me" book of a classmate, Olivia, whose mother had to change the days that her child attended the school. An "All About Me" book has pictures of a child beginning when that child is a baby. Maria finds Olivia's book almost every day and looks through it. We do not positively know if she is grieving about not seeing Olivia in her room every day, but she does seem to have Olivia "in mind."

Summary

Familiarity and friendship among toddlers may play a much more important part of their lives than researchers previously thought. Friendships are fun, and they foster empathy. Toddler and 2-year-old children were three times more likely to respond to a friend in distress than another playmate who was not their friend (Howes & Farver, 1987). When children share affection with each other then they may be better able to perceive and experience each other's emotional reactions.

Toddler Glee

Two toddlers are laughing, dancing around, and spitting on each other. What toddlers find gleeful, we may not; however, when toddlers laugh it brings a smile to our face.

When infants and toddlers laugh, show delight, and experience joy and hilarity with each other, they are demonstrating toddler glee (Lokken, 2000a, 2000b). Lokken (2000b) said that "the joy in itself is the goal . . ." (pp. 168–169). With glee, toddlers feel safe with each other and give of themselves in an emotional connection that brings smiles and laughter. When we truly laugh with another adult, we abandon caution and we feel almost as one with that person. We find the same things funny, and we are in harmony with each other. We cement our relationships through laughter. When toddlers laugh with each other, their relationships become stronger as well.

With joy as the goal, more toddler glee will erupt in programs for young children.

Prosocial Strategies

Teachers and parents can help infants and toddlers learn to comfort others, think about others' perspectives, and feel empathy for others.

Be an Observer and Documenter of Positive Social Behaviors

Prosocial behaviors may be occurring more than a teacher might think because the aggressive or hurtful behaviors cause such a stir in the home or center and prosocial behaviors often go

4.9. Toddlers gleefully dance to the music.
PHOTO: ASHANTE BUTCHER

unnoticed. Adults need to attend to those negative situations to keep children safe and teach them prosocial strategies, but they also want to attend with enthusiasm and encouragement to young children's prosocial behaviors of showing empathy, comforting, and helping others.

First, adults must notice and document these often subtle but sometimes clearly visible prosocial attitudes and behaviors. Quann and Wien's (2006) documentation of toddlers' and 2-year-olds' visible empathetic behaviors certainly helped teachers and parents appreciate the capabilities of infants and toddlers and think about ways to encourage even more of these kind, thoughtful behaviors among children.

Affirm Children

Constantly affirm infants' and toddlers' prosocial pats, hugs, helping, and guiding others. Affirmation that is specific, such as, "You helped Damont. He really liked that. You are a great helper," will encourage children to continue their prosocial behavior. With affirmation, young children will develop an identity of themselves as someone who is prosocial.

Use Continuity of Group in Programs

Because friendships are more likely to occur after children have spent time together, teachers need to reconsider the policy of moving children to another classroom every 6–12 months in child care. In addition, sometimes a child is "moved up" separately from his group when he has a birthday or when he reaches a motor milestone, such as walking. Continuity of care (when a caregiver moves "up" with a group) and continuity of group (when a group stays together) promote toddler friendships, allowing the time needed for peer relationships to develop.

Continuity of groups entails keeping groups of children together from infancy through toddlerhood. Teachers can move groups, rather than individuals, to the next age group. This requires planning, as often it is easier for an administrator in a center program to move individual children as they learn to walk, as they are out of diapers, or as a slot becomes open in the next age group. However, this is not what is best for children. Keeping a group together supports familiarity, friendship, and prosocial behavior. Peers who are familiar with each other are more likely to initiate play, be more positive, and engage in more complex

4.10. A teacher supports a toddler emotionally as he tries to comfort a peer by giving her the ball.
PHOTO: ASHANTE BUTCHER

interactions (Howes, 1988). Also, it is a scary, lonely experience for a child to move to another room without familiar faces of care teachers and peers. A child I know did not want to turn 3 years old because she knew she would move alone from the toddler to the preschool room. It seems very sad that a 2-year-old would not look forward to her birthday! It is challenging for us as adults to enter a new group—imagine what it is like for young children.

Give Children Opportunities to Play

As discussed at the end of chapter 3, in an interesting environment children choose from an interesting and well-displayed environment with supportive adults available for the children to "refuel" emotionally with a care teacher. As children choose, they naturally interact with each other.

Support Children's Communication With Each Other

Quann and Wien (2006) taught the infants and toddlers to use sign language for *stop, help,* and *more* to help children feel more self-control during peer interactions. Encourage children to use the words as well as they interact with their peers.

Help Toddlers and 2-Year-Olds Problem-Solve

Help toddlers and 2-year-olds to notice another child in distress and think about how to help the other child who is feeling blue, crying, or having difficulty with a task.

Plan—"Day to Day the Relationship Way"

Teachers can thoughtfully plan for relationships to happen each day. As adults observe the particular interests and goals of each child, they change the environment, add materials, or create other opportunities for children to build relationships with peers and adults.

4.11. These toddlers take turns opening and shutting the drawer to the cupboard that is just their size.
PHOTO: ASHANTE BUTCHER

Provide an "Aura of Emotional Support" in a Room

Conscientiously create a prosocial atmosphere in the family child care home or center home rooms. Emphasize prosocial attitudes and behavior at all times. When prosocial behavior is encouraged, the children feel the caring atmosphere.

Meet individual children's emotional needs; then they are more likely to show empathy for their peers' distress. To become prosocial with others, infants and toddlers need to feel what it is like to be treated prosocially.

Model, Model, and Model Some More

Show children how to be kind and to help others. They are learning from adults how to be with others. When you see a child in need, take another infant or toddler with you to see what is wrong and provide comfort. Model how to be prosocial—caring, helping, and comforting others.

Emphasize Perspective Taking

Understanding another's point of view is difficult for adults, but adults can listen to another's words and watch physical cues to determine how others feel. Young children are just learning about their own and other's feelings and need constant support to think about a peer's emotional state or the intentions of another. Say to one child, "I think Shawn is feeling sad. Look, he is crying. What could we do to help him feel better?"

Set Up A Prosocial Environment

Prosocial environments support children's experience of each other as kind, helpful, loyal, and empathic. Teachers can arrange the physical environment with cozy corners for two or play centers for two or three children. Duplicate toys encourage imitation and children's sense of similarity to others.

4.12. Teachers arrange an inviting water table to encourage toddler interactions.
PHOTO: ASHANTE BUTCHER

Summary

Toddlers and 2-year-olds are constructing knowledge each day about how to interact with their peers in prosocial ways. They have the capacity to care and to relate to their peers with affection and empathy. They can experience peer glee as they playfully dance to music or chase a fly around the room. Parents and professionals support prosocial development through providing loving care, modeling kindness, guiding children's caring capacities, discussing feelings, supporting children's self-regulation, supporting language development, and creating an environment of cozy corners, spaces for one or two, spaces for movement, and places for toddler rituals (such as peek-a-boo behind a curtain) and routines. Children who experience a group of children with whom they are familiar and move together, as a group, to the next room in a program or stay together while materials change to accommodate their growing interests demonstrate increased prosocial feelings and skills. Teachers and parents can value the importance of friends, seen as early as 1 year of age, in toddlers' lives and support them. They thoughtfully plan for relationships each day.

References

Brownell, C. A. (1990). Peer social skills in toddlers: Competencies and constraints illustrated by same-age and mixed-age interaction. *Child Development, 61*, 838–848.

Denham, S. A., McKinley, M., Couchoud, E. A., & Holt, R. (1990). Emotional and behavioral predictors of preschool peer ratings. *Child Development, 61*, 1145–1152.

Eisenberg, N. (1992). *The caring child*. Cambridge, MA: Harvard University Press.

Hay, D. F. (2006). Yours and mine: Toddlers' talk about possessions with familiar peers. *The British Psychological Society, 24*, 39–52.

Howes, C. (1988). Peer interaction in young children. *Monographs of the Society for Research in Child Development, 53* (1, Serial No. 217), 1–78.

Howes, C. (2000). Social development, family, and attachment relationships of infants and toddlers: Research into practice. In D. Cryer & T. Harms (Eds.), *Infants and toddlers in out-of-home care* (pp. 87–113). Baltimore: Brookes.

Howes, C., & Farver, J. (1987). Toddlers' responses to the distress of their peers. *Journal of Applied Developmental Psychology, 8*, 441–452.

Lokken, G. (2000a). The playful quality of the toddling style. *International Journal of Qualitative Education, 13*(5), 531–542.

Lokken, G. (2000b). Tracing the social style of toddler peers. *Scandinavian Journal of Educational Research, 44*(2), 163–176.

Murphy, L. B. (1936). Sympathetic behavior in young children. *Journal of Experimental Education, 5*, 79–90.

Murphy, L. B. (1937). *Social behavior and child personality: An exploratory study of roots of sympathy*. New York: Columbia University Press.

Murphy, L. B. (1992). Sympathetic behavior in very young children. *Zero to Three, 12*(4), 1–5.

National Research Council & Institute of Medicine. (2000). *From neurons to neighborhoods: The science of early childhood development*. Committee on Integrating the Science of Early Childhood Development. J. P. Shonkoff & D. A. Phillips (Eds.). Washington, DC: National Academy Press.

Pines, M. (1979, June). Good Samaritans at age two? *Psychology Today*, 66–73.

Porter, P. (2003). *Social relationships of infants in daycare*. Bloomington, MN: Educarer. Retrieved June 2005 from www.educarer.com/current-article-relationships.htm

Quann, V., & Wien, C. A. (2006, July). The visible empathy of infants and toddlers. *Young Children, 61*(4), 22–29. Available online at *Beyond the Journal—Young Children on the Web* from www.journal.naeyc.org/btj/200607/Quann709BTJ.asp

Ross, H. S., & Lollis, S. P. (1989). A social relations analysis of toddler peer relationships. *Child Development, 60*(5), 1082–1092.

Roth-Hanania, R., Busch-Rossnagel, N., & Higgins-D'Alessandro, A. (2000). Development of self and empathy in early infancy: Implications for atypical development. *Infants and Young Children, 13*(1), 1–14.

Rubin, K. H., Bukowski, W., & Parker, J. G. (1998). Peer interactions, relationships, and groups. In N. Eisenberg (Ed.), *Handbook of child psychology, Volume 3: Social, emotional, and personality development* (5th ed., pp. 619–700). New York: Wiley.

Van der Mark, I., Van IJzendoorn, M. H., & Bakermans-Kranenburg, M. J. (2002). Development of empathy in girls during the second year of life: Associations with parenting, attachment, and temperament. *Social Development, 11*(4), 451–469.

Whaley, K., & Rubenstein, T. (1994). How toddlers "do" friendship: A descriptive analysis of naturally occurring friendships in a group childcare setting. *Journal of Social and Personal Relationships, 11*, 383–400.

Wittmer, D. L., & Petersen, S. H. (2006). *Infant and toddler development and responsive program planning: A relationship-based approach.* Upper Saddle River, NJ: Prentice Hall.

Zahn-Waxler, C. (1992). Development of concern for others. *Developmental Psychology, 28*, 126–136.

Zahn-Waxler, C., & Radke-Yarrow, M. (1982). The development of altruism: Alternative research strategies. In N. Eisenberg (Ed.), *The development of prosocial behavior* (pp. 109–137). New York: Academic Press.

Zahn-Waxler, C., Radke-Yarrow, M., & King, R. A. (1979). Child rearing and children's prosocial initiations toward victims of distress. *Child Development, 50*(2), 319–330.

5

OF COURSE, THERE ARE CONFLICTS—AND THEN THERE IS BITING

PHOTO: MANZANITA FINE

> **Conflict is a central concept in virtually every major theory of human development. Moments of conflict are viewed as dynamic, critical episodes of adapting or not adapting, progressing or regressing. (Shantz, 1987, p. 283)**

When infants, toddlers, and 2-year-olds are together in groups, there will be conflicts. The first section of this chapter turns the lens toward the development, value, and challenges of conflict for older infants, toddlers, and 2-year-olds. Conflicts have value for young children as they learn to negotiate sharing the teacher, space, toys, and materials. Young children learn about *self* and *other* during these inevitable experiences in group programs.

The last part of the conflict section in this chapter focuses on strategies that teachers can use to prevent major conflicts and to support infants' and toddlers' learning during moments (or days) of disagreement. What does a teacher say to two toddlers who, with grimacing faces, are struggling over a toy, with each holding tightly to a piece of the action? How does a teacher relate to families around conflict and biting? Adults' mediating strategies, rather than power strategies, facilitate children's learning during conflict resolution.

Conflicts

Most young children have a "desire for continuity of peer interaction and for harmonious communication" and "a strong desire . . . to continue to play together" that "leads children to either avoid conflict or, if conflicts emerge, search for solutions" (Singer & Hannikainen, 2002, p. 6). However, where there are older infants, toddlers, and 2-year-olds, there will be conflict. Their beginning language skills and emerging ability to coordinate goals limit their knowledge of how to enter other children's play, how to disagree and protest, and how to resolve conflicts. They are constructing their social knowledge about how to negotiate, bargain, and cooperate.

What Are Conflicts?

Conflict is defined as protesting, resisting, or retaliating against another child (Hay & Ross, 1982). Conflicts occur when, "[o]ne person overtly opposes another person's actions or statements" (Shantz, 1987, p. 283). They are tussles—verbal or nonverbal struggles between two children. Conflict is different from aggression (i.e., intentionally harming another; Shantz, 1987). Conflicts are typically between two children, and they are relational. Certain children may engage in more conflicts with each other, depending on the relationship and experience the children have (Ross & Lollis, 1989).

Reasons for Toddlers' and 2-Year-Olds' Tussles: What Are They Thinking?

Children's goals during conflict are not always immediately apparent. A grab for a toy from another may really be an awkward (and often unsuccessful) attempt to play with the other child (Singer & Hannikainen, 2002). A lunge toward another or knocking a peer's block structure down may be an attempt to initiate or join the other in play. A child who is just beginning to toddle may start to hug another toddler, only to knock the other down and then fall on the other child. The knocked-down child protests, and a conflict ensues.

Older infants, toddlers, and 2-year-olds tussle and have disagreements over the following:

- Territory

- Object possession and ownership

- Resistance at other children entering their play

- Control of the content of their play

- Access to attractive toys

- Resistance to hurtful or aggressive behaviors from other children

- Ego testing

- Asking "What can I get away with?" "Who am I?" "Who owns what?" and "Who has the right?"

- Dominance

5.2. Two infants, barely able to sit, both want the same toy. One does not protest when the other takes it away.
Photo: Nicole Smith

(List compiled from data from Corsaro, 1997; Hawley & Little, 1999; Hay, 2006; Rubin, 2002; Shantz, 1987; Singer & Hannikainen, 2002)

Younger children have more conflict over objects than preschoolers do. In a study conducted over 20 years ago, Hay and Ross (1982) found that among 24 pairs of unacquainted 21-month-olds, 88% of the conflicts were over objects. Chen, Fein, Killen, & Hak-Ping (2001) in their study of 2-, 3-, and 4-year-olds' (400 children) peer conflicts, found that:

> Two-year-olds had a higher proportion of distribution of resources conflicts than did 3- and 4-year-olds. Conflicts about play and ideas significantly increased with age while those stemming from physical harm were low overall. Further, child-generated resolutions increased while insistence decreased significantly with age. (p. 523)

Chen et al. (2001) noted that conflicts about materials and space dropped from 77.8% for 2-year-olds to 58.7% for 3-year-olds and 46.8% for 4-year-olds. There are many reasons, then, for infant and toddler conflicts, which can be nonverbal or verbal in nature, and the reason for conflicts seems to change as children develop.

Frequency

Although it is hoped that the number of conflicts would decrease with age, there is disagreement in the literature as to whether that actually happens. In their study of 400 toddlers, 2-year-olds, and 3-year-olds, Chen et al. (2001) found that the nature or quality of conflict changes rather than the number of conflicts, whereas other researchers found that the number of conflicts decreases over time (Hay, 2006). More research is needed to observe under what conditions and settings conflict between young children decreases or increases.

Conflict and Social Competence—Do They Really Go Together?

Conflicts can be considered significant situations of communication, social learning, and problem solving. (Singer & Hannikainen, 2002, p. 5)

Conflict is different from mean-spirited aggression and is related to social competence in two ways.

The first involves the fact that socially competent children are not withdrawn or aggressive but can be rather assertive in their play. They are full of confidence and often right in the middle of the play action, resulting in more opportunities for conflict with peers (Vaughn, Vollenweider, Bost, Azria-Evans, & Snider, 2003).

A second way in which conflict is related to social competence is that young children learn valuable skills during conflict with their peers (Bayer, Whaley, & May, 1995; Chen, 2003; Vaughn et al., 2003). The negotiation and self-regulation skills necessary to prevent the conflict from escalating and interfering with play improve as these children gain experience in the art of disagreeing, resisting, or competing.

> **Conflicts are natural contexts in which children develop socially, morally, and cognitively. (Chen et al., 2001, p. 523)**

Shantz (1987) emphasizes Piaget's theory when discussing the importance of conflict in young children's lives.

> [C]onflict, particularly between those of equal power, is essential for the reduction of egocentrism. One child's objections to another's goals, for example, serve as prods to the child to reflect on her or his own reasons for holding certain positions, wanting certain things, and the like in order to justify the merits of the child's viewpoint and the logic of the reasoning. Such interpersonal conflict engenders intrapsychic conflict (cognitive conflict), to result in the ability, Piaget thought, to operate in concert with others, that is to *co*-operate, and to foster cognitive development in general. (p. 284)

Children's involvement in conflict, then, may actually play a positive role in peer development as they begin to learn that others have ideas that are different from their own ideas. However, there is potential for children progressing or regressing in social competence, depending on the child, the setting, and the adults who scaffold conflict resolution—or not.

CONFLICTS ARE QUITE SOCIAL AFFAIRS   Eckerman and Peterman (2001) noted that "conflicts can be quite social affairs" (p. 343), and they asked, "Could experience in peer conflicts aid toddlers in coming to understand distinctions between themselves and others . . .?" (p. 344).

The following summary of an incident reported by Forman and Hall (2005) supports this idea.

> *Two infants—approximately 13 months old—were riding on rocking horses near each other. A third rocking horse sat empty. As Infant 1 and Infant 2 rocked they watched each other carefully, without smiling. Infant 2 moved off her horse. She approached Infant 1 and soon pushed Infant 1 off her horse. At first, Infant 1 protested but soon slid off and went to the third horse, while keeping a close eye on Infant 2. Rocking continued, but as soon as Infant 2 moved off the preferred horse, Infant 1 swiftly moved to her initial horse and mounted it. Infant 2 went back to her initial horse, as well. When Infant 1 spied her blanket across the room, she dismounted from her horse but stayed close to it, pulling the horse across the room as she retrieved her blanket. She seemed to know that if she left her horse for a second, that quick Infant 2 would snatch it.*

These very young toddlers were learning about self and other during this mild conflict over who would have which rocking horse.

Conflicts Are Relational

Kari wanted the bright colored basket that Thomas was waving in the air. It looked so much more attractive than the one she had in her hand. She walked over, grabbed the basket, and took off. Thomas stood looking forlorn and confused. Later Thomas ran across the room and grabbed a doll out of Kari's hands.

What is going on in this example?

It seems that conflicts are relational. Hay and Ross (1982) found that, with toddlers, the outcome of a prior conflict affects the next conflict, and the child who lost the prior conflict is more likely to initiate the next one. The particular relationship between Kari and Thomas is influencing how they behave with each other.

A toddler's *experience* with another child also influences how he or she will interact with the other child. For example, Mack, a toddler in a child care center, unfortunately seemed to be the toddler that all of the other toddlers avoided, because he often hit them when he came close. The other toddlers in the room based their actions (moving away when Mack came near) on past experience with Mack. The opposite can happen, too. Friends will share more with each other.

Conflicts Are Situational

Conflicts are situated in a context. Thornberg (2006) used puppets to study preschool children's conflict management attitudes and skills and found that children's strategies are, to a greater or lesser degree, influenced by the opponent's strategies—in other words, determined by the situation and the relationship. Preschool children seemed ready to respond in kind to their opponent's strategy. If an opponent during a conflict was aggressive, the other child responded with aggression. If the opponent was not aggressive, then the other child rarely used aggressive strategies. It is important, then, that adults realize that they may just be seeing an *act* of the conflict play and need to look for the *whole* play. If a child hits back, then there may have been an initial hit from the other child.

The Strategies Children Use

As Sesto and Bridger played with blocks while sitting very close together, Sesto eyed a piece on Bridger's structure that would complete his block train. With a quick grab, he pried it from Bridger's structure and placed it on his own. Obviously upset, Bridger whined and declared loudly to Sesto, "Mine!" As Sesto ignored his pleas, Bridger tried a different tactic. He raised his voice and declared, "I need that," but the words fell into space without having their intended effect on Sesto. Finally, Bridger appealed to a teacher nearby, "Teacher, Sesto took my block." As the teacher approaches, Sesto quickly throws the piece back to Bridger.

In this example, we see how one child initiated conflict and how the other child responded by using a variety of strategies. Toddlers and 2-year-olds have a repertoire of conflict behavior that they use.

INITIATION OF CONFLICT "Children initiate conflicts by using a simple 'No,' reasoning or justifying, offering alternative proposals, postponing agreement, and evading" (Chen, 2003, p. 204). They also may use nonverbal means such as "taking, tugging, or pulling objects" to start a struggle over objects (Chen, p. 204).

Hay (2006) reports that as they grow older, children use more sophisticated ways to get objects. They may ask politely, "Can I have some of yours?" or they provide a justification while admonishing the peer, "Don't take my blanket. That's my favorite blanket." He emphasized that children learn these more socially acceptable ways from their experiences with parents, siblings, and familiar peers.

RESPONSES TO OPPOSITION   Young children can vary the content of their responses. Toddlers and 2-year-olds may try to convince a peer that she or he already has a "good-enough" toy and need not try to snatch their toys (Hay, 2006). They also may justify their actions by talking about their own needs and desires (Hay, 2006). Chen (2003, p. 204) identified ways in which toddlers and 2-year-olds respond to other children's opposition. They may insist, reason, offer alternative proposals, compromise, ignore, request an explanation, or use physical force. They also could seek adult help by tattling, whining, or simply by asking. Chen et al. (2001) also described two main types of gestures: subordinate (e.g., crying, withdrawing, and yielding) and conciliatory (e.g., cooperative propositions, apologies, symbolic offers, and sharing of objects).

Young children could also use what Brenneis and Lein (1977; cited in Shantz, 1987, p. 290) referred to as "stylistic tactics." They could raise their voice, talk faster, and emphasize certain points to indicate "absolute fortissimo" (Shantz, 1987, p. 290), or absolute determination to win.

As children grew from 2-year-olds to 4-year-olds, they solved more of their conflicts *and* solicited assistance from teachers more often (Chen et. al, 2001). Both of these strategies represent increased developmental knowledge about their own skills, how teachers might assist them, and their understanding of self and other.

INSISTENCE   One can just hear and see the insistent child who resolutely hangs on tightly to his toy and gives out a screech as another child plans to take it or a child who escalates conflict by using a well-directed blow to another child's arm in an attempt to get him to release a desired toy. Two-year-olds are more likely to be insistent about needing a grabbed object back if they are using the piece in their play (Sieminski, 2007). Fortunately, insistence decreases as children develop from 2-year-old to 4-year-old and learn to use "explanations, justifications, and conciliatory behaviors such as yielding, compromising, negotiating" (Chen et al., 2001, p. 532). A decrease in insisting on their claim to an object or an idea about play represents increased understanding that others have different opinions about matters *and* one can consider another's point of view (Chen et al., 2001).

5.3. One child insists that she does not want the other child to touch her puzzle.
PHOTO: ASHANTE BUTCHER

Dominance

Do we see dominance in peer play? Toddlers and 2-year-olds who continuously prevail in conflicts with other toddlers, while using power techniques rather than negotiation strategies, may be considered dominant. Hawley and Little (1999) observed that toddlers who were physically stronger, more mature, more cognitively advanced, more goal directed, and who had more physical and social experience in a particular group setting seemed to be more dominant. They also observed that girls were dominant more often than boys.

Gender Differences

Sims, Hutchins, and Taylor (1998) discovered that there are differences between boys and girls attending child care. Boys tended to use powerful strategies when conflicting with girls and girls use less powerful strategies when conflicting with boys. Sims et al. recommended that child care professionals watch for gender differences and support both genders to use negotiation strategies.

Adults' Strategies for Conflict Relationship Restoration With Children

As the lens turns toward the development, value, and challenges of conflict for infants and toddlers, we see that there are a variety of approaches that adults can use to prevent conflicts and support children's learning when conflicts occur.

First, however, adults may want to reflect on their own attitudes about conflict. If adults know that conflicts are an important part of young children's social learning, they will approach conflicts with a supportive attitude. Rather than becoming anxious and immediately separating children during conflict, adults will make sure children have opportunities to learn valuable negotiation, justification, and other conflict resolution skills (see Box 5.3)

Adults can consider how they respond to conflicts from a variety of approaches—leading to a value for conflict as an opportunity for supporting blossoming social skills. From a relationship-based approach, teachers' primary goal is to build relationship-building skills among infants and toddlers. In a sociocultural model (Vygotsky, 1978), children learn conflict resolution strategies from more expert adults and from peers. When adults intervene, they should do so in strategic ways that support learning among the "disputants" (Bayer et al., 1995) and also take into consideration the capabilities of the particular children engaged in conflict (Chen et al., 2001). In a social–cognitive model (Piaget, 1936/1953), children actively construct their knowledge about social relationships during conflicts. They need experience with conflicts to do so. In a social cognitive model (Bandura, 1989), children watch closely and imitate ways to solve their social problems.

Conflicts, then, are opportunities for growth among peers. Certain teacher strategies are much more effective than others in restoring children's relationships during and after conflict occurs (Singer & Hannikainen, 2002), helping children understand shared meanings (Sims, Hutchins, & Taylor, 1996), and teaching skills that enable children to regulate their own behavior.

BOX 5.3

Instead of trying to avoid and prevent disputes, why not use them as opportunities to help children develop strategies for the peaceful resolution of differences with others? (Chen, 2003, p. 203)

As always, teachers' strategies are individualized. Teachers notice children's individual goals during a conflict and their styles of handling conflict. One child withdraws in the face of another infant's shriek during tussles with toys. Another child jumps into the fray with a fountain of words or a cascade of movements. These individual and cultural styles of handling conflict influence teachers' strategies during conflict.

Strategies for Teachers

DaRos and Kovach (1998) shared the following scenario of two toddlers experiencing conflict and the possible strategies that a teacher might consider.

Matthew, a 15-month-old, is playing on the floor with a blue car. He appears to be peacefully exploring how he can make noise by spinning the car wheels with his fingers. Twelve-month-old Hamilton looks up from across the room to see where the noise originated. He sees Matthew spin the car wheels and creeps over for a better look. Hamilton watches Matthew momentarily and then lunges for the blue car. Before Hamilton can attempt a getaway, Matthew snatches the car back with a swift yank. Startled, Hamilton expresses his loss with a long, loud wail.

You are the caregiver who is watching the scene unfold from a distance. Do you:

- *Remove the car that is causing the conflict between the two toddlers?*

- *Sympathetically take sides with the child you perceive to have been victimized?*

- *Ignore the interaction, as it is one of the numerous aggravations you learn to accept in a toddler's day?*

- *Move in close proximity to the situation, knowing that it has not finished playing itself out?*

What would you do? Observing and restoring relationships with mediation strategies are strategies that teachers can use to teach toddlers and 2-year-olds how to negotiate peer conflict.

OBSERVING Sometimes observation of the conflict is a first step for teachers. However, as two toddlers yell about who had a doll first, it is difficult for a teacher not to immediately intervene, especially if she knows one of the toddlers likes to bite when he is frustrated. As children develop, however, so does their ability to resolve their own conflicts (Chen et al., 2001). Chen et al. found that, although one fourth of 2-year-olds resolved their own conflicts, one half of 4-year-olds were able to do so. Too much teacher intervention, as well as intervention that happens too quickly, may not give the children an opportunity to use increasingly sophisticated conflict prevention and resolution strategies. Observing the conflict if children are not harming each other, themselves, or the environment gives children an opportunity to learn that other children's perspectives and feelings may be different than their own.

Do adults give toddlers a chance to resolve their own conflicts by observing first or moving closer to let the young children know that a teacher is present if needed? Not so much, according to DaRos and Kovach (1998), who noted that toddlers in group care are rarely allowed to engage in conflict without adult interference. They cited research by Killen and Turiel (1991), who discovered that, in 91% of all toddler conflicts, adults determined the solution—without involving the toddler. When adults usually direct the action and prevent toddlers from engaging in conflict resolution, they prevent toddlers from trying out different strategies.

Of course, toddlers and 2-year-olds often need a teacher to support their beginning ability to self-regulate their strong emotions and understand other children's feelings, but adults' constant intervention can interfere with young children's peer relationships. In an interesting study, Williams, Ontai, and Mastergeorge (2007) found that when caregivers interrupt toddler peer interactions, they may be negatively influencing peer sociability. An interruption involves the caregiver using a behavior, vocalization, or facial expression that causes a child to turn away from peers and focus on the caregiver. The amount of caregiver interruption of peer interactions among infants and toddlers attending child care (average age, 13 months) was related to negative peer interactions at the second observation (average age, 19 months). In fact, the rate of caregiver interruption of peer interactions accounted for all significant variance between child care classrooms in peer sociability. Williams et al. concluded that "the rate at which caregivers interrupt infants' early peer interactions appears to have lasting negative effects on peer sociability 6 months later" (2007, p. 362).

Observing over time will help teachers and parents understand the goals and strategies of children and their reactions to them. Teachers can document peer happenings with video or photos, or ask others to videotape their interactions with children. Analyze the documentation with other staff and family members to see the action from the children's perspectives, and determine whether teacher support is necessary.

Observing and documenting children's actions may help an adult see a behavior in a different way. For example, when 2-year-olds try to enter other children's play, the peers often reject them. Instead of giving up, young children often nonverbally stay close, circle around, and then try again. Singer and Hannikainen (2002) pointed out that, by giving in, the child who wants to enter the play shows respect; by staying close, the child learns about the other children's activity; and by trying again, the child shows his or her interest. Too often we may intervene after the child is rejected, and if so, we may have interrupted the child's showing respect for his or her peers. Observation and analysis of the documentation help us see these situations with a new lens. If we see that peers continuously reject a child, regardless of that child's strategies or because of aggressive strategies, then teachers will support the child to gain knowledge about self and other and learn strategies for how to initiate play (Honig & Thompson, 1997).

Adults must intervene, however, when toddlers' and 2-year-olds' tussles turn to turbulence and the escalation of conflict turns to aggression. Teachers' use of relationship-building strategies scaffolds children's conflict resolution abilities in these situations.

RELATIONSHIP BUILDING AND RESTORATION THROUGH MEDIATION As was discussed previously in this chapter, children are most successful during conflicts if they use strategies that involve less power and more negotiation while also thinking of the other's perspective—not an easy task for toddlers in the midst of conflicts. Adults play an important role in helping children learn these strategies to build and maintain relationships.

Relationship restoration is a key concept. Both teachers' and children's communication can occur at the content level and at the meta-communication (relational) level (Singer & Hannikainen, 2002, discussing Bonica, 1977, and Bates, 1955, 1985). When children conflict about activity ideas or who has the toy, they are communicating at the content level. When they communicate by ignoring or rejecting other children, they are at the relational level.

> According to Bonica, a conflict has escalated into a crisis when both children are simultaneously victims and aggressors, and when children reject each other at both levels. There can be no resolution until children accept each other as individuals whose feelings have to be taken into account . . . only when they accept each other's presence can they resolve their problems at the content level. (Singer & Hannikainen, 2002, p. 7)

According to Singer and Hannikainen (2002), conflict resolution between two young children requires that teachers maintain positive affirmation for all of the involved children, support children's perspective taking, and use mediation strategies. In their study of 2- to 3-year-old children, they observed two types of teacher intervention techniques that were used equally when child conflict escalated: mediating strategies and high-power strategies.

Mediating strategies involve modification (proposing changes within the logic of children's play script), avoiding prohibition rules, and appealing to verbal expression. High power strategies to restore order involve giving directives, reminders of rules, and simple (non-) verbal objections. A high power strategy ignores children's perspectives and can even aggravate their conflicts (2002, p. 5).

The teacher's use of high-power strategies interferes with relationship *restoration* and contributes to children's lack of information and skills to handle conflict in the future. Mediating restores relationships and builds children's social skills. Mediating strategies require that teachers "use their power *for and with* the children and foster the development of 'shared power strategies' (i.e., negotiating, clarifying rules and feelings, questioning, and encouraging perspective-taking, compromising, and restoring a relationship after a fight" (Singer & Hannikainen, 2002, pp. 6–7). Mediating strategies, especially those that are children-centered rather than teacher-centered, build on young children's existing problem-solving skills, listen to children's viewpoints, ask them to clarify their feelings, and encourage them to express their wishes to each other. These strategies recognize the competencies of young children and affirm that their ideas and relationships are important.

Bayer et al. (1995) observed the strategies that teachers used in 135 toddler disputes. They found that toddler teachers used three different strategies in the face of the 274 nonaggressive oppositional toddler tussles that occurred in 12 hours of observation. Given that, in this particular study, some form of opposition occurred on average every 2.6 minutes and that teachers were intervening in a toddler dispute on average every 5.3 minutes, it was important to observe the strategies that teachers used and their effectiveness with toddlers. There were three mediating strategies used by the teachers.

1. CALL: Summon disputants' attention.
2. STOP: Use physical restraint or removal of objects.
3. ASK: Ask the disputing toddlers to identify the problem.

The teachers predominantly began with STOP, which represents high teacher control and decisions about the outcome. CALL, an attempt by the teacher to get the children's attention, did not work to encourage conflict resolution. The ASK process—which negotiated peer opposition, was more information based, and involved the children more—was the most effective strategy for conflict resolution, but this strategy was used in only 10.4% of the episodes.

Teachers use power and STOP strategies in an attempt to stop the conflict before it escalates. However, if we think of conflicts as opportunities for very young children to learn about relationships, then it is well worth a teacher's time to first observe and then decide when or whether to use strategies that encourage negotiation and relationship building. During conflicts, infants, toddlers, and 2-year-olds learn to express their feelings, understand others' feelings, contemplate shared meanings, and develop empathy for others' feelings and perspectives (Sims et al., 1996).

Conflicts and Time, Space, and Materials

Children's territorial conflicts stem from a classic problem in child care centers—the dilemma of children wanting to play together while also needing privacy. The data suggest that teachers indirectly influence the occurrence and seriousness of such conflicts by their organization of time, space, and material (Singer & Hannikainen, 2002, p. 5).

5.4. A teacher reinforces the attempt of the girl on the left to keep the child on the right from touching her pile of blocks. How could the teacher involve the children in conflict resolution?
PHOTO: ASHANTE BUTCHER

Rushing children through the day, putting too many children together in one space, and having an inflexible schedule all contribute to increased conflict among infants, toddlers, and 2-year-olds. Instead, create a schedule that is responsive to the needs of infants. Feed them and help them sleep on their own schedule. Toddlers and 2-year-olds thrive with more organized routines of "hello" time, eating, sleeping, indoor and outdoor play time, and "good-bye" time. However, teachers of these age groups must still remain flexible to meet the needs of young children who may, on one day, need more holding and, on another day, want to continue eating after the other children are finished with their lunch "because their tummies aren't full yet." This kind of responsive care that trusts children to tell you what they need; gives children a sense of efficacy; and helps them to trust their own inner feelings of hunger, need for rest, and desire for companionship.

Thoughtful arrangements of activities and opportunities in a program environment are crucial, but does having duplicates of toys and materials reduce conflict? The answer is—sometimes. The social nature of conflicts, however, means that there is more to a conflict than just two children desiring the same toy (Caplan, Vespo, Pedersen, & Hay, 1991). Because of those social reasons, conflicts can occur even when there are duplicates of toys that are easily accessible to two children. A toy can suddenly become incredibly valuable to a second child *because* the first child has it and is waving it around. As discussed earlier in this book, there are also subtle rules about possession and ownership that occur. If a toddler had a toy several minutes ago and then discarded it, that toddler might still consider the object his when another toddler picks it up. Power and dominance issues may also be at play.

The strategies discussed at the end of chapters 3 and 4 in this book also prevent conflicts. Although conflicts have value, teachers and parents probably will not want them to occur every moment of the day. Empathy for what it is like to be a toddler or 2-year-old, an understanding of infant and toddler development, and an awareness of the effect of responsive adult–child relationships and responsive environments are key elements of preventing conflicts and promoting social development.

When Conflicts End in Bites

Biting is a major concern of children, families, and teachers of infants and toddlers and often occurs in infant and toddler rooms. When conflict begins or ends with a bite or other hurtful behaviors, the room or family child care home can erupt with emotion. On the cusp of using language to express their needs, mobile infants or toddlers may use bites to convey what they cannot say: "I like you," "Get out of my way," or "Give me back my toy, I had it first." Teachers, who know the variety of reasons why young children may bite while they are learning to negotiate conflict, know that their role is to meet the needs of children and teach them what to do to become prosocial members of their peer community.

Aggression is discussed in the next chapter, but biting is discussed here because biting is a developmental phenomenon and biting typically is not done to intentionally hurt another person (aggression), but rather to obtain a desired object, express frustration, move another person out of the way, or even to express affection. The biggest reasons that infants, toddlers, and 2-year-olds bite others is that they are learning the difference between self and other, the skills of self-regulation, how to express feelings, how to show empathy and take the perspective of others, and how to express their desires and needs. They require social support and feedback to know what behavior is culturally appropriate in which context. For example, a toddler's playful nibbling is accepted by his father during roughhousing, but not accepted in his toddler classroom when he nibbles a peer in an attempt to play. In fact, the toddler's nibbles are probably going to bring shrieks of protest from a toddler peer. The nibbling toddler has to learn with whom and in what context the behavior is acceptable, and this experimentation takes time.

Biting Is OK Except for Adults, Children, Animals, and Some Objects

Children are biting all of the time—their food, their toys, their books, and sometimes another person. When adults say, "No biting," it can be confusing to young children. Adults can use other words and nonverbal strategies that are more effective in stopping the biting of others. When children are together in early care and education programs, they need support, encouragement, prompting, and relationship re-establishment strategies from sensitive and responsive adults.

Why Do Babies Bite?

Teachers and parents who observe children carefully see that there are many reasons why children might bite an adult or peers. Kaileia (14 months) is new to her infant room (which has children ages 7 weeks to 18 months) in a large center program. The teachers know that Kaileia is experiencing separation anxiety from her mother and father. She clings to them tightly when they try to say good-bye. She often sucks her thumb and cautiously watches the other children play. Kaileia's primary caregiver greets her each morning and sits on the floor near her when she plays. She tries to be the one to change Kaileia's diaper and sing songs to her before nap-time. Her teachers and her parents are surprised when she bites Mara, another toddler, when Mara takes a toy out of her hand.

Darren (20 months) is in the toddler room with children who range from 18 months to 36 months. He has been with the teachers since he was an infant and feels very comfortable in the room. Lately, he is saying, "No" to everything the teachers says, he doesn't want to take a nap, and he doesn't want to help put toys away before lunch. He says a few words and uses sign language for "milk" and "eat." The teachers watch him closely to model words for him when he wants something from his peers. Darren bites Michel, the teacher, on the arm when she picks him up to change his diaper without preparing him to leave his play and make the transition.

Why did these children bite people? There are many possible reasons. After observing and thinking about children's development and a particular child's development and individuality, teachers and parents can make an informed guess. When the teachers observed Kaileia they realized that even though they and Kaileia's parents are using gentle transition strategies, she is facing a world that is new and strange to her. Much of her familiar world has changed during the day and she may be feeling anxious. We know that she is experiencing separation anxiety. Her teachers are asking her to participate in routines that are unfamiliar to her with unfamiliar adults. Another reason might be that the rules for her behavior are different in the room with other children than they were at home. Kaileia could be asking (nonverbally), "What are the rules here?" or "What is OK to do and what is not?" Another reason may be that Kaileia has not had much experience with peers. She is just learning how to express her needs with her peers. In addition, her language is just developing and she does not have many words to express her overwhelming feelings.

Darren is developing autonomy. He wants to do everything by himself and his way. He did not like it when the teacher picked him up to diaper him. He did not want to leave the task that he had started—dumping the blocks from the basket and then putting them all back again. Also, after his teachers discussed the bite with Darren's parents they thought about how Darren explores toys by smelling, touching, and tasting them. Using his mouth is a way that Darren learns. Darren is just learning words to express himself as well. He certainly did not have the words to say to the teacher, "Not now, please, I need to finish my block play and then I will be willing to go with you." Darren is still learning about cause and effect, experimenting to see what happens when he tries different behaviors. Imitating others is also a powerful way that toddlers learn about social behavior. Darren may have observed another child biting a peer or teacher and he was able to remember the behavior to try himself when the occasion arose.

What Could Teachers and Parents Do to Prevent Biting?

Kaileia needs the adults' gentle support to ease the separation from her home to the center. It often takes infants and toddlers longer than adults think it does to feel at ease in their new environment. Kaileia needs time to learn what is culturally acceptable in this particular room with these particular peers. She needs time to play with peers and construct strategies that work. She will benefit from many opportunities with her teachers to be prosocial—to get a Kleenex for a crying peer or a child's favorite stuffed animal when a peer is sad. Her language is sure to blossom as she hears words from her peers, is read stories, and hears adults use rich, descriptive language during the day while giving her an opportunity to always take a turn in the conversation.

Adults can help Darren develop his autonomy within safe limits. He will benefit from making simple choices throughout the day. A question from a teacher such as, "Do you want juice or milk?" offers a budding individual an opportunity to maintain some control and develop his ability to make choices. Although it can be a difficult task for adults to show respect for toddlers' struggles to become separate people while still supporting the toddlers' need to "be and belong," it is one of the most important tasks that the adults will encounter. They will want Darren to be able to develop a positive sense of self-worth and to be a master at human relationships—both of which take time and patience.

Although the primary reason for Darren's biting seems to be his desire for autonomy, he will also benefit from experiences with many sensory–motor materials because he, as well as many children are, is a sensory explorer. Darren needs many opportunities to increase his language development as teachers respond to his words, explain what is happening during the day, read to him several times a day in small groups that gather around them, sing delightful songs, and chant fingerplays. As adults help Darren learn how

5.5. Opportunities to look at books are important for children's language and social learning. Here Arleta independently reads *Hands Are Not for Hitting* (Agassi & Heinlen, 2000), a book about other ways to use hands.
PHOTO: ASHANTE BUTCHER

to express feelings and notice how others are feeling, he is likely to feel less frustrated with both adults and peers.

When a Child Bites

The following strategies were adapted with permission from *Infant and Toddler Development and Responsive Program Planning: A Relationship-Based Approach* (by D. L. Wittmer & S. H. Petersen, 2006, Upper Saddle River, NJ: Prentice Hall, p. 323).

■ Use words or actions appropriate to a child's developmental level. The goal is to support both the biter and the victim emotionally, teach both children different strategies (depending on their developmental level), and restore relationships.

■ If the biter did not break the skin of the other child, then proceed as follows, calmly, kindly, and seriously.

  ■ Depending on the children's developmental level, either (a) ask, "What happened?" or (b) state the problem (of the children). For example, say, "Kevin, you took the toy from Charley. Charley, you bit Kevin."

  ■ Ask about or emphasize the perspective and feelings of the child who was hurt. Say, "_____ doesn't like it when you bite him." "You hurt him. He's crying" (pointing out how the bite's behavior affected the other child). Encourage the child who received the bite to be proactive. Help the bitten child say or sign "STOP" to the biter.

  ■ Ask about or emphasize the biter's feeling, too. "You seemed angry. You wanted the toy back."

- Ask or state what the biting child can do instead—teach the child what to do. "You can bite this cloth (or food, biting toy, etc.) or "you can tell her how you feel." Encourage the child to use sign language.

- Problem-solve with both children to reach possible solutions.

- Ask, "How can we make it better?" Encourage the child who bit to think of how to help the other child feel better. Suggest an ice pack, a favorite toy, or a Band-Aid.

- If the biter broke the skin of the other child, ask another teacher to talk with the biter—use strategies listed earlier. Immediately help the bitten child. If the skin is broken, wash it well with soap and water. If possible, bring the biter along to assist the victim (however, the victim may appropriately want the biter to stay far away). Call the parent of the child who received the bite. If the skin is broken, then the parent must take the child to a doctor.

- It is easy in the emotional moments after a biter has bitten to discount the biter as a person with feelings! However, often the biter is as frightened as the victim. If punishment for the biter is harsh, the young biter nurses his or her own hurt rather than concentrating on and helping the bite victim. If you punish or yell at the child or put the child in time-out, she will try to protect herself, think only of herself, and will not be open to learning about alternatives to biting others.

General Strategies

The following strategies were adapted with permission from *Infant and Toddler Development and Responsive Program Planning: A Relationship-Based Approach,* (by D. L. Wittmer & S. H. Petersen, 2006, Upper Saddle River, NJ: Prentice Hall, p. 323).

- Use words or actions appropriate to a child's developmental level.

  - Observe when the biting occurs. Keep records. A child may bite before lunch each day because he is hungry and frustrated because he can't eat yet. Another child may bite when other children crowd around him.

  - If one child's biting continues after several days of repeating these techniques, meet with the family and other teachers to figure out what might be causing the child to bite and then plan together to provide consistency across home and the child education program. Infants and toddlers deserve our best planning, caring, and teaching. Explore with the parents the reasons for biting. Try the solution that corresponds to the possible reasons. Work with the parents of the biter so that the guidance techniques used at home and at the center are consistent with each other.

  - Implement a program of time-in with an adult. An adult stays near the child, meets the child's emotional needs, shows the child affection and encouragement, catches her *before* she bites, teaches her alternative behavior, and teaches her how to be gentle or use sign language or words to express her needs.

  - Have a staff meeting. Review all the reasons that toddlers bite and all the techniques that they can use. Individualize strategies for a child and then work together as a team to provide caring relationships and *consistency* for that child.

  - *Before* parents become upset about the biting problem, hold a parent meeting or send a newsletter home to let parents know about the relationship restoration techniques they and the staff can use. Parents need to know why toddlers bite, that it is a common problem whenever toddlers are together in a group, and that the staff will do everything possible to ensure the safety of the children.

■   Include in the newsletter that when adults hit or bite children for biting others, the child learns that biting is okay if you are bigger and stronger than the other person is. The child will be *more* likely to bite his or her peers (especially smaller ones).

If a solution works, give yourself a big pat on the back. If a solution does not work, provide the time-in approach. If the child continues biting, bites viciously, or bites and then smiles, seek professional help and/or explore the possibility that this child needs an environment with fewer children and more one-on-one attention for a while.

Summary

Infants, toddlers, and 2-year-olds have the capacity to be prosocial *and* to engage in conflicts as they learn about themselves and others, possessions, and ownership. Conflict and social competence go hand in hand as children learn many social strategies as they engage in tussles over toys, space, or a teacher's lap. Conflicts are relational as they may occur with certain children and not others.

There are many relationship-building and restoration strategies that adults can use to help children learn from their conflicts. When conflicts end in bites, then individualized strategies developed in partnerships with the child's parents work best.

References

Agassi, M., & Heinlen, M. (2000). *Hands are not for hitting.* Minneapolis, MN: Free Spirit Publishing.

Bandura, A. (1989). Social cognitive theory. In R. Vasta, *Annals of child development, 6,* 1–60. Greenwich, CT: JAI Press.

Bayer, C., Whaley, K., & May, S. (1995). Strategic assistance in toddler disputes II. Sequences and patterns of teachers' message strategies. *Early Education and Development, 6*(4), 406–432.

Caplan, M., Vespo, J. E., Pedersen, J., & Hay, D. F. (1991). Conflict and its resolution in small groups of one- and two-year-olds. *Child Development, 62,* 1513–1524.

Chen, D. W. (2003). Preventing violence by promoting the development of competence conflict resolution skills: Exploring roles and responsibilities. *Early Childhood Education Journal, 30,* 203–208.

Chen, D., Fein, G. G., Killen, M., & Hak-Ping, T. (2001). *Early Education and Development, 12*(4), 523–544.

Cosaro, W. A. (1997). *The sociology of childhood.* Thousand Oaks, CA: Pine Forge Press.

DaRos, D. A., & Kovach, B. A. (1998). Assisting toddlers and caregivers during conflict resolutions: Interactions that promote socialization. *Childhood Education, 75*(1), 25–30.

Eckerman, C. O., & Peterman, K. (2001). Peers and infant social/communicative development. In G. Bremner & A. Fogel (Eds.), *Blackwell handbook of infant development* (pp. 326–350). Oxford, England: Blackwell.

Forman, G., & Hall, E. (2005). *Rocking horse rumble.* Retrieved September, 15, 2007, from www.videatives.com/content-new/store/product_info.php?products_id=75

Hawley, P. H., & Little, T. D. (1999). On winning some and losing some: A social relations approach to social dominance in toddlers. *Merrill-Palmer Quarterly, 45*(2), 185–214.

Hay, D. F. (2006). Yours and mine: Toddlers' talk about possessions with familiar peers. *British Journal of Developmental Psychology, 24*, 39–52.

Hay, D. F., & Ross, H. S. (1982). The social nature of early conflict. *Child Development, 53*(1), 105–113.

Honig, A., & Thompson, A. (1997). Parent information: Helping toddlers with peer group skills. *Zero to Three, 14*(5), 15–19.

Killen, M., & Turiel, E. (1991). Conflict resolution in preschool social interactions. *Early Education and Development, 2*, 240–255.

Piaget, J. (1953). *The origins of intelligence in the child.* New York: International Universities Press. (Original work published 1936)

Ross, H. S., & Lollis, S. P. (1989). A social relations analysis of toddler peer relationships. *Child Development, 60*(5), 1082–1092.

Rubin, K. (2002). *The friendship factor.* New York: Penguin Books.

Shantz, C. U. (1987). Conflicts between children. *Child Development, 58*, 283–305.

Sieminski, J. (2007). *Conflict in toddler rooms.* Unpublished manuscript.

Sims, M., Hutchins, T., & Taylor, M. (1996). Young children in child care: The role adults play in managing their conflict. *Early Childhood Development and Care, 124*, 1–9.

Sims, M., Hutchins, T., & Taylor, M. (1998). Gender segregation in young children's conflict behavior in child care settings. *Child Study Journal, 28*(1), 1–16.

Singer, E., & Hannikainen, M. (2002). The teacher's role in territorial conflicts of 2- to 3-year-old children. *Journal of Research in Early Childhood Education, 17*(1), 5–18.

Thornberg, R. (2006). The situated nature of preschool children's strategies. *Educational Psychology, 26*(1), 109–112.

Vaughn, B. E., Vollenweider, M., Bost, K. K., Azria-Evans, M. R., & Snider, J. B. (2003). Negative interactions and social competence for preschool children in two samples: Reconsidering the interpretation of aggressive behavior for young children. *Merrill-Palmer Quarterly, 49*, 245–327.

Vygotsky, L. S. (1978). *Mind in society: The development of higher psychological processes.* Cambridge, MA: Harvard University Press.

Williams, S. T., Ontai, L. L., & Mastergeorge, A. M. (2007). Reformulating infant and toddler social competence with peers. *Infant Behavior and Development, 30*, 353–365.

Wittmer, D. L., & Petersen, S. H. (2006). *Infant and toddler development and responsive program planning: A relationship-based approach.* Upper Saddle River, NJ: Prentice Hall.

6

CHILDREN WHO FEEL CHALLENGED

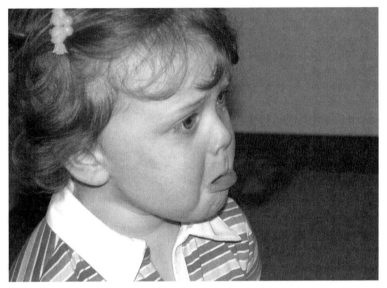

<small>PHOTO: MARILYN NOLT</small>

> **The foregoing evidence for stable individual differences in competence with peers in the first three years of life suggests that attempts to prevent peer problems from developing may need to begin rather earlier than initially thought. (Hay, Payne, & Chadwick, 2004, p. 87)**

Cara does not want to be touched by her peers. She moves away whenever a peer comes near. Lonnie squeezes herself into the tiny space between the block shelf and the puzzle shelf. Langston whimpers when another toddler takes a toy from him, and Ariel often hits other children for apparently no reason.

Infants and toddlers are capable of being social and even prosocial. However, some toddlers and 2-year-old children feel challenged by peer relationships. They feel sad, tired, afraid, rejected by peers, angry, frustrated, upset, disoriented, or confused. Teachers and family members may refer to these children as withdrawn, too shy, aggressive, traumatized, depressed, or grieving. Caring teachers worry about these children because they are generally not happy. They may be irritable or lash out at others, and some seem to want to hurt first before being hurt. They may have difficulty regulating their feelings or expressing a variety of feelings. At times, they may withdraw to a corner of the room, refuse another child's initiation to play, cling tightly to a teacher's leg, throw things, or cry for long periods. Other toddlers or 2-year-olds who may anticipate scary or hurtful responses from these children may scurry away as these children move through the room. They are often challenging to teachers and parents; meanwhile, *they* are feeling challenged emotionally by relationships and peer interactions.

The infant and toddler period is the time to identify and prevent challenging behaviors and intervene if a child is experiencing challenges. Professionals play an important role in providing quality programs that support children and families to experience rewarding relationships.

The children's characteristics—such as temperament, their experiences with relationships, and the quality of the environment they are experiencing—all play a part in whether children feel challenged with peers (Deynoot-Schaub & Riksen-Walraven, 2006; Williams, Ontai, & Mastergeorge, 2007).

Young children's early care and education experiences can enhance, advance, and increase social attitudes and skills, or they can actually *increase* the negative interactions and *decrease* positive interactions between children. When children's behavior is challenging, special training for teachers is required. Work with families is crucial. Mental health assessment and consultation can help children, families, and teachers.

An Attitude of Respect for Children's Experiences and Feelings

Understanding challenging behavior begins with an attitude of respect for what infants and toddlers are telling us with their expression of feelings and other behaviors. They are experiencing powerful emotions (Tremblay, 2004). Infants and toddlers tell us they are troubled or experiencing well-being through their play, sleep patterns, eating, affect, body tone, cries, words, and their approach and response to adult and peer relationships.

All infants' and toddlers' behavior has a source, meaning, and purpose. Through respect for young children's experiences and feelings, careful observation, dialogue with families, and thoughtful reflection, professionals can figure out how to support children as they negotiate relationship experiences, learn social skills, and develop social attitudes that influence their present and later peer behavior.

Challenges With Relationships Can Begin Early

Infants and toddlers are developing the social attitudes and skills that they need for harmonious interactions and conflict negotiation. Hay et al. (2004) identified the critical skills important for successful peer interactions as follows:

- Joint attention
- Emotion regulation
- Inhibition
- Language

■   Imitation

■   Causal understanding

Because these skills are developing in the early years, all young children will *sometimes* find peer interactions challenging. However, some children who are experiencing delays or a disability in the development of these skills will find peer interactions challenging most of the time.

We know there is a social attitude about relationships that develops early that influences young children's peer relationships. Trevarthen (2001) emphasized that human beings are social and cultural beings. They learn through communicating about their intentions, interests, and feelings with others. There is the potential for infants and toddlers to learn that relationships are meaningful, but there is also the potential to feel misunderstood, develop anger because no one hears their cries, and learn strategies that are harmful to their social experiences to gain the attention and protection of others.

When we focus our lens on infants and toddlers who find peer relationships particularly challenging, we begin to see several patterns of relating that reveal young children's skills and attitudes about social relationships—about self and other. This chapter covers how these patterns influence children's peer interactions when they are infants and toddlers and whether these patterns predict children's later social behavior. It will also address what the source of the challenge may be, in terms of child characteristics and environmental influences, and what adults can do to support social competence. The pathway to social competence definitely begins in infancy.

Children Who Experience Challenges With Self-Regulation of Emotion

Demetrio angrily threw the toy on the ground. Earlier, he had tried to climb the book shelf and fell apart when a teacher tried to guide him to the safe climbing area. Later, other toddlers moved quickly out of his way when he picked up the hammer to the xylophone and started tapping his way across the room.

In this example, Demetrio is having difficulty regulating his emotions. In chapter 2, affect or emotional regulation was emphasized as the possible foundation of social competence. When children have difficulty controlling the intensity of their emotions, have difficulty evaluating their emotions and expressing them, have a frequent negative mood, and are often disruptive and noncompliant, they are more likely to have challenges with peers (National Institute of Child Health and Human Development [NICHD] Early Child Care Research Network, 2004a). Emotion regulation includes other important aspects as well. Thompson and Goodvin (2007) in an article on "Taming the Tempest in the Teapot: Emotion Regulation in Toddlers," emphasize that

1.   Toddlers learn to regulate positive as well as negative emotions by changing the intensity or duration of the emotional response,

2.   Emotion regulation does not necessarily mean that the type of emotion changes (e.g., children may not become happy when they start out sad),

3.   The strength and duration of children's expression of emotions has to be evaluated in context (e.g., it may be appropriate for a toddler to be angry or sad),

4.   Evaluating their emotions is an important part of emotion regulation, and

5. When children are young, self-regulation does not mean that they regulate their emotions by themselves—they often rely on adults to help them.

Without adult support, young children who have difficulty with emotion regulation will still have difficulty as 4-year-olds. Two-year-olds who made aggressive overtures to others and who also had difficulty controlling their emotions were more likely to be disruptive and aggressive as 4-year-olds (Rubin, Burgess, Dwyer, & Hastings, 2003). Children who feel emotionally upset much of the time have a difficult time with peers and need adult understanding and support.

Teachers who work hard at building a child's trust in them, comfort children in distress, and respond to strong emotions with empathy help children become more self-regulated. When teachers notice and acknowledge emotions, children begin to learn to express emotions in healthy ways. Infants and toddlers need to know that caring adults will hear and understand their intense emotions. Children need the words to express their feelings and the freedom to say them.

In addition, when teachers are responsive and establish emotional chains of communication with children they learn, first, that someone cares about their feelings. They also learn to regulate emotions, experience pleasure, focus, and problem solve (Greenspan & Shanker, 2004). An emotional chain may look like the following: a toddler cries, an adult responds, the child cries harder, the adult comforts and describes the child's feelings, the child begins to calm down, the teacher problem-solves with the child, and the child begins to focus on what could happen next. Within this powerful chain of communication the child regulates strong emotions and becomes an emotional problem-solver.

Observing children carefully and providing activities that they love, such as sand and water play, will also help young children learn to focus and focus to learn.

Children Who Experience Stress

Ariel, an 8-month-old, started the day with a smile for her teacher and her peers. She played on the floor for a while with a teacher near. However, by the end of the day in child care, Ariel was irritable and difficult to comfort. She seemed to feel stressed.

Conner, a toddler, seemed fearful around other children. As the day in child care progressed, he seemed more stressed than the other toddlers who liked to play with other children.

These stories describe the results of research on morning-to-afternoon increases in cortisol level in infants (average age, 10.8 months) and 2-year-olds (average age, 29 months) who attended full-day child care (Watamura, Donzella, Alwin, & Gunnar, 2003). Cortisol, a hormone that indicates that children feel unsafe or threatened, increased in 35% of infants (20 infants) and 71% of the toddlers (35 toddlers) at child care, compared with a decrease in cortisol for 71% of the infants and 64% of the toddlers at home. Infants and toddlers who were shyer and more socially fearful with their peers were more likely to experience the increases in cortisol levels in child care settings. Children who felt more comfortable with their peers did not have increases in their cortisol levels.

Children who are more socially fearful have a more difficult time managing their negative emotions, and teachers may have difficulty giving them emotional support, thus leading to the children's (and the teachers') increased stress levels (Crockenberg, 2003).

Quality of care and other features of the environment make a difference, however. In a sample of 3- to 5-year-olds attending programs in Australia, children who attended high-quality programs showed a decrease in cortisol levels, whereas children attending poorer quality programs showed an increase across the day (Sims, Guilfoyle, & Parry, 2006). In another study of 113 children ranging in age from 18 to 40 months attending eight different child care centers, Legendre (2003) found that the cortisol levels of the children stayed stable between 9:30 a.m. and 10:30 a.m. while they were attending child care, whereas these same children's cortisol levels went down during that time when they were at home. This researcher found that large group sizes over 15 children, large numbers of caregivers in the room, less space per child, and age differences among the children that was less than 6 months contributed to the increases in cortisol levels.

It seems, then, that both a child's fear and shyness and poor quality programs contribute to young children experiencing stress in child care (Sims et al., 2006).

What can teachers do to decrease the peer stress for young children in programs? Teachers who form strong, affectionate relationships with the children mediate children's stress levels (Dettling, Parker, Lane, Sebanc, & Gunnar, 2000; Sims et al., 2006).

Chapter 7 will highlight primary care and continuity of care—two methods of care that build children's positive relationships with infants and toddlers over time.

Children Who Withdraw

Lotty, a toddler, looks on with a passive face as other children play. Meghan actively avoids all of the toddlers in the room, moving in the other direction when children come near her. Mia seems fearful when she has to be with the other children.

Rubin (2002) referred to children who withdraw from other children as *inhibited* or *hiders*. They "move away" from—rather than toward—interaction with others (Rubin, 2002). They are different from toddlers and 2-year-olds who are solitary but involved in constructive activities (Rubin, 2002). Rubin and Coplan (2004) emphasized that teachers should pay attention to, and not neglect, social withdrawal and social isolation.

Other children exhibit active peer refusal rather than passive peer avoidance (Williams et al., 2007). Both of these groups, however, may be fearful of others and new situations (Henderson, Marshall, Fox, & Rubin, 2004). Their heart rates increase when they are watching other toddlers play.

There may be a temperamental factor at play. Some children are more reticent to enter play. They need to know exactly what is happening before they step into a situation. Other children may be sensitive to touch and not want to sit close to other children or join a crowd in a group. Loud noises may bother others, so these children try to find a quiet corner in the room.

Parent styles also seem to influence the stability of inhibited behavior. Toddlers who were inhibited were still inhibited at 4 years of age if mothers made derisive comments or used intrusive control with them (Rubin, Burgess, & Hastings, 2002). If mothers were not intrusive or scornful with temperamentally shy toddlers, then the toddlers were not socially reticent at 4 years of age. Inhibited toddlers may be challenging for parents who want their children to be socially competent. Parents may believe that controlling or chiding toddlers will encourage them to interact with their peers. However, patience, support, and a gradual introduction of these toddlers to peers will have better social outcomes (Rubin, 2002).

There also may be a cultural factor. Rubin (1998), in his examination of social and emotional development from a cultural perspective, emphasized that the Chinese culture does not view shyness and inhibition as negative traits.

 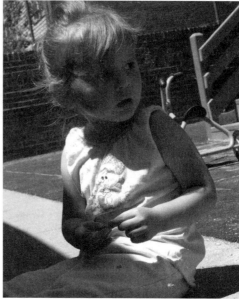

6.2 and **6.3.** Young children who withdraw from peers may be fearful and will need adult support to engage with peers.
PHOTO: ASHANTE BUTCHER

Also, toddlers and 2-year-olds who have delayed language need to be supported, as they are more likely to have behavioral difficulties. Carson, Klee, Perry, Muskina, & Donaghy (1998) found that late talkers were more depressed and withdrew more from social interactions.

Teachers who see toddlers and 2-year-olds stand by or run the other way when other children approach will want to scaffold social success. These children may be overlooked, as they are possibly quieter than other children are and they stay on the periphery of the social group (Volling & Feagans, 1995). Again, a strong, positive relationship with the teacher is important, as trust in the adult is a necessary ingredient for infants and toddlers to feel socially safe. Hold an infant who seems fearful of peers, and sit with a toddler while gradually introducing her to peers. Stay with a child as you enter an outdoor sandbox. Stay near and help the child get started with play. Use encouraging words and be patient. Set up opportunities for two children while others go outside with a different teacher.

Teachers who discuss the behavior with the child's family will gain important insights into the child's cultural experiences. Perhaps the family's goal is to create a child who is quiet and respectful of others. However, the parents may not want their child to withdraw or actively avoid other children. Listen to the family's perspective, and work collaboratively with them to support the child's social competence in a way that is culturally relevant.

Teachers can remember that there may be a fear factor to withdrawing or actively refusing peers. They can observe the child and talk with family members to determine the source and content of a child's fears. Help infants and toddlers feel safe by responding to their physical and emotional needs. Greet each child warmly in the morning, inform toddlers and 2-year-olds what will be happening next during the day, and create a comfort corner where children can go when they are feeling sad or want to be alone. Place soft animals, a quilt, and books in the comfort corner to soothe children. Be available for holding and hugs when a child shows fear. If an infant, toddler, or 2-year-old clings to adults in a program, slowly introduce the child to materials and activities. When adults do not respond to children for fear of "spoiling" them, a child's independence is *not* increased. In fact, when teachers reject children, this may lead the children to become more dependent as their fears for their own safety grow.

Children Who Are Rejected

Each time Karli, a toddler, tries to enter the small group of children in the dramatic play area in the toddler room, Jamie pushes her out.

To be rejected by others is to be unwanted, abandoned, and in a sense, discarded by others and has detrimental effects on young children. Can toddlers and 2-year-olds actually reject some of their peers?

It seems that they can. Toddlers or 2-year-olds may continuously push a certain toddler out of a dramatic play area. A toddler who is aggressive may cause other toddlers to run the other way.

Hay (2006) emphasized that the goal for responding to rejected children is to teach them prosocial behaviors rather than just eliminate behaviors that contribute to others' rejection of them. It is also important that teachers and families of young children who are often rejected work together to figure out the child's socially constructed view of relationships. Questions to ponder include:

- What are the child's goals for peer interaction?

- Does the child expect to be rejected? Where did this expectation originate?

- Which child behaviors contribute to the other children's rejection of him?

- How can the child be supported to engage prosocially with peers?

- How may the family need support to reduce the child's stress?

If a child continues to be rejected, teachers and families together can assess whether delays in language or other domains may be contributing. If so, the family has a right for the child to receive a free comprehensive assessment from the local Part C program.

Children Who Feel Aggressive and/or Hostile

While researchers and other professionals used to think that aggression developed in adolescence—they now look at the infant and toddler age period as crucial for children to develop self-control and non-aggressive attitudes.

These studies indicated that the peak age for physical aggression was not during early adulthood, adolescence, or even kindergarten, but rather between 24 and 42 months after birth. (Tremblay, 2004, p. 399)

Sardi, a toddler, hits other toddlers. When Mara takes a plastic plate that is in front of Sardi and then leaves the dramatic play area, Sardi picks up another plate, runs across the room, and hits Mara on the head.

Aggression is a concern during the infant and toddler period. We can consider the children's perspective by asking the following questions. How does aggression help children cope with their environment? What is the meaning to the children? Does it make children feel safe if they can strike out before other children strike them? Do they feel strong and powerful? Do they feel dysregulated, and hitting (or other aggressive acts) helps them to regulate their emotions and feel in control again? Have they learned that aggression is a way to get an adult to pay attention? Are they modeling adults in their lives who show them that responding to negativity with negativity is a way of life? Alternatively, do they *not* know other ways to solve their problems?

Alink et al. (2006) described two theories that may account for toddler and 2-year-old aggression. One is that "studies inspired by social learning theory emphasize the influence of the social environment on the onset and development of aggression . . ." (Alink et al., 2006, p. 954). The other is Patterson's theory that "describes the possibility that child aggressive behavior may be biologically determined and reinforcement processes may result in maintaining or increasing this behavior" (as discussed in Alink et al., 2006, p. 954). There is research to support both theories.

Definition

In the example of Sardi, the aggressive act was hitting Mara on the head. *Aggression* is typically defined as intentionally hurting another, either verbally or physically. Alink et al. (2006, citing Tremblay, 2000, 2003) did not include intention as a part of the definition of physical aggression because it is difficult to determine intention. Instead, they define *physical aggression* as follows:

> We define physical aggression as behavior that may cause physical harm to people, animals, or objects. Examples of physical aggression are hitting, kicking, and fighting. (Alink et al., 2006, p. 956)

Aggression can be proactive or reactive. Proactive aggression occurs when a child initiates aggressive behavior, and reactive aggression occurs when a child reacts to another's aggression.

Prevalence and Ages of Aggression

Experienced family members and teachers know that aggressive behavior begins early. It seems that "by 12 months of age, children have the physical, cognitive, and emotional means of physically aggressing others" (Tremblay, 2004, p. 405).

Many researchers are now seeing a pattern for the onset and incidence of aggressive behavior. As Tremblay reported, "physical aggression appears during the first year after birth (Tremblay, 2002). Its frequency increases rapidly during the second year after birth, reaches a peak between 24 and 42 months after birth, and then decreases steadily (Tremblay, 2002)" (2004, pp. 402–403). Other researchers have reported a similar pattern (Deynoot-Schaub & Riksen-Walraven, 2006; Hay, 2005; NICHD Early Child Care Research Network, 2004b), although they have reported the peak for aggressive behaviors to be 30 months of age.

In a large sample of over 2,000 Dutch parents, researchers (Alink et al, 2006) confirmed this same pattern in an increase in aggression from 12 months of age to 36 months of age. Parents of 24-month-olds and 36-month-olds reported that their children engaged in higher numbers of physical aggression than those reported by parents of 12-month-olds. Alink et al. reported that there was a rise in aggression from 12 to 24 months of age and that aggressive behavior declined after 36 months of age. The percentages of parents reporting that their children demonstrate aggression at the different ages are as follows (see Table 6.1).

6.4 and **6.5.** Toddlers may at times play well and at other times be aggressive with each other.
PHOTO: LINDA ENGER

Table 6.1. Percentage of Parents Reporting Child Aggression at 12, 24, and 36 Months

Child age group	% Mothers	% Fathers
12-month-olds	52	46
24-month-olds	80	74
36-month-olds	78	68

Alink et al. (2006) discussed possible reasons why there is an increase in aggression from 1 year of age to approximately 3 years of age. Children during this age period may experience anger, frustration, and the confusing feelings of becoming autonomous. By 3 years of age, when aggression begins to decrease, children are internalizing rules and values, their communication skills have increased, and their negotiation and persuasive skills have improved. Williams et al. (2007) pointed out that aggression can be viewed as an important stage in development that allows adults to help young children learn how to express their aggressive feelings in an appropriate manner.

The frequency of total interactions with peers also increases during this time (Deynoot-Schaub & Riksen-Walraven, 2006). This could contribute to increased negative interactions as well as positive ones. Now walking, the 1-year-olds' peer world changes dramatically as they move into their second year of life.

Because, "[i]t appears that most children will at some point hit, bite, or kick another child or even an adult" (Tremblay, 2004, p. 405), Tremblay has recommended that during the toddler and 2-year-old age period, adults should focus on helping children learn *not* to use aggression.

Stability

However, does aggression at ages 1 to 2½ years predict later aggression? Should we be worried if a 1- to 3-year-old seems more aggressive than other children? It seems that for most children, especially within families with a high number of risk factors, we should be concerned and intervene early.

Alink et al. (2006) found that there was high stability of aggression at 24 and 36 months of age. The NICHD Early Child Care Research Network (2004b), in a longitudinal study of over 1,200 children, studied the stability of aggression from 24 months of age to 8 years of age. They found that the level of aggression was quite stable for children who were rated high (18% of the sample) and low (70% of the sample) on aggression. A subsample of the 1,200 children who were moderately aggressive (12% of the sample) at 24 months of age steeply declined in aggression between 36 and 54 months of age. The researchers did not find a clear reason for the decline in aggressive behavior in this group.

The majority of children (88%) who started out with high or low levels of aggression continued their patterns throughout the years. It is interesting that there were no children who started low in physical aggression who increased to even moderate levels of aggression in adolescence. Therefore, this study seems to indicate that a goal for infant–toddler teachers and parents is to prevent or reduce aggression by 24 months of age.

In the NICHD Early Child Care Research Network (2004b) monograph, the researchers reported that increased family risk (lower income and maternal education, lower levels of observed maternal sensitivity, higher maternal reports of depressive symptoms, and higher levels of less child-centered attitudes) predicted these young children's levels of aggressive behavior. Unfortunately, for the children with high levels of aggression, their family risk did not improve over 8 years of the study.

A Canadian study found a similar pattern concerning the stability of aggression. Approximately 10,000 children (six cohorts of children studied from 1 to 6 years of age) found that 83.3% of the children infrequently or occasionally used aggression from toddlerhood to adolescence (Cote, Vaillancourt, LeBlanc, Nagin, & Tremblay, 2006). However, one sixth (approximately 17%) of the children (mostly boys) were high on aggression as toddlers and continued to be high on aggression into adolescence. These authors, too, found that the children with high levels of aggression were more likely to be from low-income families, families in which the mother did not complete high school, and families in which parents reported using hostile and ineffective parenting strategies. Cote et al. (2006) concluded that children at risk for aggressive and disruptive behavior can be spotted at 15 months based on their interaction with their peers in child care.

The stability of aggression was also studied in the Netherlands (Deynoot-Schaub & Riksen-Walraven, 2006). Seventy children attending 39 different child care centers were videotaped for 90 minutes each in their groups at 15 and 23 months of age. Both the observed child's initiations and responses to their peers' initiations, as well as their peers' initiations to them, were coded as positive or negative. Responses to other children could also include withdrawal. Negative interactions included hitting, pushing, pulling, or kicking other children; taking away objects; and using verbal or nonverbal sounds of protest. Negative behaviors at 15 months predicted negative behaviors at 23 months. Children who initiated negative behaviors toward their peers were rated as more aggressive/disruptive by their caregivers at 23 months. Teachers and parents do need to care if a child uses negative peer interaction strategies at 15 months of age are should implement strategies to meet the child's emotional needs and teach prosocial behavior.

There are researchers who have argued that aggression in toddlerhood does not mean the same thing as aggression in older children and thus is not predictive of later aggression (Vaughn, Vollenweider, Bost, Azria-Evans, & Snider, 2003; Williams et al., 2007). These researchers have emphasized that socially competent children are aggressive at times and even that aggression is an aspect of social competence. One can imagine the very sociable toddler who is always in the midst of the action and who, at times, may push or hit another toddler. Williams et al. (2007) found that toddlers who were sociable (smiled, initiated play, responded to their peers' initiations, and imitated peers), toddlers who actively refused other peers (withdrew, refused, and turned away from peers), and toddlers who passively avoided other children all used aggression at times.

Intense and proactive aggression, however, is of concern and requires intervention, as does hostile aggression (Rubin, 2002). A number of research studies indicate that children who use proactive aggression at a young age are at higher risk for later aggression.

> Loeber and Hay (1994) suggested that serious aggression in later childhood might be predicted by *intense* and *proactive* aggression in the early years. In particular, tendencies to use force in its own right, not as a means to an end, and to use it proactively, rather than in reaction to another's provocation, might qualify as precursors to later aggression (Hay, Castle, & Davies, 2000, pp. 457–458).

Eighteen- to 30-month-old British toddlers and 2-year-olds who were especially sensitive to peers' possible intentions were found to hit their peers more often and 6 months later were more likely to use force proactively (Hay et al., 2000). When these toddlers reacted to their peers who were merely pointing toward or reaching for an object as aggression, they were more likely to hit, kick, or otherwise physically assault their peers (Hay et al., 2000). Children who misinterpret their peers' intentions as negative will need additional support from adults to interpret other children's behavior as benevolent or neutral. These young children may be "on guard" to ensure their own safety. Work with families to support secure attachment, reduce stress, and build children's trust in others.

Gender Differences

In the Alink et al. (2006) study of over 2,000 children, boys were reported as more physically aggressive at 24 and 36 months of age than were girls. Rubin, Hastings, Chen, Stewart, and McNichol (1998) found that 2-year-old boys were significantly more aggressive than girls were. However, Hay, Castle, and Davies (2000) summarized research that indicates very few differences in boys and girls concerning toddler aggression. More research is needed to illuminate the conditions under which girls or boys may be more aggressive.

The Early Years Are Crucial to Prevent and Reduce Aggression

The early years are crucial for the prevention of aggression and intervention to reduce aggression. During the second year of life, children may form a pattern of aggressive behavior (Cote et al., 2006; Deynoot-Schaub & Riksen-Walraven, 2006; Gauthier, 2003; Howes & Phillipsen, 1998; NICHD Early Child Care Research Network, 2004a), and "adults must help the child to internalize controls essential to his socialization" (Gauthier, 2003, p. 304).

Pay attention to dysregulated toddlers (Rubin et al., 2003). Among toddlers who initiated conflict and aggression as toddlers, those who showed emotion/behavior undercontrol were more likely to have behavior problems at age 4. These children need ongoing comforting, understanding, patience, support, and caring encouragement to learn to control and express difficult emotions. They need "well timed supportive assistance" (Rubin, 2002, pp. 64–65). They count on parents and other adults to help them—kindly and confidently—contain and express their strong emotions in healthy and functional ways.

Families, especially those with multiple risk factors, need support to prevent their children's aggressive behavior. Parents and children may be engaged in a relationship characterized by negativity, anger, and conflict (NICHD Early Child Care Research Network, 2004b). Parents who felt alone and lonely as children may have difficulty in providing loving care for their children. Maternal depression can contribute to children's problem behaviors. Marital conflict can lead to difficulties in infants' emotional regulation, as young children feel the tension in the home and model their behavior after parents who express frequent anger (Crockenberg, Leerkes, & Lekka, 2007). Parent rejection and lack of involvement contribute to children's angry, disruptive, and aggressive (externalizing problems) behavior (Shaw & Vondra, 1995). Families with multiple risk factors will benefit from home-visiting programs, community resources, and possibly infant mental health consultation.

Child Care—Does It Contribute to Aggression?

In 1998, the NICHD Early Child Care Network reported on the results of a study of more than 1,000 children designed to answer the question of how child care affected children's outcomes. The researchers found that among children observed at 24 and 36 months old there was little evidence to indicate that "early, extensive, and continuous care was related to problematic child behavior, in contrast to results from earlier work" (1998, p. 1145). In 2001, the NICHD Early Child Care Research Network reported that "children who spent more hours in child care were rated by their caregivers at 24 and again at 36 months as more negative in peer play, but their observed peer play was not related to the quantity of care" (2001, p. 1478). For these children, family risk variables were the strongest predictors of behavior problems and other outcomes, whereas child care quality was a significant predictor of caregiver-rated social and language skills when the children were 3 years old (NICHD Early Child Care Research Network, 2002b).

For these same children in third grade, after family characteristics were taken into consideration, no negative effects concerning aggression were found for the number of hours of child care attended between birth and 24 months, the quality of child care, or the total number of hours of child care between 24 and 54 months of age (NICHD Early Child Care Research Network, 2004b).

It is important to remember, however, that the NICHD Early Child Care Research Network (2004b) reported on a group of children who remained aggressive from an early age through third grade. The NICHD study reminds us to observe individual children in the context of their home and child care programs. Only then can we determine whether aggression is occurring at a high, moderate, or low level and, if at a high level, how the environment can change to support the children. They need to feel safe, develop a sense of self-worth, receive sensitive care, and learn prosocial strategies. In addition, families may need support to reduce the number of their risk factors and increase sensitivity to the needs of the child.

Quality of care is related to other social outcomes, for example, child engagement (NICHD, 1999), skilled peer interactions (NICHD, 2001), and social skills (NICHD, 2002).

Also, in many studies completed by other researchers, poorer quality care predicts aggression and deteriorating social skills, and higher quality care predicts social competence and cooperation among peers (Clarke-Stewart, Gruber, & Fitzgerald, 1994; Honig & Park, 1993; Howes, 1988; Volling & Feagans, 1995). Detailed aspects of quality, including sensitive care, related to children's social skills are discussed in chapter 7.

Children Who Are Traumatized

To an infant or toddler, trauma comes in many forms. They may witness or experience violence in their home or neighborhood, or experience separation from a loved one. Children who experience trauma may feel fearful, unsettled, and upset. They have lost the ability to predict what will happen next. They may cry and not sleep well. They may cling tightly to favorite adults and become "human Velcro" (Schechter, Coates, & First, 2002, p. 13). Some infants and toddlers will withdraw into a world of their own. Others will become aggressive because of their frightened and angry feelings. Children whose family members are experiencing trauma will lose their "insulation of affection" (Solnit, 2002, p. 17) from their family. Traumatized children cannot interact normally with their peers when they are feeling so worried about the safety of themselves and others.

Jeree Pawl, in an article on protecting young children who have experienced trauma, emphasized the following:

> We cannot successfully protect our children if we fail to be aware of how tuned in to us they are whenever they are around us and how much what we say matters. We want them to know only what they need to know. (Pawl, 2002, p. 22)

Another expert in working with infants and toddlers who have experienced trauma emphasized the following:

> Infants and toddlers depend on trusted adults to protect them and make sense out of their world, especially when children have been exposed to potentially traumatic events. (Osofsky, 2002, p. 19)

Osofsky (2002) discussed how infants, toddlers, and 2-year-olds might react to traumatic events that affect their parents and other adults in their lives.

- One-year-olds need reassurance from adults. "They react to tensions, stress, anxiety, and fear of the trusted adult . . . . Hold them and hug them and tell them everything is going to be all right" (Osofsky, 2002, p. 19).

- "A 2-year-old will understand more that something terrible has happened, that people have been hurt, and that people are anxious and sad. Since children of this age tend to feel very powerful, they may even think they have done something to 'cause' this awful thing to happen" (Osofsky, 2002, p. 19). Tell them details in simple language. Reassure them they are safe and protected.

- In the third year, they will understand more but have difficulty knowing the difference between pretend and real. Children are likely to repeat the traumatic event through play to try to master it. If they seem stuck in their play, you may suggest a different more positive ending.

Understand that children may regress in their development. Infants who loved to explore may want to be on a teacher's lap most of the day. Toddlers who were eating with a spoon may now eat with their fingers. Two-year-olds who were learning to use a toilet will have accidents and may want their diapers back. Children who separated easily from their families at the beginning of the day may cry and scream when a parent has to leave.

Use strategies that create a kind, predictable environment. Provide consistent routines while still being flexible if, for example, a toddler cannot sleep. Create a corner in the room where one child can be alone with a teacher. Provide dolls and other play materials for 2-year-olds to reenact the trauma. Provide toys that allow children to experience cause and effect, as well as a sense of mastery. Encourage play with art materials, sand, and water that can soothe a grieving child.

However, most important, have empathy for the child's experience. Ask, "What must this be like for this child?" "Can this child predict what will happen in his or her life?" Provide protection and affection for children experiencing trauma. Hug them and let them know they are safe. Use soothing and comforting words. Be an emotional haven for them and their families. Be patient, gentle, and loving. Children who feel angry and aggressive need the opposite from adults, not more aggression and anger that continues a cycle of negative interactions. Work closely with families to support them as they strive to provide the best experiences for their children.

Abuse, Neglect, and Maltreatment

A 2-month-old held facing outward will drop his head back to look at the holder from time to time, if he's well nurtured. By the time you are a sitting baby, with good enough ordinary experiences, your very back feels safe, held. You know you are watched—that is, that you exist, are held, in someone's mind. You feel secure, and secured (Pawl, 1995, p. 5).

But what if the 2-month-old doesn't feel secure, and secured? What if she feels alone when she cries? What if a parent sometimes slaps her for crying and at other times hugs her? What if adults hurt her and frequently yell at her? Trust vanishes before it forms, and mistrust materializes in its place.

Young children who have been abused or neglected may suffer from chronic malnutrition, head injury resulting in brain damage, hearing loss, poor motor control, developmental delays, attachment disorders, lack of basic trust, "frozen watchfulness," anxiety, and aggression (Goodman & Scott, 1997). There are significantly more language delays among children who were maltreated before the age of 2 than among those who had not been maltreated (Eigsti & Cicchetti, 2004; Wiggins, Fenichel, & Mann, 2007). All of these results of abuse or neglect will influence peer behavior as well as adult–child relationships.

Strategies for Teachers

Managing strong feelings, observing whether the needs of children are met, determining children's working model of relationships, documenting the purpose of the children's behaviors, and developing a relationship plan for children with families are strategies that teachers of infants and toddlers can use when they are feeling challenged by relationships.

Reflect on Your Own Feelings

We are sad when babies feel tension, cope with a lack of continuity, and live without love. We struggle to make sense of the insensible: families without homes, children suddenly without parents, and abuse and neglect of vulnerable babies. Some adults may feel anger at the unfairness and inequity across the world. We admire babies', families', and our own resilience, yet we worry that if risk factors accumulate, the chances for a child's sense of well-being are challenged. We often feel helpless to make a difference in the lives of infants, toddlers, and their families, and we often feel a sense of urgency because of our knowledge of the importance of the early years.

All behavior has a purpose, and babies from birth to 3 years old have found ways to get their needs met. While empathizing with the challenges that babies feel, note the coping strategies of children that may sometimes seem like challenges to adults. Admire the spirit of a child who cries in the hope that someone will come to soothe her. She has not given up. Respect the coping skills of a 1-year-old who holds his hands up to a teacher to be held, even though the infant's previous care teacher did not believe in holding him for fear of spoiling him. He has not given up. Admire the feistiness of a 2-year-old who is still trying to get his needs met, even though many of those needs were not met in the past. This child has not given up. Try to put yourself in the minds and bodies of the children and determine what needs they have and the behaviors they have learned to get those needs met. Children have learned these behaviors in order to cope with their environment. We need to support the children to find more relational ways of getting their needs met.

Observe and Document With Families and Team Members

In a curriculum for service providers to help parents and other caregivers meet the social and emotional needs of young children, Kelly, Zuckerman, Sandoval, and Buehlman (2001) identified 10 needs of infants and toddlers. If any of these needs are not met, then the young child may experience relationship challenges (see Box 6.1).

Discuss these needs with team members and families. Ask: How are these needs met at home and in the program, and who meets these needs? Discuss how a child might demonstrate that his or her needs are met or unmet. If a child has an unmet need, how can programs and families work together to ensure that the need is met?

Use questions such as the following (beginning on page 134) to document specific behaviors of toddlers and to develop an intervention plan that incorporates strengths as well as peer challenges of infants and toddlers. Observe a child for a period of time (e.g., 30 minutes each day for several days) and capture through words, photos, or video the answers to one or more questions. Then use the information to plan for how to help the child express negative feelings appropriately, and use sociable and prosocial behavior.

BOX 6.1 | **The Needs of Infants and Toddlers**

1. To feel safe and secure

2. To feel worthy and loved

3. To have mutually enjoyable relationships and feel a sense of belonging

4. To feel acknowledged and understood

5. To feel noticed and receive attention

6. To feel a sense of control and predictability

7. To understand and be able to manage upset feelings

8. To feel safe and stimulated in my exploration

9. To feel competent

10. To be heard and communicate

6.6 and 6.7 Children learn about feelings by first creating a happy face and then a sad face during a song.
PHOTO: ASHANTE BUTCHER

Sociable

Ask:

- How does the child show interest in a peer(s)?

- How does the child initiate play with a peer(s)

- When and how often does a child smile at a peer(s)?

- When does the child experience glee with a peer(s)?

- When and how does the child imitate a peer(s)?

- How does the child engage in rituals, games, and reciprocal interactions with a peer(s)?

- Does the child engage in social pretend play? What are the topics of the play?
- How does each child communicate with peers?
- What emotions does the child express nonverbally and verbally?
- What do toddlers and 2-year-olds talk about when they are together?

Prosocial

Ask:

- Does the child show empathy with another child's distress?
- How does the child try to comfort another child?
- Does the child help other children, and if so, how?
- Does the child have a friend? How do the child and the peer show that they are friends?

Active refusal of peers

Ask:

- How and when does the child refuse her peers' initiatives?
- When does the child move away from peers?
- What are the child's facial expressions, gestures, and words when he refuses another child's initiations?

Withdraws from peers

Ask:

- When does the child watch a peer(s) rather than participate?
- Does the child ever pretend not to notice when a peer attempts to initiate play? How does the other child react?
- When does the child cry or fuss around peers?
- What does the child do when she withdraws?

Is rejected by peers

Ask:

- When, where, and how do peers reject the child?
- How do peers actively ignore him?

Engages in conflict with a peer(s)

Ask:

- What is the reason for the conflict?
- Who engages in conflict with the child?
- When is the child most likely to engage in conflict?
- Does the child generate any solutions to a conflict? If so, what are they?

<u>Takes from or is negative or aggressive with peers</u>

Ask:

- How and when does the child hit, push, or in other ways hurt other children?

- When and for what reason does the child take toys or other objects from peers?

- Does the child ever scare peers with noises, faces, or other actions?

- Does the child ever use verbal aggression?

Document the Purpose of Children's Behavior

Observe and document what, when, where, and how a child behaves to figure out why a child might hit, bite, withdraw, or reject peers. Through using the following chart, teachers and families can begin to understand what a child might be trying to accomplish with his behavior (see Table 6.2).

From these observations, the teachers thought about what they wished Kenneth would do in these situations. They wanted him to learn to "use his words," but they knew that he was not quite ready to do that. They taught him how to use the sign "STOP" when other children came too close to him. They practiced it with him many times during the day. At other times, the teachers focused on encouraging Kenneth to comfort other children in distress and play near one other child with a teacher nearby. The teachers gave Kenneth attention by using encouraging and affirming words with him. They held him when he needed to be held and gave him additional positive attention throughout the day. Soon Kenneth was using sign language and seemed to enjoy his peers being near.

Develop a Relationship Plan for Children With Families

Develop a relationship plan for the child with families and team members. Ask, Who has the meaningful relationships with this child? How can those with meaningful relationships with the child:

- Help children feel safe?

- Meet all of their emotional needs?

- Provide nurturing routines?

- Provide continuity of care?

- Develop trust that they will grow each day with sensitive responsive care?

- Support children's development of a positive working model of relationships?

Table 6.2. Sample Observations Used to Help Determine Reason for Behavior

What happened before the behavior?	Behavior	What happened after the behavior?
Sienna pushed Kenneth.	Kenneth bit Sienna on the arm.	Sienna cried and the teacher came to intervene.
Tommy reached in front of Kenneth to get a toy on the shelf.	Kenneth bit Tommy on the arm.	Tommy yelled and the teacher came to intervene.
Matti tried to sit near Kenneth, who was on the floor looking at a book.	Kenneth bit Matti on her shoulder.	Matti cried and the teacher came to intervene.

Provide Mental Health Referral and Supports for Families

Mental health services support relationships for children who feel challenged, as well as for families and teachers who are challenged by children. Mental health professionals in collaboration with families, teachers, and community members typically provide the services.

To know when to provide specialized emotional and social support to children and their families, professionals must recognize the fact that infants and toddlers do suffer and may be in need of specialized mental health services. Emde (2001) described four types of suffering that interfere with young children's developing healthy relationships:

- Pain and distress from trauma, abuse, or loss of a caregiver;

- Misery from neglect;

- Suffering from cumulative stress; and

- Suffering from lack of opportunity.

Young children are affected by maternal depression, domestic violence, poverty, and homelessness (Chazan-Cohen & Jerald, 2001).

Mental health supports include in-home or group therapies such as parent–child attunement therapy, consultation to a program that the child attends, one-on-one counseling for family members, and infant psychotherapy.

Emde (2001) recommended that as teachers work with mental health consultants, teachers ask the following questions to improve their relationships with the children and the children's relationships with their peers: (a) What do we want to strengthen? and (b) What do we want to prevent?

Summary

Some young children are experiencing relationship challenges because of their temperament, relationship experiences, or the settings that they encounter on a daily basis at home or in a program. Adults feel challenged by these children, and the children feel challenged by the adults and their environment. When children suffer from grief, trauma, aggression, or abuse/neglect, their sad, angry, or helpless feelings spill over to their peers. They may withdraw or lash out angrily on certain days or every day. The astute teachers and other caring adults understand the emotional and social needs of young children and attempt to meet those needs. Mental health services for the family and children who are experiencing emotional pain are sometimes needed to prevent and ameliorate present suffering and long-term effects.

References

Alink, L. R. A., Mesman, J., van Zeijl, J., Stolk, M., Juffer, F., Koot, H. M., et al. (2006). The early childhood aggression curve: Development of physical aggression in 10- to 50-month-old children. *Child Development, 774*, 954–966.

Carson, D. K., Klee, T., Perry, C. K., Muskina, G., & Donaghy, T. (1998). Comparisons of children with delayed and normal language at 24 months of age on measures of behavioral difficulties, social and cognitive development. *Infant Mental Health Journal, 19*, 59–75.

Chazan-Cohen, R., & Jerald, J. (2001). A commitment to supporting the mental health of our youngest children. *Zero to Three, 22*(1), 4–12.

Clarke-Stewart, K. A., Gruber, C. P., & Fitzgerald, L. M. (1994). *Children at home and in day care.* Hillsdale, NJ: Erlbaum.

Cote, S. M., Vaillancourt, T., LeBlanc, J. C., Nagin, D. S., & Tremblay, R. E. (2006). The development of physical aggression from toddlerhood to pre-adolescence: A nationwide longitudinal study of Canadian children (Clinical report). *Journal of Abnormal Child Psychology, 34*(1), 71–86.

Crockenberg, S. C. (2003). Rescuing the baby from the bathwater: How gender and temperament (may) influence how child care affects child development. *Child Development, 74,* 1034–1035.

Crockenberg, S., Leerkes, E., & Lekka, S. K. (2007). Pathways from marital aggression to infant emotion regulation: The development of withdrawal in infancy. *Infant Behavior and Development, 30*(1), 97–113.

Dettling, A. C., Parker, S. W., Lane, S. K., Sebanc, A., & Gunnar, M. R. (2000). Quality of care and temperament determine whether cortisol levels rise over the day for children in full-day child care. *Psychoneuroendocrinology, 25,* 819–836.

Deynoot-Schaub, M. G., & Riksen-Walraven, M. (2006). Peer interaction in child care centres at 15 and 23 months: Stability and links with children's socio-emotional adjustment. *Infant Behavior and Development, 29*(2), 276–288.

Eigsti, I. M., & Cicchetti, D. (2004). The impact of child maltreatment on expressive syntax at 60 months. *Developmental Science, 7*(1), 88–102.

Emde, R. N. (2001). A developmental psychiatrist looks at infant mental health challenges for Early Head Start: Understanding context and overcoming avoidance. *Zero to Three, 22*(1), 21–24.

Gauthier, Y. (2003). Infant mental health as we enter the third millennium: Can we prevent aggression? *Infant Mental Health Journal, 24*(3), 296–308.

Goodman, R., & Scott, S. (1997). *Child psychiatry: Key facts and concepts explained.* Oxford: Blackwell Publishing.

Greenspan, S. I., & Shanker, S. G. (2004). *The first idea: How symbols, language, and intelligence evolved from our primate ancestors to modern humans.* Cambridge, MA: Da Capo Press.

Hay, D. F. (2005). The beginnings of aggression in infancy. In R. E. Tremblay, W. W. Hartup, & J. Archer (Eds.), *Developmental origins of aggression* (pp. 107–132). New York: Guilford Press.

Hay, D. F. (2006). Yours and mine: Toddlers' talk about possessions with familiar peers. *The British Journal of Developmental Psychology, 24,* 39–52.

Hay, D. F., Castle, J., & Davies, L. (2000). Toddlers' use of force against familiar peers: A precursor of serious aggression? *Child Development, 71*(2), 457–467.

Hay, D. F., Payne, A., & Chadwick, A. (2004). Peer relations in childhood. *Journal of Child Psychology and Psychiatry, 45,* 84–108.

Henderson, H. A., Marshall, P. J., Fox, N. A., & Rubin, K. H. (2004). Psychophysiological and behavioral evidence for varying forms and functions of nonsocial behavior in preschoolers. *Child Development, 75*(1), 251–264.

Honig, A. S., & Park, K. (1993). Effects of day care on preschool sex-role development. *American Journal of Orthopyschiatry, 63,* 481–486.

Howes, C. (1988). Peer interaction in young children. *Monographs of the Society for Research in Child Development, 53* (1, Serial No. 217), 1–78.

Howes, C., & Phillipsen, L. (1998). Continuity in children's relationships with peers. *Social Development, 7*(3), 340–349.

Kelly, J. F., Zuckerman, T. G., Sandoval, D., & Buehlman, K. (2001). *Promoting first relationships. A curriculum for service providers to help parents and other caregivers meet young children's social and emotional needs.* Seattle, WA: AvenUW-NCAST Publications.

Legendre, A. (2003). Environmental features influence bioemotional reactions in day care centers. *Environment and Behavior, 35*(4), 523–549.

NICHD Early Child Care Research Network. (1998). Early child care and self-control, compliance and problem behavior at twenty-four and thirty-six months. *Child Development, 69,* 1145–1170.

NICHD Early Child Care Research Network. (1999). Child care and mother–child interaction in the first three years of life. *Developmental Psychology, 34,* 1119–1128.

NICHD Early Child Care Research Network. (2001). Child care and children's peer interaction at 24 and 36 months. *Child Development, 72*(5), 1478–1501.

NICHD Early Child Care Research Network. (2002). The interaction of child care and family risk in relation to child development at 24 and 36 months. *Applied Developmental Science, 6*(3), 144–157.

NICHD Early Child Care Research Network. (2004a). Affect dysregulation in the mother-child relationship in the toddler years: Antecedents and consequences. *Development and Psychopathology, 16,* 43–68.

NICHD Early Child Care Research Network. (2004b). Trajectories of physical aggression from toddlerhood to middle childhood. *Monographs of the Society for Research in Child Development, 4*(Serial No. 278), vii–128.

Osofsky, J. D. (2002). Helping young children and families cope with trauma in a new era. *Zero to Three, 22*(3), 18–20.

Pawl, J. (1995). The therapeutic relationship as human connectedness: Being held in another's mind. *Zero to Three, 15*(4), 1, 3–5.

Pawl, J. (2002). Protecting our children. *Zero to Three, 22*(3), 21–22.

Rubin, K. (1998). Social and emotional development from a cultural perspective. *Developmental Psychology, 34,* 611–615.

Rubin, K. (2002). *The friendship factor*. New York: Penguin Books.

Rubin, K. H., Burgess, K., Dwyer, K. M., & Hastings, P. D. (2003). Predicting preschoolers' externalizing behaviors from toddler temperament, conflict, and maternal negativity. *Developmental Psychology, 39,* 164–176.

Rubin, K. H., Burgess, K., & Hastings, P. (2002). Stability and social-behavior consequences of toddlers' inhibited temperament and parenting behaviors. *Child Development, 73*(2), 483–496.

Rubin, K. H., & Coplan, R. (2004). Paying attention to and not neglecting social withdrawal and social isolation. *Merrill-Palmer Quarterly, 50*(4), 506–535.

Rubin, K. H., Hastings, P., Chen, X., Stewart, S., & McNichol, K. (1998). Interpersonal and maternal correlates of aggression, conflict, and externalizing problems in toddlers. *Child Development, 69,* 1614–1629.

Schechter, D. S., Coates, S. W., & First, E. (2002). Observations of acute reactions of young children and their families to the World Trade Center attacks. *Bulletin of Zero to Three: National Center for Infants, Toddlers, and Families, 22*(3), 9–13.

Shaw, D. S., & Vondra, J. I. (1995). Infant attachment security and maternal predictors of early behavior problems: A longitudinal study of low-income families. *Journal of Abnormal Child Psychology, 23*(3), 335–357.

Sims, M., Guilfoyle, A., & Parry, T. S. (2006). Children's cortisol levels and quality of child care provision. *Child: Care, Health and Development, 32*(4), 453–466.

Solnit, A. J. (2002). Supporting parents, helping children: Some questions and principles. *Zero to Three, 22*(3), 16–17.

Thompson, R. A., & Goodwin, R. (2007). Taming the tempest in the teapot: Emotion regulation in toddlers. In C.A. Brownell, & C.B. Kopp (Eds.), *Socioemotional development in the toddler years. Transitions & transformations* (pp. 320–344). New York: Guilford.

Tremblay, R. E. (2000). The development of aggressive behaviour during childhood: What have we learned in the past century? *International Journal of Behavioral Development, 24,* 129–141.

Tremblay, R. E. (2003). Why socialization fails. The case of chronic physical aggression. In B. B. Lahey, T. E. Moffitt, & A. Caspi (Eds.), *Causes of conduct disorder and juvenile delinquency* (pp. 182–224). New York: Guilford Press.

Tremblay, R. E. (2002). Prevention of injury by early socialization of aggressive behavior. *Injury Prevention, 8*(Suppl. 4), 17–21.

Tremblay, R. E. (2004). Decade of Behavior Distinguished Lecture: Development of physical aggression during infancy. *Infant Mental Health Journal, 25*(5), 399–407.

Trevarthen, C. (2001). Intrinsic motives for companionship in understanding: Their origin, development, and significance for infant mental health. *Infant Mental Health Journal, 22*(1–2), 95–131.

Vaughn, B. E., Vollenweider, M., Bost, K. K., Azria-Evans, M. R., & Snider, J. B. (2003). Negative interactions and social competence for preschool children in two samples: Reconsidering the interpretation of aggressive behavior for young children. *Merrill-Palmer Quarterly, 49,* 245–327.

Volling, B., & Feagans, L. (1995). Infant day care and children's social competence. *Infant Behavior and Development, 18,* 177–188.

Watamura, S., Donzella, B., Alwin, J., & Gunnar, M. (2003). Morning-to-afternoon increases in cortisol concentrations for infants and toddlers at child care: Age differences and behavioral correlates. *Child Development, 74*(4), 1006–1021.

Wiggins, C., Fenichel, E., & Mann, T. (2007). *Literature review: Developmental problems of maltreated children and early intervention options for maltreated children.* Washington, DC: U.S. Department of Health and Human Services. Retrieved August 30, 2007, from http://aspe.hhs.gov/hsp/07/Children-CPS/litrev/index.htm

Williams, S. T., Ontai, L. L., & Mastergeorge, A. M. (2007). Reformulating infant and toddler social competence with peers. *Infant Behavior and Development, 30,* 353–365.

7

DEVELOPING A COMMUNITY OF CARING IN INFANT AND TODDLER PROGRAMS

PHOTO: NICOLE SMITH

Deidre, still sitting in her car seat after an hour in child care, was unable to get out by herself. Carl reached out to touch his peer who sat close by and a teacher, in a gruff voice, immediately told him, "No, do not touch him." Samuel was tired, and as his fusses turned to cries, teachers ignored him. Other peers became upset and started to cry as well.

Too many peers and too few teachers created relationship chaos in this infant–toddler program.

In another program, two teachers sat on the floor with three infants per teacher. Two children were sleeping, while another teacher fed a bottle to a baby, rocking her in the glider. The children on the floor seemed relaxed, as did the teachers. A teacher placed two sitting infants close to each other in order to promote peer interaction.

An appropriate number of peers and teachers created relationship harmony in this infant–toddler program.

These two examples—one in a quality program and one not—represent how caring teachers and programs contribute to children's peer relationships. The infants who were in a crowded room in which peer interactions were discouraged experienced their peers very differently than did the infants who had room to crawl, space to rest, and responsive, affectionate adults.

This chapter addresses quality from the perspective of infants, toddlers, and 2-year-olds. What does it feel like to be a baby who attends a program? How can we help them "be and belong" (Galardini & Giovannini, 2001, p. 105). How do teacher education and the program structure (including group sizes, ratios, and how the program is organized) make a difference in the peer lives of children from birth to 3 years old, their families, and the professionals who work with them?

Create a Community of Caring

A community of caring in programs for children from birth to 3 years old makes children's emotional and social development a priority (Lally et al., 2003). Caring teachers know that social and emotional development provides the foundation for learning. If young children have a sense of emotional and social well-being, they feel well and they learn well. If they feel safe and secure, they can focus on play and peers. On the other hand, if they feel sad, angry, and stressed much of the time, they will not develop social competence. A caring community makes healthy relationships the main concern of the program from the moment-to-moment teacher–child and peer interactions to the attention given to families, the structure of the day and program, and the support that teachers are given. A caring community makes a difference for young children's peer relationships.

> **Early child-care experiences appeared to influence social competence by fostering individual differences that remained stable through childhood and early adolescence. (Campbell, Lamb, & Hwang, 2000, p. 166)**

Family members, teachers, and other infant–toddler professionals can make a difference in the lives of children who spend much of their time in groups. They can create personal relationships and physical environments that help young children thrive as individuals within social relationships.

Quality Makes a Difference

"Quality" in early child care and education . . . is perceived differently when we view child care as a prominent feature of the environment of relationships in which young children develop. The importance of ensuring that relationships in child care are nurturing, stimulating, and reliable leads to an emphasis on the skills and personal attributes of the caregivers, and on improving the wages and benefits that affect staff turnover. (National Scientific Council on the Developing Child, 2004, p. 5)

Each aspect of a program affects the relationships that infants and toddlers experience from day to day with their peers in an early care and education program. Respectful and responsive adult–child interactions, close relationships with families, teacher education and training, the program organization, and administrative support are a few of the aspects of programs that make a difference (Lally, 1995; Lally et al., 2003).

Respectful and Responsive Adult–Child Interactions

"Positive, responsive caregiver behavior was the feature of child care most consistently associated with positive, skilled peer interaction in child care" (National Institute of Child Health and Human Development [NICHD] Early Child Care Research Network, 2001, p.1478). Research studies show that specific characteristics of teachers make a difference concerning peer interactions. The following list contains one or more references for each characteristic, although there are many more.

- Pleasant and enthusiastic affect—not negative, flat, or neutral (Clawson, 1997)

- Affectionate (Zanolli, Saudargas, & Twardosz, 1997)

- Consistent, reliable, and stable for children (Barnas & Cummings, 1994; Braungaart-Rieker, Garwood, Powers, & Wang, 2001)

- Emotionally available (Volling, McElwain, Notaro, & Herrara, 2002)

- Empathetic (Weil, 1992)

- Highly involved (Anderson, Warren, Nagle, Rogers, & Smith, 1981)

- Engages in mutually responsive and reciprocal interactions with children (Kochanska, 1997; NICHD Early Child Care Research Network, 2004)

- Uses positive caregiving (Howes & Smith, 1995)

- Uses strategies to support child regulation (Spinrad, Stifter, Donelan-McCall, & Turner, 2004)

- Responsive (NICHD Early Child Care Research Network, 2001)

- Sensitive (NICHD Early Child Care Research Network 2004; Warren & Simmens, 2005)

- Warm (Ispa et al., 2004)

When teachers are emotionally available, responsive, and empathetic with young children, they need not be afraid of spoiling children. One concern of adults is that children from birth to 3 years old will become demanding if adults are responsive. The opposite is true: If caregivers are not responsive they may harden children's hearts to their own and others' feelings. If adults are not responsive, children can become demanding or withdraw from relationships. Children find a way to get their needs met.

Teachers can help infants and toddlers learn how to self-regulate by comforting them when they are distressed and by building trust. As they grow, *because they have learned to trust others*, they will be able to wait a bit for snack, be calm for naptime, or sit for a story. Have conviction that, as infants and toddlers trust their favorite adults, they will feel safe to explore their world, knowing that someone "has their back" (Pawl, 1995).

Infants, toddlers, and 2-year-olds who have a sense of security (a secure attachment) with teachers are less likely to use hostile aggression and are more likely to play in a complex way with their peers (Howes, Hamilton, & Matheson, 1994). With teachers who are affectionate, young children are more likely to be affectionate (Zanolli et al., 1997). When adults are responsive to the cues of infants, toddlers, and 2-year-olds, children learn that they are good at relationships. When children receive tender care, they are more likely to show others tender care. When adults support positive interactions with peers, children will learn how to be socially competent.

Work Closely With Families

Another indicator of quality of programs is how teachers and administrators communicate with and support families. Program support for families results in more harmonious

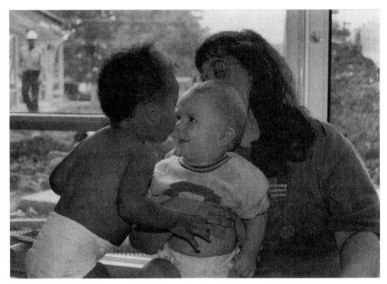

7.2. When teachers are warm and sensitive to children, peer relationships are more likely to flourish.
Photo: Janet Brown McCracken

family–child relationships, which are important for peer relationships to blossom. When young children are treated with warmth and affection at home, they are more likely to be competent and less aggressive with peers (Brook, Zheng, Whiteman, & Brook, 2001; Fagot, 1997; Jacobson & Wille, 1986; Shaw & Vondra, 1995). Maternal sensitivity and children's cognitive and language competence predicted peer competence across both home and program settings as rated by parents and teachers (NICHD Early Child Care Research Network, 2001). Infants and toddlers learn how to value relationships with sensitive and responsive care from their families. The more support that families have, the more they can provide this sensitive care.

Teacher Education and Training

The period from birth to age 3 is very important for peer prosocial development. Professional opportunities to learn the following are important:

> to know how to support the "relationship embeddedness of the child (for example, facilitating development of what is mutual and shared), as well as the individuality of the child (facilitating development of what is creative and unique in each child" (Emde, 2001, p. viii).

Teacher education programs must teach knowledge of peer social development, a value for peer relationships, knowledge of how to see the value of and mediate peer conflicts, skills for supporting children with relationship challenges, and skills concerning how to set up a relationship-based, responsive program.

The Program Organized for Social Relationships

> All programs place a high value on a network of relationships. This includes valuing a structure that has continuity of staff and a connectedness for children who are in a community of relationships that, in turn, are trusting and emotionally supportive. (Emde, 2001, p. vii)

MULTI-AGE OR AGE SEGREGATED An age-old question emerges again: Will peer relationships flourish better in same-age groups or multi-age groups? The evidence seems to support multi-age groups. Toddlers and 2-year-olds in multi-age groups engage in more complex play (Howes & Farver, 1987).

More recently, Logue (2006) described how teachers observed to learn about the differences in social behavior of toddlers and preschoolers in same-age and multi-age groupings. The teachers were concerned because when children from birth to age 3 years were divided into same-age groups, the young children seemed to use their bodies to solve problems, and with the high levels of physical contact among the toddlers, there were too many injuries (despite teachers' vigilance). The preschoolers were very competitive with each other. They were not being given the opportunity to be "nurturers" (2006, p. 72).

The teachers reconfigured the 31 children ranging in age from 2 to 5 years old as multi-age groups with a 1:4 teacher–child ratio and group sizes of eight children. Teachers found the following:

■ "Aggressive behaviors, such as hitting, kicking, spitting, and taking and demanding objects, were significantly reduced in multiage groups compared to behaviors in same-age groups.

■ "Children shared objects more often in multiage groups, as evidenced by the higher rates of offering objects.

■ "Language activity also varied across types of settings. Children imitated language and conversed at higher rates in multiage groups compared to their previous activity in same-age groups" (Logue, 2006, p. 74).

The preschool children's impulse control became stronger. One preschooler said to the teacher when a toddler grabbed her toy, "He took my toy and I want to hit him." This gave the teacher the opportunity to help the preschooler problem-solve and control strong negative emotions.

Logue (2006), the author of the study, concluded that toddlers are not inherently aggressive; rather, the size and age composition of the groups in which they participate may contribute to aggression.

When a community of caring and healthy relationships is the teachers' goal, then experimenting with different age configurations is worth the effort.

LOWER RATIOS AND SMALL GROUP SIZES The ratios and group sizes influence how teachers provide care, a compassionate and engaging curriculum, responsive routines, and the aspects of programs that support or challenge peer interactions and relationships. In 12 classrooms serving 194 preschool children, there were fewer teacher–child interactions in larger classes (Clawson, 1997). For toddlers and preschoolers positive caregiving was more likely when child–adult ratio and group sizes were smaller (NICHD Early Child Care Research Network, 2000). When there is positive caregiving, infants and toddlers have good models for relationships, and as teachers meet their needs, they are able to interact more positively with peers.

CONTINUITY OF CARE When teachers in programs provide continuity of care, children are more positive with peers. With continuity of care, one or several teachers move with children as they age to a new room, rather than each child or a group of children transitioning to a new room by themselves; or, teachers stay with children in the same room and change the materials and environment to be developmentally and individually appropriate. Infants and toddlers establish close relationships with their teachers and benefit in many ways (Cryer, Hurwitz, & Wolery, 2000; Essa, Favre, Thweatt, & Waugh, 1999). Children are less negative and more positive with peers when they experience continuity of care (NICHD Early Child Care Research Network, 2001). Continuity of group—keeping a group of peers together throughout their early years in care and education programs—is also important for positive peer relationships (Howes & Phillipsen, 1998).

A PEER-RICH ENVIRONMENT AND MATERIALS An environment, materials, and time for children to interact are important elements that promote positive peer relationships. Specific aspects of environments that make a difference for peer interactions, peer relationships, prosocial behavior, and reduction of conflict were shared in the previous chapters. In this chapter, a summary of important facets of a peer-rich environment is highlighted and demonstrated with photos.

Provide child-size equipment and create areas for two or three children to interact with each other. A table for two creates opportunities for cooperation and prosocial interactions (see photos 7.4 and 7.5).

7.3. A toddler and caregiver spend valuable time together in a program with low adult–child ratios.
PHOTO: ASHANTE BUTCHER

7.4 and **7.5.** Toddlers are more likely to share when they have an opportunity to sit at a table for two.
PHOTO: ASHANTE BUTCHER

Provide duplicates of materials. Two tubs encourage two children to play near each other, each sitting in his/her own space (see photo 7.6).

Spaces for children to gather and follow each other encourage games with shared meaning.

7.6. These two girls enjoy each other's company.
PHOTO: ASHANTE BUTCHER

7.7. Three children begin a game of "follow the leader."
PHOTO: ASHANTE BUTCHER

7.8 and **7.9.** Large equipment, such as a loft and slide, allows several infants and toddlers to play with each other.
PHOTO: ASHANTE BUTCHER

7.10. Young toddlers need individual time or small group time with teachers, too.
PHOTO: MANZANITA FINE

Floor space with infants placed near each other encourages interest and peer awareness. As teachers observe children's interests and the spaces, equipment, and materials that promote positive peer interactions, they can create more peer opportunities, while remembering that infants and toddlers need individual or informal small group time with responsive teachers, too.

Administrative Support for Relationships

Anna, a child care and early education teacher, felt supported by her director. The director used ZERO TO THREE's model of reflective supervision to develop close relationships with the staff. The director believed in the importance of teacher–child and teacher–family relationships, so she supported continuity of care in the program. Anna knew that her director was always advocating for higher pay and benefits for the staff. Manzanita, on the other hand, did not feel supported and each day felt like quitting her job. She loved the infants, but she did not feel that she could do a good job because there were too many infants per teacher and the group sizes were large. Her director constantly moved Manzanita around to other rooms when another teacher was absent for the day, so it was difficult to maintain the relationships that she

knew were so important for infants and families. The children moved on to another room every
6 months—again making it difficult to really know the children and families.

Administrators in programs make a difference in the development of relationship-based care and education. If an administrator believes in the importance of relationships, then he or she establishes a community of caring in the program. With each policy decision, the administrator asks, "How does this policy reflect our value for relationships at all levels in the organization?"

A Society That Cares for Its Youngest

When an infant cries, is she heard? When an infant smiles, does someone mirror that smile back? When a toddler wants to sit on a teacher's lap, is there a lap that welcomes him? When an infant's or toddler's curiosity and motivation to learn are blossoming are there interesting materials with which to play? When a child behaves in a way that is consistent with her culture, do teachers respect her individuality? Are there opportunities for infants to be near other infants, for toddlers to play with and imitate each other, and for 2-year-olds to create complementary games and be gleeful with each other? All of these happen in relationship-based programs. However, a responsive program is much easier to create if the program receives support from the community and if public policies are in place that recognize and facilitate children's social and emotional development as key factors to the children's well-being and future social and academic success. This support occurs in a society that truly cares for its youngest citizens.

A society that cares for its youngest is one that focuses on three areas: (a) healthy functioning in all domains, (b) strong families, and (c) positive learning experiences (ZERO TO THREE, 2007b). Peer relationships are a part of all three of these areas.

Public policies influence how families and programs can support children, socially, emotionally, physically, and financially.

> **While almost every social policy from welfare reform to education to substance abuse and mental health treatment affects infants and toddlers, the impact of these policies on very young children is seldom sufficiently addressed. (ZERO TO THREE, 2007a)**

For example, maternal and infant health policies, such as availability and affordability of health care, influence how well young children feel when they are together (CDC National Center for Health Statistics, 2006). Child welfare systems such as child protective services influence whether infants, toddlers, and families are given the help they need to survive and thrive. Funding and licensing policies for child care and early education programs influence group sizes, ratios, salaries for teachers, and teacher/caregiver training, which then have a direct effect on the quality of adult–child, family, and peer relationships. All of these policies influence children's social competence.

Partnerships between child care and education programs for infants and toddlers and community resources will provide services that support families, assess and provide services and supports for children for delays and disabilities, link families to needed resources, and train teachers/caregivers in responsive, relationship-based care and education. All of these partnerships influence children's social competence.

A society that cares will make every effort to ensure that infants and toddlers receive a relationship-based start—one that builds on their relational capacity and the inherent need of humans to be a part of a social group.

Summary of the Book

The research on the importance of social and emotional development for infants, toddlers, and 2-year-olds has implications for the quality of programs provided for children from birth to 3 years old. When emotional and social competence is the goal then caring programs are a must.

In caring programs the most important strategy is for teachers to "see":

- That infants, toddlers, and 2-year-olds have a remarkable capacity to form satisfying relationships with peers.

- How much peer interactions and relationships mean to the children themselves.

- How each child discovers self through others and other through their interactions with adults and peers.

- That families and teachers have an important role to play in supporting young children's peer relationships.

In the early years with their peers, children learn the difference between self and other and that others have wishes and needs that may be different from their own. Toddlers and 2-year-olds share meaning that gives them great joy and satisfaction—jumping up and down, chasing a fly, or playing follow the leader and peek-a-boo. Children learn through social relationships, social constructivism, social–cultural experiences, and social learning. They are social beings who learn early in their lives what relationships will be like.

We want them to have social dispositions, play and negotiation skills, and affection for others. We want to build on their relational capacity—an ability to relate to family members, peers, and other important adults in their lives. We want to support their "intrinsic motives for companionship" (Trevarthen, 2001, p. 95). We want them to be able to learn to express their feelings in helpful ways and manage difficult feelings. We know that emotional competence is the pathway to social competence (Denham et al., 2003). Empathy and perspective taking may be the two most important feelings and skills in helping children develop. This starts with adults feeling empathy for, and taking the perspective of, the children.

Adults make a difference in helping children feel that relationships are worthwhile, feel that they are good at "doing" relationships, and develop the skills necessary for social competence. Adults are the ones who help children manage negative emotions and experience positive ones. Adults thoughtfully scaffold peer possibilities, interactions, and relationships. Teachers organize environments and plan activities with relationships as a priority. They promote children's well-being and peer relationships by reducing stress and giving infants and toddlers the gift of their attention, their comfort for children's distress, and their encouragement of learning within the context of a relationship-based program.

Adults must act when children are feeling challenged, as we know that the very structure of the brain is formed in the early years. Trevarthen (2001) emphasized that children's motivation to communicate and relate can lead to challenges when their motivation is thwarted or interrupted because of lack of intuitive communication partners. Teachers can work with families and their team members to develop a caring community for children and their families who are feeling challenged.

Teachers and other adults have a powerful role to help young children feel effective at getting their needs met, learn that others have feelings, and know that those feelings matter. Teachers and families can experience the joy of helping young children feel their connection with humanity and the value for social relationships.

References

Anderson, C. W., Warren, C., Nagle, R. J., Rogers, W. A., & Smith, J. W. (1981). Attachment to substitute caregivers as a function of center quality and caregiver involvement. *Child Development, 52*, 53–61.

Barnas, M. V., & Cummings, E. M. (1994). Caregiver stability and toddlers' attachment-related behaviors towards caregivers in day care. *Infant Behavior and Development, 17*(2), 141–147.

Braungart-Rieker, J. M., Garwood, M. M., Powers, B. P., & Wang, X. (2001). Parental sensitivity, infant affect, and affect regulation: Predictors of later attachment. *Child Development, 72*, 252–270.

Brook, J. S., Zheng, L., Whiteman, M., & Brook, D. (2001). Aggression in toddlers: Associations with parenting and marital relations. *Journal of Genetic Psychology, 162*, 228–241.

Campbell, J. J., Lamb, M. E., & Hwang, C. P. (2000). Early child-care experiences and children's social competence between 1½ and 15 years of age. *Applied Developmental Science, 4*, 166–175.

CDC National Center for Health Statistics. (2006). Retrieved February 1, 2008, from www.cdc.gov/nchs/data/factsheets/Infanthlth.pdf

Clawson, M. A. (1997, April). *Contributions of regulatable quality and teacher-child interaction to children's attachment security with day care teachers* (Report no. ED406014 PS025232). Paper presented at the 62nd Biennial Meeting of the Society for Research in Child Development, Washington, DC.

Cryer, D., Hurwitz, S., & Wolery, M. (2000). Continuity of caregiver for infants and toddlers in center-based child care: Report on a survey of center practices. *Early Childhood Research Quarterly, 15*(4), 497–514.

Denham, S., Balir, K. A., DeMulder, E., Levitas, J., Sawyer, K., Auerbach-Major, S., & Queenan, P. (2003). Preschool emotional competence: Pathway to social competence? *Child Development, 74*, 238–257.

Emde, R. N. (2001). Foreword. In L. E. Gandini & C. P. Edwards (Eds.), *Bambini: The Italian approach to infant/toddler care* (pp. vii–xv). New York: Teachers College Press.

Essa, E. L., Favre, K., Thweatt, G., & Waugh, S. (1999). Continuity of care for infants and toddlers. *Early Development and Care, 148*, 11–19.

Fagot, B. I. (1997). Attachment, parenting, and peer interactions of toddler children. *Developmental Psychology, 33*, 489–499.

Galardini, A., & Giovannini, D. (2001). Pistoia: Creating a dynamic, open system to serve children, families, and community. In L. Gandini & C. P. Edwards (Eds.), *Bambini: The Italian approach to infant/toddler care* (pp. 89–105). New York: Teachers College Press.

Howes, C., & Farver, J. (1987). Toddlers' responses to the distress of their peers. *Journal of Applied Developmental Psychology, 8*, 441–452.

Howes, C., Hamilton, C. E., & Matheson, C. (1994). Children's relationship with peers: Differential associations with aspects of the teacher–child relationship. *Child Development, 65*, 253–263.

Howes, C., & Phillipsen, L. (1998). Continuity in children's relationships with peers. *Social Development, 7*(3), 340–349.

Howes, C., & Smith, E. W. (1995). Relations among child care quality, teacher behavior, children's play activities, emotional security, and cognitive activity in child care. *Early Childhood Research Quarterly, 10*, 381–404.

Ispa, J. M., Fine, M. A., Halgunseth, L. C., Harper, S., Robinson, J., Boyce, L., et al. (2004). Maternal intrusiveness, maternal warmth, and mother–toddler relationship outcomes: Variations across low-income ethnic and acculturation groups. *Child Development, 75*, 1613–1631.

Jacobson, J., & Wille, D. (1986). The influence of attachment pattern on developmental changes in peer interaction from the toddler to the preschool period. *Child Development, 57*, 338–347.

Kochanska, G. (1997). Mutually responsive orientation between mothers and their young children: Implications for early socialization. *Child Development, 68*, 139–143.

Lally, J. R. (1995). The impact of child care policies and practices on infant/toddler identity formation. *Young Children, 51*(1), 58–67.

Lally, J. R., Griffin, A., Fenichel, E., Segal, M., Szanton, E., & Weissbourd, B. (2003). *Caring for infants and toddlers in groups: Developmentally appropriate practice.* Washington, DC: ZERO TO THREE.

Logue, M. E. (2006). Teachers observe to learn differences in social behavior of toddlers and preschoolers in same-age and multiage groupings. *Young Children, 61*(3), 70–76.

National Scientific Council on the Developing Child. (2004, Summer). *Young children develop in an environment of relationships* (Working Paper No. 1). Retrieved April 23, 2006, from www.developingchild.net/pubs/wp/Young_Children_Environment_Relationships.pdf

NICHD Early Child Care Research Network. (2000). Characteristics and quality of child care for toddlers and preschoolers. *Applied Developmental Science, 4*, 116–135.

NICHD Early Child Care Research Network. (2001). Child care and children's peer interaction at 24 and 36 months. *Child Development, 72*, 1478–1501.

NICHD Early Child Care Research Network. (2004). Affect dysregulation in the mother-child relationship in the toddler years: Antecedents and consequences. *Development and Psychopathology, 16*, 43–68.

Pawl, J. (1995). The therapeutic relationship as human connectedness: Being held in another's mind. *Zero to Three, 15*(4), 1, 3–5.

Shaw, D. S., & Vondra, J. I. (1995). Infant attachment security and maternal predictors of early behavior problems: A longitudinal study of low-income families. *Journal of Abnormal Child Psychology, 23*(3), 335–357.

Spinrad, T. L., Stifter, C. A., Donelan-McCall, N., & Turner, L. (2004). Mothers' regulation strategies in response to toddlers' affect: Links to later emotion self-regulation. *Social Development, 13*(1), 40–55.

Trevarthen, C. (2001). Intrinsic motives for companionship in understanding: Their origin, development, and significance for infant mental health. *Infant Mental Health Journal, 22*(1–2), 95–131.

Volling, B., McElwain, N. L., Notaro, P., & Herrara, C. (2002). Parents' emotional availability and infant emotional competence: Predictors of parent–infant attachment and emerging self-regulation. *Journal of Family Psychology, 16*, 447–465.

Warren, S. L., & Simmens, S. J. (2005). Predicting toddler anxiety/depressive symptoms: Effects of caregiver sensitivity on temperamentally vulnerable children. *Infant Mental Health Journal, 26*(1), 40–55.

Weil, J. L. (1992). *Early deprivation of empathic care.* Madison, CT: International University Press.

Zanolli, K. M., Saudargas, R. A., & Twardosz, S. (1997). The development of toddlers' responses to affectionate teacher behavior. *Early Child Research Quarterly, 12*, 99–116.

ZERO TO THREE. (2007a). *Infant-toddler policy agenda.* Retrieved February 1, 2008, from http://zttcfn.convio.net/site/PageServer?pagename=ter_pub_infanttodller

ZERO TO THREE. (2007b). *Policy priorities.* Retrieved August 15, 2007, from www.zerotothree.org/site/PageServer?pagename=pub_policypriorities

About the Author

Donna S. Wittmer, PhD, was a Fellow of ZERO TO THREE in 1982–1983. She obtained her doctorate in child, family, and community studies at Syracuse University in 1985; taught behavioral pediatrics at the State University of New York Health Sciences Center from 1982 to 1990; and directed a grant that provided developmental services to the Onondaga Indian Nation from 1985 to 1990. Beginning in 1990, she taught early childhood/early childhood special education at the University of Colorado Denver for 17 years, and for 8 of those years was coordinator of the program. She has conducted research on infant–toddler social interactions, prosocial development, teacher–child interactions, and the social skills of preschool children, and has presented at ZERO TO THREE, NAEYC, Early Head Start, and DEC conferences. Donna serves on the faculty for the Expanding Quality in Infant-Toddler Care Initiative in Colorado and was the lead author of the *RELATE*—a self-reflection and coaching tool to improve the quality of infant–toddler child care. She is the co-author, with Sandra Petersen, of the book *Infant and Toddler Development and Responsive Program Planning—A Relationship-Based Approach* (Merrill Prentice Hall, 2006); *Endless Opportunities for Infant and Toddler Curriculum— A Relationship-Based Approach* (Merrill Prentice Hall, 2008); and the chapter "Programs for Infants and Toddlers" in S. Feeney, A. Galper, & C. Seefeldt's book *Continuing Issues in Early Childhood Education, Third Edition* (Merrill, 2008). She is now a grandmother and is enjoying the new role immensely.